ANGELS
FEAR

BANTAM NEW AGE BOOKS

This important imprint includes books in a variety of fields and disciplines and deals with the search for meaning, growth and change. They are books that circumscribe our times and our future.

Ask your bookseller for the books you have missed.

ANIMAL DREAMING by Jim Nollman
THE ART OF BREATHING by Nancy Zi
BEYOND EINSTEIN: THE COSMIC QUEST FOR THE THEORY OF THE UNIVERSE by Dr. Michio Kaku and Jennifer Trainer
BEYOND THE QUANTUM by Michael Talbot
BEYOND SUPERNATURE by Lyall Watson
THE CASE FOR REINCARNATION by Joe Fisher
THE COMPLETE CRYSTAL GUIDEBOOK by Uma Silbey
THE COSMIC CODE by Heinz R. Pagels
CREATIVE VISUALIZATION by Shakti Gawain
THE DANCING WU LI MASTERS by Gary Zukav
DON'T SHOOT THE DOG: HOW TO IMPROVE YOURSELF AND OTHERS THROUGH BEHAVIORAL TRAINING by Karen Pryor
ECOTOPIA by Ernest Callenbach
EMMANUEL'S BOOK by Pat Rodegast and Judith Stanton
AN END TO INNOCENCE by Sheldon Kopp
ENTROPY by Jeremy Rifkin with Ted Howard
FOCUSING by Dr. Eugene T. Gendlin
HANDS OF LIGHT by Barbara Ann Brennan
THE HEART OF HEALING by Bruce Davis and Genny Wright Davis
THE HOLE IN THE SKY by John Gribbin
I CHING: A NEW INTERPRETATION FOR MODERN TIMES by Sam Reifler
IF YOU MEET THE BUDDHA ON THE ROAD, KILL HIM! by Sheldon Kopp
IN SEARCH OF SCHRÖDINGER'S CAT by John Gribbin
IN SEARCH OF THE BIG BANG: QUANTUM PHYSICS AND COSMOLOGY by John Gribbin
IN SEARCH OF THE DOUBLE HELIX: QUANTUM PHYSICS AND LIFE by John Gribbin
INFINITY AND THE MIND by Rudy Rucker
KUNDALINI FOR THE NEW AGE/Editor Gene Keiffer
THE LIVES OF A CELL by Lewis Thomas
MAGICAL CHILD by Joseph Chilton Pierce
MAGICAL CHILD MATURES by Joseph Chilton Pierce
THE MEDUSA AND THE SNAIL by Lewis Thomas
METAMAGICAL THEMAS: QUESTING FOR THE ESSENCE OF MIND AND PATTERN by Douglas R. Hofstadter
MIND AND NATURE by Gregory Bateson
MINDING THE BODY, MENDING THE MIND by Joan Borysenko
THE MIND'S I by Douglas R. Hofstadter and Daniel C. Dennett
NATURAL ESP: THE ESP CORE AND ITS RAW CHARACTERISTICS by Ingo Swann
THE NEW STORY OF SCIENCE by Robert M. Augros and George N. Stanciu
THE OMEGA POINT: THE SEARCH FOR THE MISSING MASS AND THE ULTIMATE FATE OF THE UNIVERSE by John Gribbin
ORDER OUT OF CHAOS by Ilya Prigogine and Isabelle Stengers
ORIGINS: A SKEPTIC'S GUIDE TO THE CREATION OF LIFE ON EARTH by Robert Shapiro
OUT OF WEAKNESS: HEALING THE WOUNDS THAT DRIVE US TO WAR by Andrew Bard Schmookler
PERFECT SYMMETRY by Heinz R. Pagels
PROSPERING WOMAN by Ruth Ross
THE REENCHANTMENT OF THE WORLD by Morris Berman
SCIENCE, ORDER AND CREATIVITY by David Bohm and F. David Peat
SHAMBHALA: THE SACRED PATH OF THE WARRIOR by Chogyam Trungpa
SPACE-TIME AND BEYOND (THE NEW EDITION) by Bob Toben and Fred Alan Wolf
STAYING SUPPLE by John Jerome
SYMPATHETIC VIBRATIONS: REFLECTIONS ON PHYSICS AS A WAY OF LIFE by K. C. Cole
SYNCHRONICITY: THE BRIDGE BETWEEN MATTER AND MIND by F. David Peat
THE TAO OF LEADERSHIP by John Heider
THE TAO OF PHYSICS (REVISED EDITION) by Fritjof Capra
TO HAVE OR TO BE? by Erich Fromm
THE TURNING POINT by Fritjof Capra
THE WAY OF THE SHAMAN: A GUIDE TO POWER AND HEALING by Michael Harner
ZEN AND THE ART OF MOTORCYCLE MAINTENANCE by Robert M. Pirsig

ANGELS FEAR

Towards an

Epistemology of the Sacred

GREGORY BATESON

MARY CATHERINE BATESON

BANTAM BOOKS
TORONTO · NEW YORK · LONDON · SYDNEY · AUCKLAND

*This edition contains the complete text
of the original hardcover edition.*
NOT ONE WORD HAS BEEN OMITTED.

ANGELS FEAR

*A Bantam Book / published by arrangement with
Macmillan Publishing Company*

PRINTING HISTORY
*Macmillan edition published May 1987
Bantam edition / November 1988*

Material excerpted in the glossary taken from Mind and Nature: A Necessary
Unity *by Gregory Bateson. Copyright © 1979 by Gregory Bateson. Reprinted by
permission of the Publisher, E.P. Dutton, a division of New American Library.*

*Bantam New Age and the accompanying figure design as well as the statement
"the search for meaning, growth and change" are trademarks of Bantam Books,
a division of Bantam Doubleday Dell Publishing Group, Inc.*

Library of Congress Cataloging-in-Publication Data

Bateson, Gregory.
  Angels fear.

  Includes index.
  1. Philosophy.   2. Anthropology.   3. Knowledge,
Theory of.   4. Religion.   I. Bateson, Mary Catherine.
II. Title.
B72.B37 1988   100   88-47528
ISBN 0-553-34581-8 (pbk.)

Published simultaneously in the United States and Canada

PRINTED IN THE UNITED STATES OF AMERICA

CW   0 9 8 7 6 5 4 3 2 1

This book is for
LOIS BATESON
and
BARKEV KASSARJIAN.
Without them we would not
have been ourselves.

Full fathom five thy father lies;
    Of his bones are coral made;
Those are pearls that were his eyes:
    Nothing of him that doth fade,
But doth suffer a sea-change
Into something rich and strange.
Sea-nymphs hourly ring his knell:
                  Ding-dong.
Hark! now I hear them, —Ding-dong, bell.

—SHAKESPEARE, *The Tempest*

Contents

Acknowledgments   xi

I   Introduction (MCB & GB)   1

II   The World of Mental Process (GB)   16

III   Metalogue: Why Do You Tell Stories? (MCB)   31

IV   The Model (GB)   36

V   Neither Supernatural nor Mechanical (GB)   50

VI   Metalogue: Why Placebos? (MCB)   65

VII   Let Not Thy Left Hand Know (GB)   69

VIII   Metalogue: Secrets (MCB)   82

IX   Defenses of Faith (GB)   88

X   Metalogue: Are You Creeping Up? (MCB)   100

XI   The Messages of Nature and Nurture (GB)   110

XII   Metalogue: Addiction (MCB & GB)   125

XIII   The Unmocked God (GB)   135

XIV   Metalogue: It's Not Here (MCB)   145

XV   The Structure in the Fabric (GB)   151

XVI   Innocence and Experience (GB & MCB)   167

XVII   So What's a Meta For? (MCB)   183

XVIII   Metalogue: Persistent Shade (MCB)   201

Glossary   206

Notes on Chapter Sources   213

Index   216

Acknowledgments

It was six years ago that I undertook to complete the book my father was working on at the time of his death, and a great deal has happened in the interval. My first thanks should go to those who have waited patiently for a work they were already anxiously looking forward to, my father's widow, Lois Bateson, other family members, my father's publisher, and common friends and colleagues, who have exercised great restraint in pressing for completion.

A number of institutions have played a role in making this work possible, particularly in providing the settings and contexts for Gregory's work and thought: the Esalen Institute, the Camaldolese Hermitage in Big Sur, San Francisco Zen Center, the Lindisfarne Association. The Institute for Intercultural Studies has formal disposition of my father's literary estate and provided me with a computer on which the manuscript was typed. Amherst College facilitated this work by permitting me to go off salary and put necessary distance between myself and that institution, making concentrated work and creative thought possible.

This book has had the same agent, John Brockman, and editor, William Whitehead, since it was first conceived, and these two have been highly supportive in keeping it alive through changes in both authorship and publisher. Other individuals who played an important role include Lois Bateson, my brother, John Bateson, at whose home in British Columbia several chapters were composed, Joseph and Jane Wheelwright. More recently, I have benefited from help and suggestions from

Rodney Donaldson, Richard Goldsby, Jean Houston, David Sofield, William Irwin Thompson, and Francisco Varela, each of whom has contributed a valuable perspective, whether for change or for restraint.

Most of my work on this book has been done in Cambridge, Massachusetts, with the support of my most enlivening critic, my husband, Barkev Kassarjian. I have also relied on the companionship of a large, sweet Akita puppy who tirelessly assures me that epistemology is indeed a matter of relationship and comforts me for the vagaries of the computer.

MCB

Cambridge, Massachusetts
August 1986

ANGELS
FEAR

I Introduction (MCB & GB)

I. SETTING THE CONTEXT (MCB)

In 1978, my father, Gregory Bateson, completed the book titled *Mind and Nature: A Necessary Unity* (Dutton, 1979). Under the threat of imminent death from cancer, he had called me from Tehran to California so we could work on it together. Almost immediately, as it became clear that the cancer was in extended remission, he started work on a new book, to be called *Where Angels Fear to Tread*, but often referred to by him as *Angels Fear*. In June 1980 I came out to Esalen, where he was living, having heard that his health was again deteriorating, and he proposed that we collaborate on the new book, this time as coauthors. He died on July 4, without our having had the opportunity to begin work, and after his death I set the manuscript aside while I followed through on other commitments, including the writing of *With a Daughter's Eye* (Morrow, 1984), which was already under way. Now at last, working with the stack of manuscript Gregory left at his death—miscellaneous, unintegrated, and incomplete—I have tried to make of it the collaboration he intended.

It has not seemed to me urgent to rush this work forward. Indeed, I have been concerned on my own part to respect the warning buried in Gregory's title: not, as a fool, to rush in. The real synthesis of Gregory's work is in *Mind and Nature*, the first of his books composed to com-

1

municate with the nonspecialist reader. *Steps to an Ecology of Mind* (Chandler, 1972, and Ballantine, 1975) had brought together the best of Gregory's articles and scientific papers, written for a variety of specialist audiences and published in a multiplicity of contexts, and in the process Gregory became fully aware of the potential for integration. The appearance of *Steps* also demonstrated the existence of an audience eager to approach Gregory's work as a way of thinking, regardless of the historically shifting contexts in which it had first been formulated, and this moved him along to a new synthesis and a new effort of communication.

Where Angels Fear to Tread was to be different. He had become aware gradually that the unity of nature he had affirmed in *Mind and Nature* might only be comprehensible through the kind of metaphors familiar from religion; that, in fact, he was approaching that integrative dimension of experience he called the *sacred*. This was a matter he approached with great trepidation, partly because he had been raised in a dogmatically atheistic household and partly because he saw the potential in religion for manipulation, obscurantism, and division. The mere use of the word *religion* is likely to trigger reflexive misunderstanding. The title of the book therefore expresses, among other things, his hesitation and his sense of addressing new questions, questions that follow from and depend upon his previous work but require a different kind of wisdom, a different kind of courage. I feel the same trepidation. This work is a testament, but one that passes on a task not to me only but to all those prepared to wrestle with such questions.

In preparing this book, I have had to consider a number of traditions about how to deal with a manuscript left uncompleted at the time of a death. The most obvious and scholarly alternative was that of scrupulously separating our voices, with a footnote or a bracket every time I made an editorial change and a *sic* every time I refrained when my judgment suggested that a change was needed. However, since it was Gregory's own intention that we complete this manuscript together, I decided not to follow the route of the disengaged editor, so I have corrected and made minor alterations in his sections as needed. The original manuscripts will, of course, be preserved, so that if the work proves to merit that kind of attention, someone someday can write a scholarly monograph about the differences between manuscripts and published text that incorporates the work of us both. I will limit my scrupulosity to the preservation of the sources. After some hesitation, I decided not to supplement the materials Gregory had designated for possible use in this book by drawing extensively on his other writings, but I have made omissions and choices, as Gregory would have. Material that partly duplicates previous publications, however, has often been retained for its contribution to the overall argument.

On the other hand, where my additions or disagreements were truly substantive, I have not been prepared simply to slip them in, writing prose that the reader might mistake for Gregory's own. This would be to return to the role of amanuensis, the role I was cast in for *Mind and Nature*, in which I merged all of my contributions in his, as wives and daughters have done for centuries. The making of this book has itself been a problem of ecology and of epistemology, because Gregory's knowing was embedded in a distinctive pattern of relationship and conversation.

Thus, it seemed important that when I made significant additions, it should be clear that these, right or wrong, were my own. I have chosen to do this partly in the form of inserted sections, set in square brackets, and partly in the form of what Gregory called metalogues. Over a period of nearly forty years, Gregory used a form of dialogue he had developed between "Father" and "Daughter," putting comments and questions into the mouth of a fictionalized "Daughter," asking the perennial question, "Daddy, why . . . ," to allow himself to articulate his own thinking. Over a period of about twenty years, we actually worked together, sometimes on written texts, sometimes in public dialogue or dialogue within the framework of a larger conference, and sometimes across the massive oak table in the Bateson household, arguing our way towards clarity. The fictional character he had created, who initially incorporated only fragmentary elements of fact in our relationship, grew older, becoming less fictional in two ways: "Daughter" came to resemble me more fully, and at the same time I modeled my own style of interaction with Gregory on hers.

This was a gradual process. Part of the dilemma I faced in deciding how to deal with the materials Gregory left was that he never defined what he was doing in relation to me. He attributed words to a character named "Daughter," words that were sometimes real and sometimes imagined, sometimes plausible and sometimes quite at odds with anything I might have said. Now I have had to deal with an uncompleted manuscript left by him, using my own experience of the occasions we worked together and my understanding of the issues as guides. The lines given to "Father" in these metalogues are sometimes things Gregory said in other contexts, often stories he told repeatedly. But these did not, as conversations, ever occur as presented here. They are just as real—and just as fictional—as the metalogues Gregory wrote himself. Like Gregory, I have found the form sufficiently useful and flexible not to observe stringently his original requirement that each metalogue exemplify its subject matter in its form, but, unlike his metalogues, the ones in this book were not designed to stand separately. Nevertheless, it seems important to emphasize that the father-daughter relationship continues to be a rather precise vehicle for issues that Gregory wanted to address because it functions as a reminder that the conversation is always moving between intellect and emotion, always dealing with relationship and communication, within and between systems. Above all, the metalogues contain the questions and comments I would have raised had we worked on this manuscript together, as well as my best approximation of what Gregory would have said. I have also allowed myself near the end to emerge from the child role of the metalogues and to write in my own present voice. Each section of the book is labeled "GB" or "MCB," but this should be understood to be very approximate, meaning no more than "primarily GB" or "primarily MCB." The section of Notes on Chapter Sources provides further detail.

At the top of the stack of materials Gregory had accumulated for the book was a draft introduction, one of several, that began with this story:

"In England when I was a boy, every railroad train coming in from a long run was inspected by a man with a hammer. The hammer had a very small head and a very long handle, rather like a drumstick, and it was indeed designed to make a sort of music. The man walked down the whole length of the train, tapping every hotbox as he walked. He was testing to find out if any one was cracked and would therefore emit a discordant sound. The integration, we may say, had to be tested again and again. Similarly, I have tried to tap every sentence in the book to test for faults of integration. It was often easier to hear the discordant note of the false juxtaposition than to say for what harmony I was searching."

I only wish that in drafting an introduction Gregory had been describing something he had actually done rather than something he still aspired to do. Gregory was working in an interval of unknown length while his cancer was in remission. He was living at Esalen, an environment where he had warm friendships but not close intellectual collaborations. Even though the "counterculture" has faded in the 1980s, Gregory's occasional references to it provide a clarifying contrast, for the shifting population and preoccupations of Esalen underlined his essential alienation. Always, for Gregory, the problem was to get the ideas and the words right, but his life-style in that last period, without a permanent base or a steady source of income, required that he keep on producing, reiterating, and recombining the various elements of his thought as he sang for his supper, but without doing the tuning or making the integration that they needed. It also meant that Gregory, always sparing in his reading, was more cut off than ever before from ongoing scientific work. He combined great and continuing originality with a store of tools and information acquired twenty years earlier. In effect, his groping poses a challenge to readers to make their own creative synthesis, combining his insights with the tools and information available today, advances in cognitive science, molecular biology, and systems theory that are nonetheless still subject to the kinds of muddle and intellectual vulgarity he warned against.

There is no way that I can make this manuscript into what Gregory wanted it to be, and at some level I doubt that Gregory could have done so or that we could have done it together. Certainly what he wanted was still amorphous at the time of his death, the thinking still incomplete. But although the ideas were not yet in full flower, they were surely implicit in the process of growth. Surely, too, the richest legacy lies in his questions and in his way of formulating questions.

In the autumn after the completion of *Mind and Nature*, living at Esalen, Gregory wrote several poems, one of which seems to me to express what he felt he had attempted in the work just completed, and perhaps an aspiration for the work that lay ahead.

The Manuscript

So there it is in words
Precise
And if you read between the lines
You will find nothing there
For that is the discipline I ask
Not more, not less

Not the world as it is
Nor ought to be—
Only the precision
The skeleton of truth
I do not dabble in emotion
Hint at implications

> Evoke the ghosts of old forgotten creeds
>
> All that is for the preacher
> The hypnotist, therapist and missionary
> They will come after me
> And use the little that I said
> To bait more traps
> For those who cannot bear
>> The lonely
>>> Skeleton
>>>> of Truth

Because Gregory's manuscript did not yet correspond to this aspiration, I could not read it as the poem commands. It has not been possible for me to avoid reading between the lines—indeed, that has often been the only way I could proceed. Often, too, working within the context of a metalogue, I have deliberately admitted emotion and evocation. In fact, Gregory's own language was often highly evocative. His ambition was to achieve formalism, but as he groped and ruminated, he often relied on less rigorous forms of discourse.

The poem is important here, however, not only for what it asserts about method and style, but because it proposes a context for interpretation. In this poem, Gregory was expressing real caution and irritation. A great many people, recognizing that Gregory was critical of certain kinds of materialism, wished him to be a spokesman for an opposite faction, a faction advocating the kind of attention they found comfortable to things excluded by atomistic materialism: God, spirits, ESP, "the ghosts of old forgotten creeds." Gregory was always in the difficult position of saying to his scientific colleagues that they were failing to attend to critically important matters, because of methodological and epistemological premises central to Western science for centuries, and then turning around and saying to his most devoted followers, when they believed they were speaking about these same critically important matters, that the way they were talking was nonsense.

In Gregory's view, neither group was able to talk sense, for nothing sensible could be said about these matters, given the version of the Cartesian separation of mind and matter that has become habitual in Western thought. Again and again he returns to his rejection of this dualism: mind without matter cannot exist; matter without mind can exist but is inaccessible. Transcendent deity is an impossibility. Gregory wanted to continue to speak to both sides of our endemic dualism, wanted indeed to invite them to adopt a *monism*, a unified view of the world that would allow for both scientific precision and systematic attention to notions that scientists often exclude.

As Gregory affirmed in his poem, he had a sense of his thinking as skeletal. This is a double claim: on the one hand, it is a claim of formalism and rigor; on the other hand, it is a claim to deal with fundamentals, with what underlies the proliferation of detail in natural phenomena. However, it was not dry bones that he aspired to outline but the functioning framework of life, life that in the widest sense includes the entire living planet throughout its evolution.

In attempting to rethink these issues, Gregory had arrived at a strategy of redefinition, a strategy of taking words like "love" or "wisdom," "mind" or "the sacred"—the words for matters that the nonmaterialists feel are important and that scientists often regard as inaccessible to study—and redefining them by invoking the conceptual tools of cybernetics. In his writing, technical terms occur side by side with the words of ordinary language, but these less daunting words are often redefined in unfamiliar ways. (A glossary has been provided at the end of the book.)

Inevitably, this attracted several kinds of criticism: criticism from those most committed to the orthodoxy of the meaninglessness of these terms, asserting that they are impermissible in scientific discourse; criticism from those committed to other kinds of religious and philosophical orthodoxy, arguing that these terms already have good, established meanings which Gregory failed to understand and respect; and, finally, the criticism that to use a term in an idiosyncratic way or to give it an idiosyncratic definition is a form of rhetorical dishonesty—one for which Alice taxed Humpty Dumpty.

In fact, Gregory was endeavoring to do with words like "mind" or "love" what the physicists did with words like *force*, *energy*, or *mass*, even though the juxtaposition of a rigorous definition with fuzzy popular usage can be a continual source of problems. It is a pedagogue's trick, counting on the redefined term to be at once memorable and grounded, to be relevant both to general discourse and matters of value. But what is most important to Gregory is that his understanding of such words as "mind" should be framed in precision, able to coexist with mathematical formalism.

The central theme of *Mind and Nature* was that evolution is a *mental* process. This was shorthand for the assertion that evolution is systemic and that the process of evolution shares key characteristics with other systemic processes, including thought. The aggregate of these characteristics provided Gregory with his own definition for the words "mental" and "mind," words that had become virtually taboo in scientific discourse. This allowed him to emphasize what interested him most about thought and evolution, that they are in an important sense analogous: they share a "pattern which connects," so that a concentration on their similarities will lead to significant new insight with regard to each, particularly the way in which each allows for something like anticipation or purpose. The choice of such a word as "mind" is deliberately evocative, reminding the reader of the range of issues proposed by these words in the past and suggesting that these are properly matters for passion.

Similarly, Gregory has found a place to stand and speak of "God," somewhere between those who find the word unusable and those who use it all too often to argue positions that Gregory regarded as untenable. Playfully, he proposed a new name for the deity, but in full seriousness he searched for an understanding of the related but more general term "the sacred," moving gingerly and cautiously onto holy ground, "where angels fear to tread." Given what we know about the biological world (that knowledge that Gregory called "ecology," with considerable cybernetic revision of the usage of this term by members of the contemporary biological profession), and given what we are able to understand about "knowing" (what Gregory called "epistemology," again within a cybernetic framework), he was attempting to clarify what one might mean by "the sacred." Might the concept of the sacred refer to matters intrinsic to description, and thus be recognized as part of "necessity"? And if a viable clarity could be achieved, would it allow important new insight? It seems possible that a mode of knowing that attributes a certain sacredness to the organization of the biological world might be, in some significant sense, more accurate and more appropriate to decision making.

Gregory was quite clear that the matters discussed in *Mind and Nature*, the various ways of looking at the biological world and at thought, were necessary preliminaries to the challenge of this present volume, although they are not fully argued here. In this book he approached a set of questions that were implicit in his work over a very long period, again and again pushed back: not only the question of "the sacred," but also the question of "the aesthetic," and the question of "consciousness."

This was a constellation of issues which, for Gregory, needed to be addressed in order to arrive at a theory of action in the living world, a cybernetic ethics, and it is this that I have listened for above all in his drafts. Imagining himself at the moment of completion, Gregory wrote, "It was still necessary to study the resulting sequences and to state in words the nature of their music." This is necessary still, and can in some measure be attempted, for the implicit waits to be discovered, like a still-unstated theorem in geometry, hidden within the axioms. Between the lines? Perhaps. For Gregory did not have time to make sure that the words were complete.

II. DEFINING THE TASK (GB)

The actual writing of this book has been a research, an exploration step by step into a subject matter whose overall shape became visible only gradually as coherence emerged and discord was eliminated.

It is easier to say what the book is not about than to define the harmony for which I was searching. It is not about psychology or economics or sociology, except insofar as these are chiaroscuro within some larger body of knowledge. It is not exactly about ecology or anthropology. There is the still wider subject called epistemology, which transcends all the others, and it seems that the glimpses of an order higher than that of any of these disciplines have come when I have touched on the *fact* of anthropological and ecological order.

The book, then, is a comparative study of matters that arise from anthropology and local epistemology. As anthropologists we study the ethics of every people and go on from there to study comparative ethics. We try to see the particular and local ethics of each tribe against a background of our knowledge of ethics in other systems. Similarly it is possible, and begins to be fashionable, to study the epistemology of every people, the structures of knowing and the pathways of computation. From this kind of study it is natural to go on to compare the epistemology implicit in one cultural system with that in other systems.

But what is disclosed when comparative ethics and comparative epistemology are set side by side? And when both are combined with economics? And when all is compared with morphogenesis and comparative anatomy?

Such comparison will inevitably drive the investigator back to the elemental details of what is happening. He must make up his mind about the universal *minima* of the overlapping of all these fields of study. The minima are not parts of any one field; they are not parts even of behavioral science at all. They are parts, if you will, of *necessity*. Some are what Saint Augustine called Eternal Verities, others are perhaps what Jung called archetypes. These fundamentals, which must underlie all of our thought, are the subject matter of the next section.

Of course, the anthropologist and the epistemologist, the psychologist and the students of history and economics will all have to deal, each in his or her field of concentration, with every one of these Eternal Verities. But the verities are not the subject matter of any special field and are, indeed, commonly concealed and avoided by the concentration of attention upon the problems proper to each specialized field.

Many before me, aware of these higher levels of order and organization and sense, including Saint Augustine himself, have attempted to share their discoveries with those who came after. There is a vast literature of such sharing. In particular, every one of the great religions has contributed texts to the unraveling of these matters—or sometimes to their further obfuscation.

Again, many of the contributions of the past have been made within the historically unique context of science, and yet today the intellectual preoccupation with quantity, the artificiality of experiment, and the dualism of Descartes combine to make these matters even more difficult of access than they have been heretofore. Science, for good reason, is impatient of muddled definitions and foggy confusions of logical typing, but in attempting to avoid these dangers, it has precluded discussion of matters of first—indeed of primary—importance.

It is, alas, too true, however, that muddleheadedness has helped the human race to find "God." Today, in any Christian, Buddhist, or Hindu sermon, you are likely to hear the mystic's faith extolled and recommended for reasons that should raise the hackles of any person undrugged and unhypnotized. No doubt the discussion of high orders of regularity in articulate language is difficult, especially for those who are untrained in verbal precision, so they may be forgiven if they take refuge in the cliché "Those who talk don't know, and those who know don't talk." If the cliché were true, it would follow that all the vast and often beautiful mystical literature of Hinduism, Buddhism, Taoism, and Christianity must have been written by persons who did not know what they were writing about.

Be that as it may, I claim no originality, only a certain timeliness. It cannot now be wrong to contribute to this vast literature. I claim not uniqueness but membership in a small minority who believe that there are strong and clear arguments for the *necessity* of the sacred, and that these arguments have their base in an epistemology rooted in improved science and in the obvious. I believe that these arguments are important at the present time of widespread skepticism—even that they are today as important as the testimony of those whose religious faith is based on inner light and "cosmic" experience. Indeed, the steadfast faith of an Einstein or a Whitehead is worth a thousand sanctimonious utterances from traditional pulpits.

In the Middle Ages, it was characteristic of theologians to attempt a rigor and precision that today characterize only the best science. The *Summa theologica* of Saint Thomas Aquinas was the thirteenth-century equivalent of today's textbooks of cybernetics. Saint Thomas divided all created things into four classes: *(a)* those which just are—as stones; *(b)* those which are and live—as plants; *(c)* those which are and live and move—as animals; and *(d)* those which are and live and move and think—as men. He knew no cybernetics and (unlike Augustine) he was no mathematician, but we can immediately recognize here a prefiguring of some classification of entities based upon the number of logical types represented in their self-corrective and recursive loops of adaptation.

Saint Thomas's definition of Deadly Sin is marked with the same latent sophistication. A sin is recognized as "deadly" if its commission promotes further committing of the same sin by others, *"in the manner of a final cause."* (I note that, according to this definition, participation in an armaments race is among the sins that are deadly.) In fact, the mysterious "final causes" of Aristotle, as interpreted by Saint Thomas, fit right in with what modern cybernetics calls *positive feedback*, providing a first approach to the problems of purpose and causality [especially when causality appears not to flow with the flow of time].

One wonders whether later theology was not in many ways less so-phisticated than that of the thirteenth century. It is as if the thought of Descartes (1596–1650), especially the dualism of mind and matter, the *cogito*, and the Cartesian coordinates, were the climax of a long deca-dence. The Greek belief in final causes was crude and primitive, but it seemingly left the way open for a monistic view of the world, a way that later ages closed and finally buried by the dualistic separation of mind and matter, [which set many important and mysterious phenomena out-side of the material sphere that could be studied by science, leaving mind separate from body and God outside of the creation and both ignored by scientific thinking].*

For me, the Cartesian dualism was a formidable barrier, and it may amuse the reader to be told how I achieved a sort of monism—the conviction that mind and nature form a necessary unity, in which there is no mind *separate from* body and no god separate from his creation— and how, following that, I learned to look with new eyes at the integrated world. That was not how I was taught to see the world when I began work. The rules then were perfectly clear: in scientific explanation, there should be no use of mind or deity, and there should be no appeal to final causes. All causality should flow with the flow of time, with no effect of the future upon the present or the past. No deity, no teleology, and no mind should be postulated in the universe that was to be explained.

This very simple and rigorous creed was a standard for biology that had dominated the biological scene for 150 years. This particular brand of materialism had become fanatical following the publication of William Paley's *Evidences of Christianity* (in 1794, fifteen years before Lamarck's *Philosophie zoologique* and sixty-five years before *On the Origin of Species*). To mention "mind" or "teleology" or the "inheritance of acquired characters" was heresy in biological circles in the first forty years of the present century. And I am glad I learned that lesson well.

So well that I even wrote an anthropological book, *Naven*,† within the orthodox antiteleological frame, but, of course, the rigorous limitation of the premises had the effect of displaying their inadequacy. It was clear that upon those premises the culture could never be stable but would go into escalating change to its own destruction. That escalation I called *schismogenesis* and I distinguished two principal forms it might take, but I could not in 1936 see any real reason why the culture had survived so long, [or how it could include self-corrective mechanisms that *anticipated* the danger]. Like the early Marxists, I thought that escalating change must always lead to climax and destruction of the status quo.

I was ready then for cybernetics when this epistemology was proposed by Norbert Wiener, Warren McCulloch, and others at the famous Macy Conferences. Because I already had the idea of positive feedback (which I was calling schismogenesis), the ideas of self-regulation and negative

---

*Square brackets indicate an insert by MCB.

†*Naven: A Study of the Culture of a New Guinea Tribe from Three Points of View* (Cambridge, England: Cambridge UP, 1936). 2d ed., with additional "Epilogue 1958" (Stanford, Calif.: Stanford UP, 1958).

feedback fell for me immediately into place. I was off and running with paradoxes of purpose and final cause more than half-resolved, and aware that their resolution would require a step beyond the premises within which I had been trained.

In addition, I went to the Cybernetics Conferences with another notion which I had developed during World War II and which turned out to fit with a central idea in the structure of cybernetics. This was the recognition of what I called *deutero-learning*, or learning to learn.*

I had come to understand that "learning to learn" and "learning to deal with and expect a given kind of context for adaptive action" and "character change due to experience" are three synonyms for a single genus of phenomena, which I grouped together under the term *deutero-learning*. This was a first mapping of behavioral phenomena onto a scheme closely related to Bertrand Russell's hierarchy of logical types† and, like the idea of schismogenesis, was easily attuned to the cybernetic ideas of the 1940s. [The *Principia* of Russell and Whitehead provided a systematic way of handling logical hierarchies such as the relationship between an item, the class of items to which it belongs, and the class of classes. The application of these ideas to behavior laid the groundwork for thinking about how, in learning, experience is generalized to some class of contexts, and about the way in which some messages modify the meaning of others by labeling them as belonging to particular classes of messages.]

The significance of all this formalization was made more evident in the 1960s by a reading of Carl Jung's *Seven Sermons to the Dead*, of which the Jungian therapist Jane Wheelwright gave me a copy.‡ I was at the time writing a draft of what was to be my Korzybski Memorial Lecture§ and began to think about the relation between "map" and "territory." Jung's book insisted upon the contrast between *Pleroma*, the crudely physical domain governed only by forces and impacts, and *Crea-*

---

*See G. Bateson, "Social Planning and the Concept of Deutero-Learning," *Steps*, 159–76 (Chandler ed.), and elsewhere.

†Alfred North Whitehead and Bertrand Russell, *Principia Mathematica*, 3 vols., 2d ed. (Cambridge, England: Cambridge UP, 1910–13).

‡Carl Gustav Jung's *Septem Sermones ad Mortuos* was privately published in 1916. There has been a more recent British edition (Stuart and Watkins, 1967), but the work is most accessible as a supplement to some editions of *Memories, Dreams, Reflections*, ed. Aniela Jaffe (New York: Pantheon, 1966 and later editions only).

§See my essay "Form, Substance and Difference," in *Steps*, 454–71 (Chandler ed.).

tura, the domain governed by distinctions and differences. It became abundantly clear that the two sets of concepts match and that there could be no maps in Pleroma, but only in Creatura. That which gets from territory to map is *news of difference*, and at that point I recognized that news of difference was a synonym for information.

When this recognition of difference was put together with the clear understanding that Creatura was organized into circular trains of causation, like those that had been described by cybernetics, and that it was organized in multiple levels of logical typing, I had a series of ideas all working together to enable me to think systematically about mental process as differentiated from simple physical or mechanistic sequences, without thinking in terms of two separate "substances." My book *Mind and Nature: A Necessary Unity* combined these ideas with the recognition that mental process and biological evolution are necessarily alike in these Creatural characteristics.

The mysteries that had challenged biology up to the epoch of cybernetics were, in principle, no longer mysterious, though, of course, much remained to be done. We now had ideas about the general nature of information, purpose, stochastic process, thought, and evolution, so that at that level it was a matter of working out the details of particular cases.

In place of the old mysteries, a new set of challenges emerged. This book is an attempt to outline some of these, [in particular, to explore the way in which, in a nondualistic view of the world, a new concept of the sacred emerges]. It is intended to begin the task of making the new challenges perceptible to the reader and perhaps to give some definition to the new problems. Further than that I do not expect to go. It took the world 2,500 years to resolve the problems that Aristotle proposed and Descartes compounded. The new problems do not appear to be easier to solve than the old, and it seems likely that my fellow scientists will have their work cut out for them for many years to come.

The title of the present book is intended to convey a warning. It seems that every important scientific advance provides tools which look to be just what the applied scientists and engineers had hoped for, and usually these gentry jump in without more ado. Their well-intentioned (but slightly greedy and slightly anxious) efforts usually do as much harm as good, serving at best to make conspicuous the next layer of problems, which must be understood before the applied scientists can be trusted not to do gross damage. Behind *every* scientific advance there is always a matrix, a mother lode of unknowns out of which the new partial answers have been chiseled. But the hungry, overpopulated, sick, ambitious, and competitive world will not wait, we are told, till more is known, but must rush in where angels fear to tread.

I have very little sympathy for these arguments from the world's "need." I notice that those who pander to its needs are often well paid. I distrust the applied scientists' claim that what they do is useful and necessary. I suspect that their impatient enthusiasm for action, their rarin'-to-go, is not just a symptom of impatience, nor is it pure buccaneering ambition. I suspect that it covers deep epistemological panic.

II   The World of

Mental Process (GB)

BEFORE we proceed further, I want to elaborate on the contrast made by Carl Gustav Jung* between Creatura and Pleroma. This will give us an alternative starting point for epistemology, one that will be a much healthier first step than the separation of mind from matter attributed to René Descartes. In place of the old Cartesian dualism, which proposed mind and matter as distinct substances, I want to talk about the nature of mental process, or *thought*, in the widest sense of that word, and the relationship between "thought" and the material world.

I am going to include within the category *mental process* a number of phenomena which most people do not think of as processes of thought. For example, I shall include the processes by which you and I achieve our anatomy—the injunctions, false starts and self-corrections, obediences to circumstance, and so on, by which the differentiation and development of the embryo is achieved. "Embryology" is for me a mental process. And I shall also include the still more mysterious processes by which it comes about that the formal relations of *our* anatomy are recognizable in the anthropoid ape, the horse, and the whale—what zoologists call *homology*—i.e. along with embryology I shall include *evolution* within the term "mental process."

*In *Septem Sermones ad Mortuos*. In later works, e.g. in *Answer to Job*, Jung uses these words in such a way as to include his archetypes within Pleroma. I believe that this latter usage is more in step with classical and medieval thought, but I also believe that Jung's earlier way of talking provides a clearer base for epistemology.

Along with those two big ones—biological evolution and embryology—I include all those lesser exchanges of information and injunction that occur inside organisms and between organisms and that, in the aggregate, we call *life*.

In fact, wherever *information*—or *comparison*—is of the essence of our explanation, *there*, for me, is mental process. Information can be defined as a *difference that makes a difference*. A sensory end organ is a comparator, a device which responds to difference. Of course, the sensory end organ is material, but it is this *responsiveness to difference* that we shall use to distinguish its functioning as "mental." Similarly, the ink on this page is material, but the ink is not my thought. Even at the most elementary level, the ink is not signal or message. The *difference* between paper and ink is the signal.

It is, of course, true that our explanations, our textbooks dealing with nonliving matter, are full of information. But this information is all *ours*; it is part of *our* life processes. The world of nonliving matter, the Pleroma, which is described by the laws of physics and chemistry, itself contains no description. A stone does not respond to information and does not use injunctions or information or trial and error in its internal organization. To respond in a behavioral sense, the stone would have to use energy contained within itself, as organisms do. It would cease to be a stone. The stone is affected by "forces" and "impacts," but not by differences.

I can describe the stone, but it can describe nothing. I can use the stone as a signal—perhaps as a landmark. But *it* is not the landmark.

I can give the stone a name; I can distinguish it from other stones. But it is not its name, and it cannot distinguish.

It uses and contains no information.

"It" is not even an *it*, except insofar as I distinguish it from the remainder of inanimate matter.

What happens to the stone and what it does when nobody is around is not part of the mental process of any living thing. For that it must somehow make and receive *news*.

You must understand that while Pleroma is without thought or information, it still contains—is the matrix of—many other sorts of regularities. Inertia, cause and effect, connection and disconnection, and so on, these regularities are (for lack of a better word) *immanent* in Pleroma. Although they can be translated (again for lack of a better word) into the language of Creatura (where alone language can exist), the material world still remains inaccessible, the Kantian *Ding an sich* which you cannot get close to. We can speculate—and we have speculated very carefully and very creatively about it—but in the end, at the last analysis, everything we say about Pleroma is a matter of speculation, and such mystics as William Blake, for example, frankly deny its existence.

In summary then, we will use Jung's term *Pleroma* as a name for that unliving world described by physics which in itself contains and makes no distinctions, though we must, of course, make distinctions in our description of it.

In contrast, we will use *Creatura* for that world of explanation in which the very phenomena to be described are among themselves governed and determined by difference, distinction, and information.

[Although there is an apparent dualism in this dichotomy between Creatura and Pleroma, it is important to be clear that these two are not in any way separate or separable, except as levels of description. On the one hand, all of Creatura exists within and through Pleroma; the use of the term *Creatura* affirms the presence of certain organizational and communicational characteristics which are themselves not material. On the other hand, knowledge of Pleroma exists only in Creatura. We can meet the two only in combination, never separately. The laws of physics and chemistry are by no means irrelevant to the Creatura—they continue to apply—but they are not sufficient for explanation. Thus, Creatura and Pleroma are not, like Descartes' "mind" and "matter," separate substances, for mental processes require arrangements of matter in which to occur, areas where Pleroma is characterized by organization which permits it to be affected by information as well as by physical events.

[We can move on from the notion of mental process to ask, what, then, is "a mind"? And if this is a useful notion, can one usefully make a plural and speak of "minds" which might engage in interactions which are in turn mental? The characterization of the notion of "a mind" was one of the central thrusts of *Mind and Nature*, where a series of criteria were laid out for the identification of "minds." The definition anchors the notion of a mind firmly to the arrangement of material parts:

1. *A mind is an aggregate of interacting parts or components.*
2. *The interaction between parts of mind is triggered by difference.*
3. *Mental process requires collateral energy.*
4. *Mental process requires circular (or more complex) chains of determination.*

5. *In mental process, the effects of difference are to be regarded as trans-forms (i.e. coded versions) of events which preceded them.*
6. *The description and classification of these processes of transformation disclose a hierarchy of logical types immanent in the phenomena.**

[If you consider these criteria, you will recognize that they fit a number of complex entities that we are used to talking about and investigating scientifically, such as animals and persons and, in fact, all organisms. They also apply to parts of organisms that have a degree of autonomy in their self-regulation and functioning: individual cells, for instance, and organs. Then, you can go on to notice that there is no requirement of a clear boundary, like a surrounding envelope of skin or membrane, and you can recognize that this definition includes only some of the characteristics of what we call "life." As a result, it applies to a much wider range of those complex phenomena called "systems," including systems consisting of multiple organisms or systems in which some of the parts are living and some are not, or even to systems in which there are no living parts. What is described here is a something that can receive information and can, through the self-regulation or self-correction made possible by circular trains of causation, maintain the truth of certain propositions about itself. These two provide the rudiments of identity—unlike the stone, the mind we are describing is an "it." There is, however, no reason to assume that it will be either conscious or capable of self-replication, like some of the minds we count among our friends and relatives. A given mind is likely to be a component or subsystem in some larger and more complex mind, as an individual cell may be a component in an organism, or a person may be a component in a community. The world of mental process opens into a self-organizing world of Chinese boxes in which information generates further information.

[This book is above all concerned with certain characteristics of the *interface* between Pleroma and Creatura and also with interfaces between different kinds of mental subsystems, including relations between persons and between human communities and ecosystems. We will be especially concerned with the way in which our understanding of such interfaces underlies epistemology and religion, bearing in mind that because what *is* is identical for all human purposes with what can be known, there can be no clear line between epistemology and ontology.]

When we distinguish Creatura from Pleroma by some first, primary

*p. 92.

act of distinguishing, we are founding the science of *Epistemology*, rules of thought. And our Epistemology is a *good* epistemology insofar as the regularities of Pleroma can be correctly, appropriately translated in our thought, and insofar as our understanding of Creatura, namely of all of embryology, biological evolution, ecology, thought, love and hate, and human organization—all of which require rather different kinds of description than those we use in describing the inanimate material world—can grow and sit on top of (can be comfortably deductive from) that primary step in Epistemology.

I think that Descartes' first epistemological steps—the separation of "mind" from "matter" and the *cogito*—established bad premises, perhaps ultimately lethal premises, for Epistemology, and I believe that Jung's statement of *connection* between Pleroma and Creatura is a much healthier first step. Jung's epistemology starts from comparison of difference—*not* from matter.

So I will define Epistemology as the science that studies the process of knowing—the interaction of the capacity to respond to differences, on the one hand, with the material world in which those differences somehow originate, on the other. We are concerned then with an *interface* between Pleroma and Creatura.

There is a more conventional definition of epistemology, which simply says that epistemology is the philosophic study of how knowledge is *possible*. I prefer my definition—how knowing is *done*—because it frames Creatura within the larger total, the presumably lifeless realm of Pleroma; and because my definition bluntly identifies Epistemology as the study of phenomena at an interface and as a branch of natural history.

Let me begin this study by mentioning a basic characteristic of the interface between Pleroma and Creatura, which will perhaps help to define the direction of my thinking. I mean the universal circumstance that the interface between Pleroma and Creatura is an example of the contrast between "map" and "territory"—is, I suppose, the primary and most fundamental example. This is the old contrast to which Alfred Korzybski* long ago called attention, and it remains basic for all healthy epistemologies and basic to Epistemology.

Every human individual—every organism—has his or her personal habits of how he or she builds knowledge, and every cultural, religious, or scientific system promotes particular epistemological habits. These

Science and Sanity (New York: Science P, 1941).

individual or local systems are indicated here with a small *e*. Warren McCulloch used to say that the man who claimed to have direct knowledge—i.e. no epistemology—had a bad one.

It is the task of anthropologists to achieve comparisons between the many and diverse systems and perhaps to evaluate the price that muddled systems pay for their errors. Most local epistemologies—personal and cultural—continually err, alas, in confusing map with territory and in assuming that the rules for drawing maps are immanent in the nature of that which is being represented in the map.

All of the following rules of accurate thought and communication apply to the properties of maps, that is, to mental process, for in the Pleroma there are no maps, no names, no classes, and no members of classes.

The map is not the territory.

The name is not the thing named.

The name of the name is not the name. (You remember the White Knight and Alice? Alice is rather tired of listening to songs and, offered yet another, she asks its name. "The name of the song is called 'Haddocks' Eyes,' " says the White Knight. "That's the name of the song, is it?" says Alice. "No, you don't understand," says the White Knight, "that's not the name of the song, that's what the name is *called*."*)

The item in the class is not the class (even when the class has only one item).

The class is not a member of itself.

Some classes have no members. (If, for example, I say, "I never read the small print," there is no class of events consisting of my reading the small print.)

In the Creatura, all is names, maps, and names of relations—but still the name of the name is not the name, and the name of the relation is not the relation—even when the relation between A and B is of the kind we denote by saying that A is the name of B.

These constraints are *Eternal*. They are necessarily true, and to recognize them gives something resembling freedom—or shall we say that it is a necessary condition of skill. It will be interesting to compare them with other basic components of Epistemology such as Saint Augustine's

---

*Lewis Carroll, *Alice Through the Looking Glass* (New York: New American Library, 1960), 212. GB here uses the example from *Alice* to make a transition from Korzybski to the theory of logical types.

Eternal Verities or Jung's archetypes, and see where these fall in relation to the interface.

Now, Saint Augustine was not only a theologian, he was also a mathematician. He lived in Hippo in North Africa and was probably more Semite than Indo-European, which means in the present context that he may very well have been quite at home in algebraic thought. It was, I gather, the Arabs who introduced the concept "any" into mathematics, thus creating algebra, for which we still use an Arabic word.

These verities were rather simple propositions, and here I quote Warren McCulloch,* to whom I owe much: "Listen to the thunder of that saint, in almost A.D. 500: 'Seven and three are ten; seven and three have always been ten; seven and three at no time and in no way have ever been anything but ten; seven and three will always be ten. I say that these indestructible truths of arithmetic are common to all who reason.' "

Saint Augustine's Eternal Verities were crudely or bluntly stated, but I think the saint would go along with the more modern versions: e.g. that the equation

$$x + y = z$$

is soluble, and *uniquely* soluble—there is only one solution—for all values of x and y, provided that we agree on the steps and tricks which we must use. If "quantities" are appropriately defined *and if* "addition" is appropriately defined, *then* $x + y = z$ is uniquely soluble. And z will be of one substance with x and y.

But, oh my, what a long step it is from the blunt statement "Seven plus three equals ten" to our cautious generalization hedged with definitions and conditions. We have in a certain sense pulled the whole of arithmetic over the line that was to divide Creatura from Pleroma. That is, the statement no longer has the flavor of naked truth and instead is clearly an artifact of human thought, indeed of the thought of particular humans at particular times and places.

Is it then so, that Saint Augustine's Eternal Verities are *only* spin-offs from peculiar ideas or customs cherished at various times by various human cultural systems?

I am an anthropologist by trade and training, and ideas of *cultural relativity* are a part of anthropological orthodoxy . . . but how far can cultural relativity go? What can the cultural relativist say about the Eternal

*Warren McCulloch, *Embodiments of Mind* (Cambridge, Mass.: MIT P, 1965), 3.

Verities? Does not arithmetic have roots in the unchanging, solid rock of Pleroma? And how can we talk about such a question?

Is there then such a subject of inquiry as Epistemology, with a capital E? Or is it all a matter of local and even personal epistemologies, any one of which is as good, as *right*, as any other?

These are the kinds of questions that arise when we try to survey the interface between Pleroma and Creatura, and it is clear that arithmetic somehow lies very close to that line.

But do not dismiss such questions as "abstract" or "intellectual," and therefore meaningless. For these abstract questions will lead us to some very immediately human matters. What sort of question are we asking when we say, "What is heresy?" or "What is a sacrament?" These are deeply human questions—matters of life and death, sanity and insanity, to millions of people—and the answers (if any) are concealed in the paradoxes generated by the line between Creatura and Pleroma . . . the line which the Gnostics, Jung, and I would substitute for the Cartesian separation of mind from matter . . . the line that is really a bridge or pathway for messages.

Is it possible to be Epistemologically *wrong*? Wrong at the very root of thought? Christians, Moslems, Marxists (and many biologists) say *yes*— they call such error "heresy" and equate it with spiritual death. The other religions—Hinduism, Buddhism, the more frankly pluralistic religions— seem to be largely unaware of the problem. The possibility of Epistemological error does not enter their epistemology. And today in America it is almost heresy to believe that the roots of thought have any importance, and it is undemocratic to excommunicate a man for Epistemological errors. If religions are concerned with Epistemology, how shall we interpret the fact that some have the concept of "heresy" and some do not?

I believe that the story goes back to the most sophisticated religion that the world has known—that of the Pythagoreans. Like Saint Augustine, they knew that Truth has some of its roots (not all) in numerology, in numbers. The history is obscure, probably because it is difficult for us to see the world through Pythagorean eyes, but it seems to be something like this: Egyptian mathematics was pure arithmetic and always particular, never making the jump from "seven and three are ten" to "x plus y equals z." Their mathematics contained no *deductions* and no proofs as we would understand the term. The Greeks had proofs from about the fifth century B.C., but it seems that mere deduction is a toy until the discovery of proof of an impossibility by *reductio ad absurdum*. The Pythagoreans had a whole string of theorems (which are not taught in schools today) about the relations between odd and even numbers. The climax of this study was the proof that the isosceles right triangle, with sides of unit length, is insoluble—that $\sqrt{2}$ cannot be either an odd or an even number, and therefore cannot be a number or be expressed as a ratio between two numbers. *

This discovery hit the Pythagoreans squarely between the eyes and became a central secret (but why secret?), an esoteric tenet of their faith. Their religion had been founded on the discontinuity of the series of musical harmonics—the demonstration that that discontinuity was indeed *real* and was firmly founded upon rigorous deduction.

And now they faced an impossibility proof. Deduction had said *no*.

As I read the story, from then on it was inevitable to "believe," to "see" and "know" that a contradiction among the higher generalizations will always lead to mental chaos. From this point on, the idea of heresy, the notion that to be wrong in Epistemology could be lethal, was inevitable.

All this sweat and tears—and even blood—was to be shed on quite abstract propositions whose Truth seemed to lie, in some sense, outside the human mind.

As I see it, the propositions that Augustine and Pythagoras were interested in and which Augustine called Eternal Verities are, in a sense, latent in Pleroma—only waiting to be *labeled* by some scientist. If, for example, a man is pouring lentils or grains of sand from one container into another, he is not aware of any numbering of the units, but still within the crowd of lentils or grains it is true—or would be true if somebody got in there and did some counting (perhaps the ghost of Bishop Berkeley might be willing to do it for us, just to make sure that the truth is still the same when *we* are not there)—that *seven plus three equals ten* among the lentils.

In this sense there is a whole slew of regularities out there in Pleroma, unnamed, ready to be picked up. But the distinctions and differences that would be used in an analysis have not been drawn, in the absence of organisms to whom the differences can make a difference. (Bishop Berkeley always forgot the grass and the squirrels in the woods, for whom the falling tree made a *meaningful* sound!)

*Gregory seems to have become interested in this material as the result of an article by Curtis Wilson, "On the Discovery of Deductive Science," *The St. John's Review* (January 1980): 21–31.

I want to make very clear the contrast between Pleromatic regularities and those regularities that exist inside mental and organized systems—the necessary limitations and patterns of mental process, such as those of coding and logical typing.

McCulloch's famous double question: "What is a number that a man may know it: and what is a man that he may know a number?"* takes on a very different coloring, presents new difficulties, when we substitute some archetype for the utterly impersonal concept "number." The Jungian archetypes have a certain claim to transcend the purely local, but they belong squarely in the realm of Creatura.

What is a *father* that a man, a woman, or a child may know him; and what is a man, or woman, or child, that he or she may know a father?

Let me offer you an example, what in field anthropology we would call a native text—a crucial cultural utterance:

> Our Father which art in heaven,
> Hallowed be thy name.

The epistemology latent in that text is enough to keep us busy for a long while.

The words themselves are sanctified—hallowed, to use their own idiom—by the gospel narrative (Matt. 6:9), according to which Jesus recommended this prayer to his disciples for myriad repetition. In every Christian ceremony, these words are in a strange way the rock upon which the whole structure stands—the words are the familiar theme to which the ritual continually returns, not as to a logical premise but rather as music returns to a theme or phrase from which it is built.

For while the quasi-Pleromatic verities of Augustine and Pythagoras have roots in logic or mathematics, we are now looking at something different.

"Our Father . . ."

This is the language of metaphor, and a very strange language it is.

First we need some contrasting data to show that we are in the realm of epistemology with a small *e*. (If you would seek for an absolute Epistemology among the metaphors, you must go one or perhaps two stories higher—straight on and up the stairs . . .)

In Bali, when a shaman, or *balian*, goes into a state of altered consciousness, he or she speaks with the voice of a god, using the pronouns

*Embodiments of Mind, 1–18.

appropriate to the god, and so on. And when this voice addresses ordinary adult mortals, it will call them "Papa" or "Mama." For the Balinese think of the relationship between gods and people as between children and parents, and in this relationship it is the gods who are the children and the people who are the parents.

The Balinese do not expect their gods to be *responsible*. They do not feel cheated when the gods are capricious. Indeed, they enjoy minor caprice and charm as these are exhibited by gods temporarily incarnate in shamans. How unlike our dear Job!

This particular metaphor, then, between fatherhood and godhead, is by no means eternal or universal. In other words, the "logic" of metaphor is something very different from the logic of the verities of Augustine and Pythagoras. Not, you understand, "wrong," but totally different. [It may be, however, that while particular metaphors are local, the *process of making metaphor* has some wider significance—may indeed be a basic characteristic of Creatura.]

Let me point up the contrast between the truths of metaphor and the truths that the mathematicians pursue by a rather violent and inappropriate trick. Let me spell out metaphor into syllogistic form: Classical logic named several varieties of syllogism, of which the best known is the "syllogism in Barbara." It goes like this:

> Men die;
> Socrates is a man;
> Socrates will die.

The basic structure of this little monster—its skeleton—is built upon classification. The predicate ("will die") is attached to Socrates by identifying him as a member of a class whose members share that predicate.

The syllogisms of metaphor are quite different, and go like this:

> Grass dies;
> Men die;
> Men are grass.

[In order to talk about this kind of syllogism and compare it to the "syllogism in Barbara," we can nickname it the "syllogism in grass."] I understand that teachers of classical logic strongly disapprove of this way of arguing and call it "affirming the consequent," and, of course, this pedantic condemnation is justified if what they condemn is *confusion* between one type of syllogism and the other. But to try to fight all syllogisms in grass would be silly because these syllogisms are the very stuff of which natural history is made. When we look for regularities in the biological world, we meet them all the time.

Von Domarus long ago pointed out that schizophrenics commonly talk and act in terms of syllogisms in grass,* and I think he, too, disapproved of this way of organizing knowledge and life. If I remember rightly, he does not notice that poetry, art, dream, humor, and religion share with schizophrenia a preference for syllogisms in grass.

But whether you approve or disapprove of poetry, dream, and psychosis, the generalization remains that biological data make sense—are connected together—by syllogisms in grass. The whole of animal behavior, the whole of repetitive anatomy, and the whole of biological evolution—each of these vast realms is within itself linked together by syllogisms in grass, whether the logicians like it or not.

It's really very simple—in order to make syllogisms in Barbara, you must have *identified classes*, so that subjects and predicates can be differentiated. But, apart from language, there are no named classes and no subject-predicate relations. Therefore, syllogisms in grass must be the dominant mode of communicating interconnection of ideas in all preverbal realms.

I think the first person who actually saw this clearly was Goethe, who noted that if you examine a cabbage and an oak tree, two rather different sorts of organism, but still both flowering plants, you would find that the way to talk about how they are put together is different from the way most people naturally talk. You see, we talk as if the Creatura were really Pleromatic: we talk about "things," notably leaves or stems, and we try to determine what is what. Now Goethe discovered that a "leaf" is defined as that which grows on a stem and has a bud in its angle; what then comes out of that angle (out of that bud) is again a stem. The correct units of description are not leaf and stem but the relations between them.

*E. von Domarus, "The Specific Laws of Logic in Schizophrenia," *Language and Thought in Schizophrenia*, ed. J. S. Kasanin (Berkeley: U of California P, 1944). GB developed these ideas in response to criticism by Nick Humphrey ("New Ideas, Old Ideas," *The London Review of Books*, 6 December 1979) of the argument of *Mind and Nature*, which may be said to have the following structure:

Evolution is stochastic (able to achieve novelty by a
    combination of random and selective processes);
Mental process (such as thought) is stochastic;
Evolution is a mental process.

These correspondences allow you to look at another flowering plant—a potato, for instance—and recognize that the part that you eat in fact corresponds to a stem.

In the same way, most of us were taught in school that a noun is the name of a person, place, or thing, but what we should have been taught is that a noun can stand in various kinds of relationship to other parts of the sentence, so that the whole of grammar could be defined as relationship and not in terms of things. This naming activity, which probably other organisms don't indulge in, is in fact a sort of Pleromatizing of the living world. And observe that grammatical relationships are of the preverbal kind. "The ship struck a reef" and "I spanked my daughter" are tied together by grammatical analogy.

·

I went to see the nice little pack of wolves in Chicago at the Brookfield Zoo, ten of them lying asleep all day and the eleventh one, the dominant male, busily running around keeping track of things. Now what wolves do is to go out hunting and then come home and regurgitate their food to share with the puppies who weren't along on the hunt. And the puppies can signal the adults to regurgitate. But eventually the adult wolves wean the babies from the regurgitated food by pressing down with their jaws on the backs of the babies' necks. In the domestic dog, females eventually wean their young from milk in the same way. In Chicago they told me that the previous year one of the junior males had succeeded in mounting a female. Up rushed the lead male—the alpha animal—but instead of mayhem all that happened was that the leader pressed the head of the junior male down to the ground in the same way, once, twice, four times, and then walked off. The communication that occurred was metaphoric: "You puppy, you!" The communication to the junior wolf of how to behave is based on a syllogism in grass.

But let us go back to the Lord's Prayer:

> Our Father which art in heaven,
> Hallowed be thy name.

Of course, my assertion that all preverbal and nonverbal communication depends upon metaphor and/or syllogisms in grass does not mean that all verbal communication is—or should be—logical or nonmetaphoric. Metaphor runs right through Creatura, so, of course, all verbal communication necessarily contains metaphor. And metaphor when it is dressed in words has added to it those characteristics that verbalism can achieve: the possibility of simple negation (there is no *not* at the preverbal level), the possibility of classification, of subject-predicate differentiation, and the possibility of explicit context marking.

Finally there is the possibility, with words, of jumping right out of the metaphoric and poetic mode into *simile*. What Vaihinger called the *as if* mode of communication becomes something else when the *as if* is added. In a word, it becomes *prose*, and then all the limitations of the syllogisms that logicians prefer, Barbara and the rest, must be precisely obeyed.

The Lord's Prayer might then become:

It is as if you or something were alive and personal, and if that were so, it would perhaps be appropriate to talk to you in words. So, although, of course, you are not a relative of mine, since you only *as if* exist and are, as it were, in another plane (in heaven), etc. . . . .

And you know, in human ethnography, the creativeness of human minds is capable of that extreme, and most surprisingly, that extreme can itself constitute a religion—among behaviorists for example. In a currently fashionable metaphor, the right hemisphere can applaud (and be reassured in) the prosy, cautious logic of the left.

The very act of translation—from grass to Barbara, from metaphor to simile, and from poetry to prose—can itself become *sacramental*, a sacred metaphor for a particular religious stance. Cromwell's troops could run around England, breaking the noses and even heads and genitals off the statues in the churches, *in a religious fervor*, simultaneously stressing their own total misunderstanding of what the metaphoric-sacred is all about.

I used to say—have said many times—that the Protestant interpretation of the words "This is my Body—This is my Blood" substitutes something like "This stands for my Body—This stands for my Blood." This way of interpretation banished from the Church that part of the mind that makes metaphor, poetry, and religion—the part of the mind that most belonged in Church—but *you cannot keep it out*. There is no doubt that Cromwell's troops were making their own (horrible) poetry by their acts of vandalism—in which indeed they smashed the metaphoric genitals *as if* they were "real" in a left brain sense—

What a mess. But nonetheless, we cannot simply discard the logic of metaphor and the syllogism in grass, for the syllogism in Barbara would be of little use in the biological world until the invention of language and the separation of subjects from predicates. In other words, it looks as though until 100,000 years ago, perhaps at most 1,000,000 years ago, there were no Barbara syllogisms in the world, and there were only Bateson's kind, and still the organisms got along all right. They managed to organize themselves in their embryology to have two eyes, one on each side of a nose. They managed to organize themselves in their evolution so there were shared predicates between the horse and the man, which zoologists today call homology. It becomes evident that metaphor is not just pretty poetry, it is not either good or bad logic, but is in fact the logic upon which the biological world has been built, the main characteristic and organizing glue of this world of mental process that I have been trying to sketch for you.

III   *Metalogue:*

Why Do You Tell Stories?

(MCB)

DAUGHTER: Daddy, why do you talk about yourself so much?

FATHER: When we are talking, you mean? I'm not sure that I do. Certainly there is a lot about myself that never comes up.

DAUGHTER: That's right, but you tell the same stories again and again. For instance, you presented your epistemology for the introduction by telling how you arrived at it, and now you've been telling about going to the zoo in Chicago. And I've heard you tell a hundred times about going to the San Francisco Zoo and watching the otters at play, but you never talk about what you played with as a child. Did you ever have a puppy to play with when you were a little boy? What was its name?

FATHER: Whoa, Cap. That's a question that's just going to remain unanswered. But you're quite right that even when I tell stories out of my experience, it's not my own history I'm talking about. The stories are *about* something else. The otter story is about the notion that in order for two organisms to play, they have to be able to send the signal "this is play." And that leads to the realization that that kind of signal, the metacommunication or the message about the message, is going to be part of their communication all the time.

DAUGHTER: Well, but we're two organisms. And we have that same problem you're always talking about, of figuring out whether we are playing or exploring or what. What does it tell me that you don't talk about you when you were little, and you don't talk about you and me when I was little, you want to talk about otters. In the *zoo*.

FATHER: But I don't want to talk about otters, Cap. I don't even want to talk about play. I want to talk about talking about play—how the otters go about it and how we might try to go about it.

DAUGHTER: Talking about talking about talking. Cosy. So this has turned into an example of logical types, all piled up. The otter story is a story about metamessages, and the stories of you growing up in a positivistic household are about learning—because it was in thinking about learning and learning to learn that you began to realize the importance of the logical types. Messages about messages, learning about learning. I must say, even though the logic boys say they have new and better models of logical types that you don't take account of, you get a lot of mileage—a lot of insight—out of using them, when almost nobody else does.

But, Daddy, can you just go along at the top of the pile? I don't think you can talk about talking about talking without *talking*, and I mean talking about something specific, something solid and real. If you tell a story about play when I'm not part of it, does that mean we're not playing?

FATHER: Playing we may be, but you're nipping at my heels in this particular game. Look, we're getting into a tangle. You have to distinguish the logical types in the words of our conversation from the overall structure in the communication, of which the verbal conversation is only part. But one thing you can be sure of is that the conversation isn't about "something solid and real." It can *only* be about ideas. No pigs, no coconut palms, no otters or puppy dogs. Just ideas of pigs and puppy dogs.

DAUGHTER: You know, I was giving a seminar one evening at Lindisfarne, Colorado, and Wendell Berry was arguing that it is possible to know the material world directly. And a bat flew into the room and was swooping around in a panic, making like Kant's *Ding an sich*. So I caught it with somebody's cowboy hat and put it outside. Wendell said, "Look, that bat was really in here, a piece of the real world," and I said, "Yes, but look, the *idea* of the bat is still in here, swooping around representing alternative epistemologies, and the argument between me and Wendell too."

FATHER: Well, and it is not irrelevant that Wendell is a poet. But it's also true that since we're all mammals, whatever word games we play

we are talking about relationship. Professor X gets up at the blackboard
and lectures about the higher mathematics to his students, and what
he is saying all the time is "dominance, dominance, dominance."
And Professor Y stands up and covers the same material, and what
he is saying is "nurturance, nurturance," or maybe even "dependency,
dependency," as he coaxes his students to follow his argument.

DAUGHTER: Like the mewing cat you're always talking about that isn't
saying "milk, milk" but "dependency, dependency." Hmm. You
wouldn't want to comment on the nationality of your two professors,
would you?

FATHER: Brat. What is even more interesting is that someone like Konrad
Lorenz can be talking about communication of relationships among
geese, and he turns into a goose up there at the blackboard, the way
he moves and holds himself, and it's a much more complicated
account, a much richer account of the geese than we have had here
about otters. . . .

DAUGHTER: And *he's* talking to the audience about dominance and so
on at the same time. A man talking about a goose talking about a
relationship that's also about the man's relationship to the other men
. . . oh dear. And everybody in the room is supposed to pretend that
it isn't happening.

FATHER: Well, the other ethologists get pretty resentful of Lorenz. They
talk as if he were cheating, somehow.

DAUGHTER: What is cheating anyway?

FATHER: Mmm. In conversation it is "cheating" to shift logical types in
ways that are inappropriate. But I would argue that for Lorenz to
move like a goose or to use empathy in the study of geese is appropriate—the way he moves is part of the empathy. But I run into the
same problem: people say I'm cheating when I use the logic of metaphor to speak about the biological world. They call it "affirming the
consequent" and seem to feel that anyone who does so should have
their knuckles rapped. But really it seems to me to be the only way
to talk sense about the biological world, because it is the way in which
that world, the Creatura, is itself organized.

DAUGHTER: Hmm. Empathy. Metaphor. They seem similar to me. It
seems to me as if making those things against the rules—calling them
cheating—is like the kind of constraints you have in a relay race.
You know, one hand tied behind your back, or your legs in a sack.

FATHER: Quite.

Well, but Daddy, I want to get back to the subject. I want
~~/~~ why you are always telling stories about yourself. And most
~~or ~~ stories you tell about me, in the metalogues and so on, aren't
true, they're just *made up*. And here I am, making up stories about
you.

FATHER: Does a story have to have *really happened* in order to be true?
No, I haven't said that right. In order to communicate a truth about
relationships, or in order to exemplify an idea. Most of the really
important stories aren't about things that really happened—they are
true in the present, not in the past. The myth of Kevembuangga,
who killed the crocodile that the Iatmul believe kept the universe in
a random state—

DAUGHTER: Look, let's not get into that. What I want to know is, why
do you tell so many stories, and why are they mainly about yourself?

FATHER: Well, I can tell you that only a few of the stories in this book
are about me, and only apparently so at that. But as for why I tell a
lot of stories, there's a joke about that. There was once a man who
had a computer, and he asked it, "Do you compute that you will
ever be able to think like a human being?" And after assorted grindings
and beepings, a slip of paper came out of the computer that said,
"That reminds me of a story . . ."

DAUGHTER: So human beings think in stories. But maybe you're cheating
on the word "story." First the computer uses a phrase that's used for
introducing one kind of story . . . and a joke is a kind of story . . . and
you said that the myth of Kevembuangga is not about the past but
about something else. So what is a story really? And are there other
kinds of stories, like sermons in the running brook? How about trees,
do they think in stories? Or do they tell stories?

FATHER: But surely they do. Look, just give me that conch over there
for a minute. Now, what we have here is a whole set of different
stories, very beautiful stories indeed.

DAUGHTER: Is that why you put it up on the mantelpiece?

FATHER: This that you see is the product of a million steps, nobody knows
how many steps of successive modulation in successive generations
of genotype, DNA, and all that. So that's one story, because the shell
has to be the kind of form that can evolve through such a series of
steps. And the shell is made, just as you and I are, of repetitions of
parts and repetitions of repetitions of parts. If you look at the human
spinal column, which is also a very beautiful thing, you'll see that

no vertebra is quite like any other, but each is a sort of modulation of the previous one. This conch is what's called a right-handed spiral, and spirals are sort of pretty things too—that shape which can be increased in one direction without altering its basic proportions. So the shell has the narrative of its individual growth pickled within its geometric form as well as the story of its evolution.

DAUGHTER: I know—I looked at a cat's-eye once and saw the spiral, so I guessed it had come from something alive. And that's a story about our talking that did get into a metalogue.

FATHER: And then, you see, even though the conch has protrusions that keep it from rolling around the ocean floor, it's been worn and abraded, so that's still another story.

DAUGHTER: You mentioned the spinal column too, so that the stories of human growth and evolution are in the conversation as well. But even when you don't actually mention the human body, there are common patterns that become a basis for recognition. That's what I meant—part of what I meant—when I said years ago that each person is his own central metaphor. I like the conch because it's like me but also because it's so different.

FATHER: Hello, snail. Well, so I tell stories, and sometimes Gregory is a character in the story and sometimes not. And often the story about a snail or a tree is also a story about myself and at the same time a story about you. And the real trick is what happens when the stories are set side by side.

DAUGHTER: Parallel parables?

FATHER: Then there is that class of stories we call *models*, which are generally rather schematic and which, like the parables presented by teachers of religion, exist precisely to facilitate thought about some other matter.

DAUGHTER: Well, but before you go off on models, I want to point out that the stories about snails and trees are also stories about you *and* me, in combination. And I'm always responding to the stories you don't tell as well as the ones you do, and doing my best to read between the lines. But now you can tell me about models or even about Kevembuangga if you want to. That's safe enough—I've heard it before.

IV   The Model (GB)

I HAVE OFFERED the reader a distinction between Creatura and Pleroma, and it is now necessary to begin clarifying the relationship between that distinction and such concepts as "form," "structure," or "verities," or, on the other hand, such concepts as "events," or "process."

I suggested in *Mind and Nature* that we look at what goes on in the biosphere—the world of mental process—as an interaction between these two, *structure* (or form) on the one hand and *process* (or flux) on the other, or rather as an interaction between the elements of life to which these two notions refer.

William Blake says in *The Marriage of Heaven and Hell,* "Reason is the bound or outward circumference of Energy," and we may loosely equate his "reason" with our "structure," and his "energy" with our "process," the flux of events which is held—for the moment—within limits.

Blake was a contemporary of Thomas Young (1773–1829), who adopted *energy* into physics as a technical term: "the product (now half the product) of the mass or weight of a body into the square of the number expressing its velocity" (*OED*). But Blake probably knew nothing of this definition. For him, *energy* was more like *passion* or *spiritual vigor*. It is an irony of language that the older usage and the more restricted physical definition have become fused together in such nonsensical notions as "psychological energy," so that physical energy is now the Procrustean model for liveliness, excitement, motive, and emotion. Freud even went so far as to adopt the conservation of energy as a metaphor explaining certain aspects of human vigor, and thought of these matters in crudely quantitative terms, imagining some sort of budget of psychological energy.

A model of the interaction between structure and process underlies much of the argument of this book, and it will be critical to understand the relationship between these notions and the problems of knowledge or description.

A model has several uses: first, to provide a language sufficiently schematic and precise so that *relations* within the subject that is being modeled can be examined by comparing them with relations within the model. Occidental languages, in general, do not lend themselves to the discussion of relations. We start by naming the parts and after that the relations between the parts appear as predicates attached usually to a single part—not to the two or more parts among which the relation existed. What is required is precise talk about relations, and a model will sometimes facilitate this. That is the first purpose of a model.

A second purpose of a model appears when we have a vocabulary of relations, for then the model will *generate questions*. One can then look at the subject which is being modeled with these specific questions in mind—and perhaps find answers to them.

Finally, a model becomes a tool for comparative study of different fields of phenomena. It is above all the tool of *abduction*, drawing from phenomena in different fields that which is shared among them.

Now to clarify some of the meanings of this model of structure versus process, I shall describe an example, a specific ecological niche, using these concepts. Then I shall begin to explore the formal resemblances and differences between the example and the various levels of learning, the social processes of character formation, and so on.

The niche which I have selected for this first attempt is a schematic human residence containing a resident with human history behind him, a house furnace with thermostatic control, and an environment to which the system may be supposed to lose heat in an irregular manner.

I have chosen this particular example because it and the relations which it contains are familiar to most readers, though few could draw a blueprint for the heating system of their houses. Except for professionals, we do not know much about the quantitative aspects of insulation, the heat produced by furnaces, the delay of thermostatic switches, and the like. But we are aware of the circularity of the chains of causation in such systems. Thus, this is probably the simplest familiar example to illustrate how structure and process can be seen to operate together in a self-corrective system. The house with thermostatic control is particularly interesting because it contains a digital on-off system to control the continuously varying quantity called temperature.

We start, then, with a familiar item on the wall of the dining room. This item is called the *bias* of the thermostat. Thanks to the bias of the system, the resident has more control over his niche than a bird has over its nest or a weevil over the soft place under the bark of a tree where it makes its home.

This bias is a small box with an ordinary thermometer on the outside, which the resident can see and which will tell him the temperature of the house in the immediate vicinity of the bias. This thermometer does not affect the heating system of the house *except through the resident*, if and when he looks at it.

The same little box also contains another thermometer, which is not usually visible. This thermometer is a tongue, made of two metal strips placed face-to-face. These strips are of different metals with contrasting thermal characteristics, so that one metal expands more than the other when heated. As a result, when the combination is heated, it must bend; the degree of its bending is then a measure of the temperature at that moment. The bending and unbending of the combined metals also throw an electric switch which turns the house furnace on when the temperature goes below a certain level and turns it off above a certain level.

This device composed of two metals does not measure temperature relative to, say, a centigrade or Fahrenheit scale, as we usually think of a thermometer. What it does measure is temperature relative to upper and lower *thresholds* which are determined by the resident, who, by turning a small knob, can "set" the thermostat. When he turns that knob, he moves the other half of the electric contact either towards or away from the end of the metal tongue, so that a greater or lesser change of temperature will be required to throw the switch. By turning the knob, the resident thus changes the limits between which the temperature can vary before the furnace is switched on or off, moving both thresholds upward or downward.

There is usually a pointer attached to the knob which points to a Fahrenheit or centigrade scale and indicates the middle temperature around which the thermostatic system is supposed to fluctuate. This information is misleading insofar as it suggests that the middle temperature is what controls the thermostat. The thermostat knows nothing of this middle temperature and is controlled by the thresholds for maximum or minimum. We may even say that the temperature of the house is *not controlled* when it is in the middle range between thresholds. In other words, the system is what the engineers call "error activated," although the pointer attached to the adjustable knob would seem to suggest that it is "goal activated." This small epistemological lie—this falsification of *how* we know what we think we know—is characteristic of the culture in which we live, with its strong emphasis on appetitive orientation.

This little box in the dining room, the bias, is interesting in that the box is at the *interface*—the meeting place—between the world of the resident and the world of the machines. The normal thermometer and the pointer on the setting knob provide information addressed to the resident. The remainder of the system, with its own sense organ and efferent pathways, is addressed to the inner workings of the heating system.

We are now in a position to think about the ecology and epistemology of this system, which will also serve as an example of what is meant elsewhere by "system." Imagine that the resident is away from home, leaving the mechanical system to operate unattended. The setting of the bias cannot change itself and the temperature of the house will continue to fluctuate within the set limits, the pair of fixed points between which it has "freedom."

The setting "asserts" these fixed points and it is this assertion that I shall call *structure*.

Between these limits there is a *gap*, undescribed in the "structure" of the system. This gap is inevitable and necessary. It can be made smaller by increasing the resolving power of the thermometer and bringing the upper and lower limits closer together. In the end, however, the gap remains. We are at a point where the discontinuous functioning of a digital, on-off mechanism meets an analogic, quantitative, and continuously varying characteristic of that which is to be described or controlled. At this point and at all such points, the description will have a gap, and, precisely at these points, our language and the pointers on our machines commonly conspire to hide the fact of the gap. We do not say that the value of the variable which we seek to limit is "between five units and six units," we say it is "5.5 units plus or minus half a unit." But the world of flux knows nothing of the middle point.

Of course, this does not mean that we should give up the use of analogic devices and measurement because all such attempts to put salt on Nature's tail must always fail of complete accuracy. Still less should we give up the device of counting and digital classification. Cratylus, the disciple of Heraclitus (in Greece, in about 500 B.C.), attempted this when his master, Heraclitus, said, "All is flux," and "Into the same river no man can step twice." Cratylus, perhaps in ironic caricature, gave up the use of language and went around pointing with his fingers. The silly man never had any disciples because he could never explain with his fingers why he wanted to reduce human communication to the level of that of dogs and cats. If he could have talked *about* all this, he might have discovered the theory of logical types 2,500 years before Russell and Whitehead.

In the absence of the resident, what is at present happening in the house may be represented in a diagram thus:

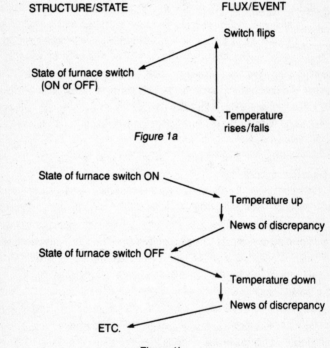

STRUCTURE/STATE   FLUX/EVENT

Switch flips

State of furnace switch
(ON or OFF)

Temperature
rises/falls

Figure 1a

State of furnace switch ON

Temperature up

News of discrepancy

State of furnace switch OFF

Temperature down

News of discrepancy

T
I
M
E

ETC.

Figure 1b

FIGURE 1A: *House thermostat.* Note that this diagram has been drawn to emphasize the circular quality of the sequence. An alternative format would space events out over time, separating successive settings and successive states: FIGURE 1B.

While the resident is away, there is only one component of what I am calling structure, the bias of the thermostat. It cannot change its own setting, so all the rules and circumstances of such a change are irrelevant. The house fluctuates between the existing set limits.

Now let us suppose that the resident returns. The temperature of the house impinges uncomfortably upon his skin, but at first he says, "Oh, well, the thermostat will fix it." An hour or two later he says, "This house is still too cold." He then goes and alters the setting of the bias. [Over time, he may even develop personal habits in varying the bias.]

The diagram must now be expanded by the addition to the system of another similar triangle. The resident received information from a *sample* of the working of the first triangle, and this information was such as to pass some threshold level in him. The first triangle now functions as a component of the second, so that an aggregate of events in the subsystem, here enclosed in dotted line and presented below, is determining events in the larger system. We may now represent the combined system thus:

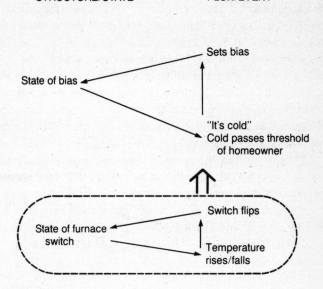

FIGURE 2: House thermostat with householder.

[The relationship between these two diagrams illustrates several matters that concern us here. We are looking at a hierarchically organized, self-corrective system, in which correction occurs in two different ways, in one case adjusting the furnace switch, in the other case resetting the bias. The heating system by itself receives information through its sense organ in the form of a difference—the difference between actual temperature and the specified threshold—and responds, but there will be no carryover from one event of self-correction to the next. In the system which includes the householder, however, the householder does not change the setting because of a specific deviation, but because he observes over time that the range of fluctuation does not fit his comfort and so he changes the range. The switching on and off of the thermostat has no permanent effect, but the system is changed when it is reset. It may be changed yet again, this time at a still higher level, if the householder changes his habits of resetting.]

The relationship between these two diagrams is reminiscent of the relationship between two methods of achieving precision in an adaptive action, which Horst Mittelstaedt discriminated and described as *calibration* and *feedback*.* These terms are closely related to the terms "structure" and "process" as I use them, but Mittelstaedt uses his terms separately, not assuming that the phenomena must always exist in combination. In my terminology, structure could not stand alone, since there must always be that material matrix in which structure is immanent as well as a flow of events, the process channeled by the structure. However, since Mittelstaedt's terms can be meaningfully used in separation, his ideas are to that extent simpler and provide a convenient next step in the formalizing with which I am concerned.

Mittelstaedt used the example of two methods of shooting: If a man is shooting with a rifle, he will look along the sights of the weapon, noting the error in its placement, correcting that error, perhaps overcorrecting and correcting again until he is satisfied. He will then press the trigger and the rifle will fire. This is the feedback method. Its prime characteristic is the use of *error correction* in each separate act of shooting.

---

*See "The Analysis of Behavior in Terms of Control Systems," *Transactions of the Fifth Conference on Group Processes* (New York: Josiah Macy, Jr., Foundation, 1958), 45–84. See also M. C. Bateson, *Our Own Metaphor: A Personal Account of a Conference on Conscious Purpose and Human Adaptation* (New York: Knopf, 1972), 136–37.

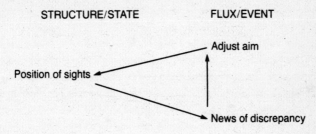

STRUCTURE/STATE   FLUX/EVENT

Adjust aim

Position of sights

News of discrepancy

FIGURE 3. Shooting with a rifle

If, on the other hand, a hunter is using a shotgun to kill a flying bird, he will not have time to correct and recorrect his aim. He will have to depend upon the "calibration" of his eyes, brain, and muscle. As he sees the bird rise, he will take in a complex aggregate of information, upon which his brain and muscles will compute, controlling the rise of his gun to a position aimed slightly in front of the moving bird. As the gun reaches that position, he will fire. In the whole single action there is a minimum of error correction. However, the marksman will do well to practice. He may spend hours shooting skeet, gradually becoming more skillful as he uses the outcome of previous completed acts of shooting to change the setting and coordination of his hands and eyes and brain. The prime characteristic of the calibration method is the absence of error correction in the single act and the use of a large sample of acts to achieve a better setting or calibration of the internal mechanisms of response.

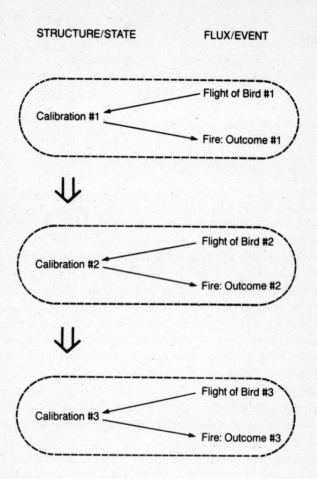

STRUCTURE/STATE   FLUX/EVENT

Flight of Bird #1
Calibration #1
Fire: Outcome #1

Flight of Bird #2
Calibration #2
Fire: Outcome #2

Flight of Bird #3
Calibration #3
Fire: Outcome #3

FIGURE 4: Shooting with a shotgun

The information used by the man with the rifle is of a different *logical type* from that used by the man with the shotgun. The former uses the news of particular error in the unique event; the latter must learn from the class or classes of error in the repeated experience of practice. The class is of higher logical type than its members.

The reader will note immediately that this contrast can have important implications for character formation and education. Zen discipline, for example, makes use of the experience provided by prolonged practice, [and frequently frustrates error correction until some broader—or deeper—change in calibration can be achieved. In fact, the relation between Mittelstaedt's concepts and those used in this book becomes clear when we consider them in terms of different types of learning. The house heating system channels events and responds to differences but is not itself changed, an example of zero-learning. Similarly, the idealized rifleman in the diagram (unlike a real hunter) makes a fresh start at aiming by error correction every time he picks up his gun.]

The other example used by Mittelstaedt was the behavior of the praying mantis that catches passing flies on the wing with a very swift reaching out of one or both claws. Mittelstaedt was interested in the precision of this action and in how it might be learned, but he found that his animals were unable to use experience to correct their calibration, which was presumably set by genetics—"hard programmed." [But when the householder is at home, his system may be altered as a result of the experience of a sequence of cycles, and similarly the calibration of the hunter with the shotgun is changed by a sequence of experiences. The hunter learns by practice.]

What is happening when the music teacher scolds the pupil for "not practicing enough"? The matter is a little complicated, and only now, as I write this, do I begin to understand a process which gave me agony when I was a boy. I was learning to play the violin, and I was a compulsive little boy. (Educators will note that when we say that a person is "compulsive," we often mean that he or she uses or attempts to use self-correction in the individual act when success depends upon calibration—automatic or spontaneous skill—acquired by longer practice. You cannot learn to shoot a shotgun by handling it as you would handle a rifle.) I tried very hard, when playing, to play *right*. In other words, I attempted to use error correction in the single action of each note. The result was unmusical.

The contrast between the use of the rifle and that of the shotgun arises from the fact that the rifleman can correct his aim *in medias res*, in the middle of his still-uncompleted action. He corrects an uncommitted error. The man with a shotgun must judge his performance *after* the action is complete. At the moment of shooting, the hunter with the shotgun has less flexibility than the rifleman because he is relying on the economics of habit formation. The bird either falls or flies away, and the hunter must add the spin-off from one more unit of experience to the memory bank upon which calibration depends.

[Both sets of diagrams, the two of a house-heating system and the two of different ways of shooting, demonstrate logical type differences. In both cases where we move up to a second logical level *(Figures 2 and 4)*, the event that occurs is not only a change applicable to the specific instance (as in *Figures 1 and 3*), but a long-term change in the system that will affect future events—a change in structure.] It is to such changes that we refer by the word "learning," but in order to construct a coherent theory I include under that rubric all events in which some organism or other system receives information, and this is why the notion zero-learning is needed. In fact, the human rifleman, unlike the praying mantis, does learn from practice, but this is not indicated in the "pure case" shown in the diagram. At the same time, I then include within the term everything from the simplest and most transitory case—the firing of a single sensory end organ—to the receipt of complex chunks of information which might determine the creature's character, religion, competence, or epistemology. I also include internal learning, i.e. changes in the characteristics of the creature's processes of learning achieved by changes in interaction between different parts of mind.

From this wide definition the next step is to achieve some classification of learnings and some explanation of this classification, which shall constitute what I call Learning Theory.* [The development of such a theory involves grouping together a number of phenomena often distinguished from each other, such as adaptation, addiction, and habit formation, and then distinguishing between different kinds of learning in terms of logical type. Above the level of zero-learning, learning consists in change in systemic characteristics as a result of experience—form affected by flux, structure affected by process. But notably in organisms such change is typically made in pursuit of some *constancy*, some previously defined goal.]

This definition of learning raises questions regarding cases of "learning" or "hysteresis,"† which are to be found among purely physical

---

*Previous essays of mine on this subject include "Social Planning and the Concept of Deutero-Learning" and "The Logical Categories of Learning and Communication," both in *Steps*, and "The Message of Reinforcement," in *Language Behavior*, compiled by J. Akin, G. Myer, and J. Stewart (The Hague: Mouton, 1971), 62–72.

†"The failure of a property that has been changed by an external agent to return to its original value when the cause of the change is removed." *American Heritage Dictionary*.

phenomena. One of the best known of these is the case of the Chladni figures. A thin metal plate supported at a single point is peppered all over with a fine powder and then stroked somewhere on the edge with a fiddle bow; the resulting vibration will be unevenly distributed throughout the plate so that the powder will leave those parts of the plate where amplitude is greatest and will collect where the amplitude is least. The resulting patterns are named for Chladni, a nineteenth-century Italian physicist who studied them. Such a plate is capable of many such patterns, depending upon the point of bowing (corresponding to the multiple harmonics of a stretched string held still at varying points by the musician's fingertip). Some of these patterns are easier to produce than others, and the plate is said to "remember" what patterns of vibration it was made to give yesterday, so that those patterns can be more easily produced today.

Similarly, of course, the owner of a precious Stradivarius will not let some novice play it, lest the novice produce squawks and squeaks which the instrument will reproduce in the concert hall.

This matter of the hysteresis of resonance patterns has become of great interest as a result of recent suggestions of Karl Pribram that memory is, at least in part, achieved by something like hologram formation in the brain. A "mental hologram" is, if I understand it aright, a complex, four-dimensional pattern of resonance in a three-dimensional neural network.

An easy way out would suggest that these phenomena are not to be classed as "learning" or do not involve the reception of "information." But I am strongly of the opinion that the brain probably does in fact depend upon acquired resonance patterns and that we cannot just shrug off the acquisition of such patterns in other contexts as "not true learning." We should rather be prepared to change our definition of "learning" or of "information" to accommodate these phenomena. [The phenomena we describe must always have an aspect that can be described physically, and we may want to look at the physical changes involved in learning within organisms, as well as at nonorganic learning or learning by systems containing complex combinations of organic and nonorganic components—like the householder with his heating system.]

Before we move on from the set of examples considered in this chapter, another similarity between the diagrams should be examined, and that is the occurrence of *triads*. The study of "learning" in psychological laboratories is usually also shaped around a triad, a rather mysterious triad of events called "stimulus, response, and reinforcement," which allows one component to be a comment upon a relation between two others. In the present context, it is natural to ask whether this triad is somehow related to the triangles in the diagrams above. And beyond that, to ask whether the triad of the learning experiments and the triangles of the diagrams which I have drawn are in some sense "real" or whether they are mere artifacts of the laboratory or of the theorist's paranoia. Do such triads occur in all examples of learning, and indeed is such a triad recognizable in the case of Chladni figures, holograms, and the like?

The triadic pattern involved in learning is held together by the nature of "reinforcement." This is precisely the name of any message or experience that will attach *value* ("good" or "bad"; "right" or "wrong"; "success" or "failure"; "pleasure" or "pain"; etc.) to an association or linkage between any other two or more components in a sequence of interaction. It is not a "piece" of behavior that is reinforced; reinforcement is a comment on a relation *between* two or more events in a sequence. [The identity of different parts of the triad depends on how sequences are punctuated, which is subject to various kinds of distortion and may vary from person to person.] Some persons impose upon their world the premise that "right" and "wrong" are attributes of items rather than of relations between items. These people would define "reinforcement" in terms different from the above. Legal codes seem to do this in the belief that actions are easier to define than relations and associations between actions. I suspect that such shortcuts are commonly wrong and/or dangerous.

Let me distinguish two categories of learning, each with many members but such that the difference between the two is a difference of logical typing, i.e. such that what is learned in learnings of one category is contained within the learning of higher and more inclusive categories. For examples, consider a rat in a relationship with an experimenter, learning to get food by pressing a bar whenever he hears a particular buzzer, or a child being taught by an adult to play the piano. There are two sorts of learning in each of these examples. There is the particular task to be learned: for the rat, "Press this bar and get food"; for the child, "Press these keys in this order and get approval."

And for each there is learning of a higher logical type. For the rat, "The world contains many contexts such that my right action will bring food," or still more generally, "The world contains many contexts for purposive action." The rat is becoming a manipulative rat.

For the child, the sequence is rather more complicated. True, the perceptions of the rat are available to the child: "There are contexts I can manipulate to get approval." In addition there is the very interesting question of the relation between the unit of action that brings success or failure on the outside and the unit of action that is susceptible to corrective action by the self. Should I correct the way I play every note? Or should I correct some variable in the *sequence* of notes?

In the discussion of the contrast between shooting with a rifle and shooting with a shotgun, it was plain that the weapons differed in the opportunity each gave for self-correction. The rifle allows the marksman to see his error as he looks along the sights during the single act of aiming. The shotgun permits the learner to judge only after the shot is fired, but in order to learn he must *practice*.

But this, too, is a matter of learning—or could become one. As a boy, I spent terrible hours from the age of nine to eighteen trying to learn to play the violin and, so far as music was concerned, I learned precisely the wrong thing. By continually trying to correct the individual note, I prevented myself from learning that the music resides in the larger sequence.

As I write this, in the woods of British Columbia, my little tape recorder plays Bach's *Goldberg Variations*. The fidelity is not perfect and the harpsichord sounds even more soft than usual. But I wonder about the composition. It begins with a statement, which Bach calls the "aria." This is followed by separate variations, thirty of them, till finally the sequence works its way back to repeating the original aria. Did Bach write the thirty variations and then set them in an order? Or did each variation somehow propose its follower?

Be that as it may, this dilemma—whether to treat the learning as change in calibration or as a problem in self-correction from moment to moment—seems to be present in all arts. Is it the first virtue of art to present this problem? To force the player and the listener, the painter and the viewer, and so on, to surrender to that necessity which marks the boundary between conscious self-correction and unconscious obedience to inner calibration? [Perhaps too this kind of shift of logical types will be seen to resemble some of the kinds of experience we label "religious."] For me, in learning to play the violin, those were regions where I feared to tread. Are there, then, regions that angels inhabit but fools fear to enter?

V *Neither Supernatural*

nor Mechanical (GB)

BEFORE we can attempt to discover what it is to hold something sacred, certain barriers must at least be mapped. Every speaker in such a discussion must make clear where he or she stands on a number of topics related to basic premises of this civilization as well as to religion and the sacred.

[It seems that the particular focus of the epistemological perplexity in which we all live today is the beginning of a new solution to the body-mind problem. A first step towards a solution is contained in the discussion of Jung's distinction between Pleroma and Creatura, such that mind is an organizational characteristic, not a separate "substance." The material objects involved in the residential heating system—including the resident—are so arranged as to sustain certain mental processes, such as responding to differences in temperature, and self-correction. This way of looking, which sees the mental as organizational and as accessible to study, but does not reduce it to the material, allows for the development of a monistic and *unified* way of looking at the world. One of the key ideas developed at the conference on Conscious Purpose and Human Adaptation,* some fifteen years ago, was that every religion and many other kinds of systems of thought can be seen as proposing a solution or partial solution to the body-mind problem, the recurrent difficulty of

---

*M. C. Bateson, *Our Own Metaphor* (New York: Knopf, 1972), 33.

seeing how material objects can display or respond to such qualities as beauty or value or purpose.] Of the several ways of thinking about body-mind, many are what I would regard as unacceptable solutions to the problem, and these of necessity give rise to a whole variety of superstitions, which seem to fall into two classes.

There are those forms of superstition that place explanations of the phenomena of life and experience outside the body. Some sort of separate supernatural agency—a mind or spirit—is supposed to affect and partly control the body and its actions. In these belief systems it is unclear how the mind or spirit, itself immaterial, can affect gross matter. People speak of the "power of mind over matter," but surely this relationship between "mind and matter" can obtain only if either mind has material characteristics or matter is endowed with mental characteristics such as "obedience." In either case the superstition has explained nothing. The difference between mind and matter is reduced to zero.

There are in contrast those superstitions that totally deny mind. As *mechanists* or materialists try to see it, there is nothing to explain that cannot be covered by lineal sequences of cause and effect. There shall be no information, no humor, no logical types, no abstractions, no beauty or ugliness, no grief or joy. And so on. This is the superstition that man is a machine of some kind. Even placebos would not work on such a creature!

But the life of a machine, even of the most elaborate computers we have so far been able to make, is cramping—too narrow for human beings—and so our materialists are always looking for a way out. They want *miracles*, and my definition of such imagined or contrived phenomena is simple: Miracles are dreams and imaginings whereby materialists hope to escape from their materialism. They are narratives that precisely—too precisely—confront the premise of lineal causality.

These two species of superstition, these rival epistemologies, the supernatural and the mechanical, feed each other. In our day, the premise of external mind seems to invite charlatanism, promoting in turn a retreat back into a materialism which then becomes intolerably narrow. We tell ourselves that we are choosing our philosophy by scientific and logical criteria, but in truth our preferences are determined by a need to change from one posture of discomfort to another. Each theoretical system is a cop-out, tempting us to escape from the opposite fallacy.

The problem is not, however, entirely symmetrical. I have, after all, chosen to live at Esalen, in the midst of the counterculture, with its incantations, its astrological searching for truth, its divination by yarrow root, its herbal medicines, its diets, its yoga, and all the rest. My friends here love me and I love them, and I discover more and more that I cannot live anywhere else. I am appalled by my scientific colleagues, and while I disbelieve almost everything that is believed by the counterculture, I find it more comfortable to live with that disbelief than with the dehumanizing disgust and horror that conventional occidental themes and ways of life inspire in me. They are so successful and their beliefs are so heartless.

The beliefs of the counterculture and of the human potential movement may be superstitious and irrational, but their reason for being and indeed the reason for the growth of that whole movement in the 1970s was a good reason. It was to [generate that buffer of diversity that will] protect the human being against obsolescence.* The older beliefs have ceased to provide either explanation or confidence. The integrity of leaders in government, industry, and education who live by the old beliefs has become suspect.

This dimly felt obsolescence is central to—at the root of—the epistemological nightmare of the twentieth century. It should now be possible to find a more stable theoretical stance. We need such a stance to limit the excesses both of the materialists and of those who flirt with the supernatural. And further, we need a revised philosophy or epistemology to reduce the intolerance that divides the two camps. "A *plague on both your houses!*" Mercutio exclaims as he dies.

And I assert that we know enough today to expect that this improved stance will be unitary, and that the conceptual separation between "mind" and "matter" will be seen to be a by-product of—a spin-off from—*an insufficient holism*. When we focus too narrowly upon the parts, we fail to see the necessary characteristics of the whole, and are then tempted to ascribe the phenomena which result from wholeness to some supernatural entity.

People who read what I have written too often get from my writing some support for supernatural ideas which they certainly entertained before they read my work. I have never knowingly provided such support, and the false impression which, it seems, I give is a barrier between them and me. I do not know what to do except to make abundantly clear what

---

*Note that Gregory discusses this issue in an appendix to *Mind and Nature* from a somewhat different point of view.

opinions I hold regarding the supernatural on the one hand and the mechanical on the other. Very simply, let me say that I despise and fear both of these extremes of opinion and that I believe both extremes to be epistemologically naive, epistemologically wrong, and politically dangerous. They are also dangerous to something which we may loosely call mental health.

My friends urge me to listen to more stories of the supernatural, to subject myself to various sorts of "experience," and to meet more practitioners of the improbable. They say I am being narrow-minded in this connection. Indeed so. After all, I am by bent and training skeptical, even about sense data. I do believe—really I do—that there is some connection between my "experience" and what is happening "out there" to affect my sense organs. But I treat that connection not as matter-of-course but as very mysterious and requiring much investigation. Like other people, I normally experience much that does not happen "out there." When I aim my eyes at what I think is a tree, I receive an image of something green. But that image is not "out there." To believe that is itself a form of superstition, for the image is a creation of my own, shaped and colored by many circumstances, including my preconceptions.

With regard to the supernatural, I believe that the data in many cases simply are not as represented and do not support—much less prove—what it is claimed they should prove. I also believe that the claims made are so unlikely to be valid, so difficult to believe, that very strong evidential proof would be needed. The matter has been put in words stronger than mine:

> No testimony is sufficient to establish a miracle, unless the testimony be of such a kind, that its falsehood would be more miraculous than the fact which it endeavors to establish: And even in that case there is a mutual destruction of arguments, and the superior only gives us an assurance suitable to that degree of force, which remains, after deducting the inferior.*

It is that "mutual destruction of arguments" which most convinces me that there are not believably at the present time any miracles in which it is easier to believe than to doubt the attesting evidence.

The trouble is that belief in a claimed miracle must always leave the believer open to *all* belief. By accepting two contradictory kinds of explanation (both the ordered and the supernatural), he sacrifices all criteria

*David Hume, "Of Miracles" in *An Inquiry Concerning Human Understanding, Essays and Treatises*, vol. 2 (Edinburgh, 1804), 121.

of the incredible. If some proposition is both true and false, then *all* propositions whatsoever are and *must* be both true and false. All questions of belief or doubt then become meaningless. It is in this context that the concept of *heresy* assumes its importance. However, if heresy be defined as internally contradictory opinion about some major premise of life and religion, then belief in the supernatural is ultimately "heresy."

An example will perhaps make this matter more clear. I recently attended a séance at which a professed (and professional) psychic painted about twenty pictures in about two hours. These pictures he signed with the names of various deceased and famous artists—Picasso, Monet, Toulouse-Lautrec, Matisse, Rembrandt, etc. And indeed each painting was recognizably in the style of the artist whose name was "signed" on it. The psychic claimed that the spirit of the deceased artist controlled him in the act of painting and that, without such control, he himself did not know how to draw.

Some days later, a little girl, four years old, defaced with a marking pen one of these paintings, which was signed "Monet." The members of the community were duly horrified. I suggested, however, that this sequence of events proved the reality of ghosts. Clearly Monet, somewhere in the land of the dead, had become aware, by ESP, of the monstrous impersonation which had been perpetrated upon him, and had come back to earth in a rage, where he had possessed the little girl, guiding her hand as she defaced the picture. I pointed out that the defacing marks were surely "genuine Monet" and should fetch several thousand dollars at auction. Or was the whole picture a "genuine Monet"? Either hypothesis is as credible (or incredible) as the other. The introduction of the supernatural into the scheme of explanation destroys all belief and all disbelief, leaving only a state of mind, completely gaga, but which some find pleasant.

The great variety of supernaturalist superstitions with which we are currently blessed seems to depend on a rather small number of misconceptions. Thus, I believe that the receipt of information, whether by organisms or machines, always occurs by way of material pathways and end organs which are, in principle, identifiable. This rules out such variants of extrasensory perception as telepathy, distance perception, second sight, etc. It also excludes that superstition called "the inheritance of acquired characteristics." It does not, of course, exclude the possibility that men, animals, or machines may have organs of sense of which we are still unaware. But in discussion with friends who believe in ESP, I find that any simple explanation of what they assert is not at all what they hope for.

Other species of superstition are built on contradictions similar to the notion of communication without a channel, such as the belief in things or persons possessing no material being, yet interacting with the material world. Thus, there are those who describe "out-of-body experiences," in which a nonmaterial something (a something which is not a something) is supposed to leave the body in a literal spatial sense, to have percepts and experiences while out on such a trip (although lacking sensory end organs), and to return to the body providing the owner of the body with narratable information about the trip. I regard all such accounts as either dreams or hallucinations or as frank fiction. Similarly, the belief in anthropomorphic supernaturals asserts the existence and ability to influence the course of events of persons who have no location or material existence. Thus, I do not believe in spirits, gods, devas, fairies, leprechauns, nymphs, wood spirits, ghosts, poltergeists, or Santa Claus. (But to learn that there is no Santa Claus is perhaps the beginning of religion.)

Some supernatural notions appear to be based in materialistic science but are not; on examination, they prove not to have those properties that belong to the world of matter. Of all examples of physical quantities endowed with mental magic, "energy" is the most pernicious. This once neatly defined concept of quantitative physics with real dimensions has become in the talk and thinking of my antimaterialistic friends the explanatory principle to end them all.

My position and the reason why so many prefer to believe otherwise may be clarified by an exploration of the relation between religion and magic. I believe that all spells, meditations, incantations, suggestions, procedures of sympathetic and contagious magic, and the like, do indeed work—but they work upon the practitioner (as does "psychic energy"). But I presume that none of these procedures has any effect at all upon any other person unless that other participates in the spell or suggestion or at least has information or expectation that such spell or procedure has been performed.

But where these conditions are met and the other person is partly aware of what is being done and aware of its purposes aimed at himself or herself, I am sure that magical procedures can be very effective either to kill or cure, to harm or bless.

I do not believe that such magical procedures have relevant effects upon inanimate things.

So far so good. I accept no story of action at a distance without communication. But I observe in passing that when the target person participates, the procedure becomes not magic but religion, albeit of a somewhat simple kind.

In general, magical procedures seem to bear formal resemblance both to science and to religion. Magic may be a degenerate "applied" form of either. Consider such rituals as rain dances or the totemic rituals concerned with man's relationship to animals. In these types of ritual the human being invokes or imitates or seeks to control the weather or the ecology of wild creatures. But I believe that in their primitive state these are true religious ceremonials. They are ritual statements of unity, involving all the participants in an integration with the meteorological cycle or with the ecology of totemic animals. This is religion. But the pathway of deterioration from religion to magic is always tempting. From a statement of integration in some often dimly recognized whole, the practitioner turns aside to an appetitive stance. He sees his own ritual as a piece of purposive magic to make the rain come or to promote the fertility of the totemic animal or to achieve some other goal. The criterion that distinguishes magic from religion is, in fact, *purpose* and especially some extrovert purpose.

Introvert purpose, the desire to change the self, is a very different matter, but intermediate cases occur. If the hunter performs a ritual imitation of an animal to cause that animal to come into his net, that is surely magic; but if his purpose in imitating the animal is perhaps to improve his own empathy and understanding of the beast, his action is perhaps to be classed as religious.

My view of magic is the converse of that which has been orthodox in anthropology since the days of Sir James Frazer. It is orthodox to believe that religion is an evolutionary development of magic. Magic is regarded as more primitive and religion as its flowering. In contrast, I view sympathetic or contagious magic as a product of decadence from religion; I regard religion on the whole as the earlier condition. I find myself out of sympathy with decadence of this kind either in community life or in the education of children.

[The difficulty in all of this is to clarify the sense in which ideas and images do participate in certain kinds of causal chains, although they have neither location nor material being, and to relate this to their embodiment in material arrangements, like ink on paper or synaptically linked brain cells. The *idea* of Santa Claus, communicated through appropriate material networks, can persuade the ten-year-old to clean up his room.]

It is becoming fashionable today to collect narratives about previous incarnations, about travel to some land of the dead, and about existence in some such place, etc. It is, of course, true that many effects of my actions may persist beyond the time of "my" death. My books may continue to be read, but again, this karmic survival does not seem to be what my friends want me to believe. As I see it, after death, the pattern and organization of the living creature are reduced to very simple forms and do not come together again. "And if thou art at death the food of worms,/How great thy use, how great thy blessing." I can write words on the blackboard and wipe them out. When wiped out, the writing is lost in an entropy of chalk dust. The ideas are something else, but they were never "on" the blackboard in the first place. It must be remembered that at least half of all ideation has no referent in a physical sense whatsoever. It is the ground that every figure must have. The hole in the bagel defines the *torus*. When the bagel is eaten, the hole does not remain to be reincarnated in a doughnut.

Another form of superstition, exemplified by astrology and divination and by the Jungian theory of synchronicity, seems to arise from the fact that human opinion is strongly biased against the probability of coincidence. People are commonly surprised by coincidences that are not improbable, for coincidences are much more common than the layman expects. Few coincidences justify the pleased surprise with which they are greeted by those who want to find a supernatural base for them.

If things turn out to coincide with our desires, or with our fears, or with other things, we are sure that this was no accident. Either "luck" was on our side or it was against us. Or perhaps our fears *caused* things to be as they are. And so on. But indeed the efficacy of prayer and/or meditation as a technique for changing ourselves would seem to give an experiential basis for superstitions of this kind. People do not easily distinguish between changes in the self and changes in the world around them. For the rest, I find it hard to be interested in coincidence.

It is of interest that harboring superstition of one kind may lead to another. Notably, for example, Arthur Koestler, starting from Marxism, achieved a repudiation of that metaphysical belief and progressed to a belief in synchronicity. *Facilis descensus Averno;* the descent to hell is easy. Koestler then progressed to arguing for the inheritance of acquired characteristics in *The Case of the Midwife Toad*.* To believe in heredity of this kind is to believe in the transmission of patterned information without receptor.

It is notable also that belief in certain kinds of superstition moves rapidly to a willingness to indulge in trickery to reinforce that belief. [Indeed, the ethnography of shamanism is replete with examples in which the shaman, genuinely believing in his or her magical powers, still uses elaborate and practiced sleight of hand to help out the supernatural. There is sometimes a confusion between different kinds of validity,] as when right-brain notions, which have their own kind of validity, are treated as if they have the validity of left-brain thinking.

To repudiate the established ways of thought and control is, however, a very different matter from criticizing elements in the counterculture. I can make a list of items in the counterculture with which I do not agree, as I have done here, because a lack of tight integration or consistency is one of their principal characteristics. To quote Kipling, "In the Neolithic Age": "There are nine and sixty ways of constructing tribal lays,/And—every—single—one—of—them—is—right!" But my objections to the established system are of a different order. I cannot make a list of the pieces. My objection is not to pieces but is a response to the entire way in which many otherwise sensible components of culture such as money or mathematics or experimentation have been fitted together.

More important than all the species of supernaturalist superstition listed above, I find that there are two basic beliefs, intimately connected, which are both obsolete and dangerous, and which are *shared* by contemporary supernaturalists and by prestigious and mechanistic scientists. The mass of superstition now fashionable even among behavioral scientists and physicists springs from a combination of these two fundamental and erroneous beliefs. It is a strange fact that both of these beliefs are connected to the same giant of philosophic thought, René Descartes. Both beliefs are quite familiar.

The first is the idea that underlies the whole range of modern superstition, namely that there are two distinct explanatory principles in our world, "mind" and "matter." As such dichotomies invariably must, this famous Cartesian dualism has spawned a whole host of other splits as monstrous as itself: mind/body; intellect/affect; will/temptation; and so

*(New York: Vintage Books, 1971).

on. It was difficult in the seventeenth century to imagine any nonsupernatural explanation of mental phenomena, and at that time it was already apparent that the physical explanations of astronomy were going to be enormously successful. It was therefore quite natural to fall back upon age-old supernaturalism to get the problems of "mind" out of the way. This accomplished, the scientists could proceed with their "objective" inquiries, disregarding or denying the fact that the organs of sense, indeed our whole range of approaches to the study of "matter," are very far from being "objective."

Descartes' other contribution also bears his name and is taught to every child who enters a scientific lab or reads a scientific book. Of all ideas about how to think like a scientist, the idea of using intersecting coordinates, the so-called Cartesian coordinates, to represent two or more interacting variables or represent the course of one variable over time, has been among the most successful. The whole of analytic geometry sprang from this idea, and from analytic geometry the calculus of infinitesimals and the emphasis upon *quantity* in our scientific understanding.

Of course, there can be no cavil at all that. And yet, "by the pricking of my thumbs," I am sure that it was no accident that the same man who invented the coordinates, which are among the most materialistic and hard-nosed of scientific devices, also dignified dualistic superstition by asserting the split between mind and matter.

The two ideas are intimately related. And the relation between them is most clearly seen when we think of the mind/matter dualism as a device for removing one half of the problem for explanation from that other half which could more easily be explained. Once separated, mental phenomena could be ignored. This act of subtraction, of course, left the half that could be explained as excessively materialistic, while the other half became totally supernatural. Raw edges have been left on both sides and materialistic science has concealed this wound by generating its own set of superstitions. The materialist superstition is the belief (not usually stated) that *quantity* (a purely material notion) *can determine pattern*. On the other side, the antimaterialist claims *the power of mind over matter*. That quantity can determine pattern is the precise complement for the power of mind over matter, and both are nonsense.

The belief that quantities can determine patterns is surprisingly pervasive and influential. It is, of course, a basic premise in contemporary economics and therefore one of the factors which determines international chaos as well as ecological disaster on the home front. I believe that this kind of ascription of the mental to the physical so that the physical becomes now the supernatural contains the ultimate in nonsense. It is now quantities that carry the divine onus of creating pattern—presumably out of nothing.

Consider on the other hand the popular verbal cliché "the power of mind over matter." This little monster contains three combined concepts, "power," "mind," and "matter." But power is a notion derived from the world of engineers and physicists. It is of the same world as the notions of energy or matter. It would therefore be quite consistent and sensible to speak, say, of the power of a magnet over a piece of iron. All three items—the magnet, the iron, and the power—come out of the same universe of discourse. The magnet and the iron and the power can meet each other in the same statement. But *mind*, since Descartes split the universe in two, does not belong in that world. So in order to give physical power to mind, we must give it materialistic existence. Alternatively, we might *mentalize* matter and talk about "the obedience of matter to mind." One way or another the two concepts must be made to meet in one conceptual world. The phrase "power of mind over matter" does not bridge the gulf between mind and matter; it only invokes a miracle to bring the two things together. And, of course, once a basic contradiction is admitted into a system of explanation, anything is possible. If some x is both equal and unequal to some y, then all x's are both equal and unequal to all y's and to each other. All criteria of the incredible are lost.

In any case, the combination of the two ideas we have attributed to Descartes blossomed out into an emphasis upon quantity in scientific explanation which distracted men's thought from problems of contrast, pattern, and gestalt. The world of Cartesian coordinates relies on continuously varying quantities, and while such analogic concepts have their place in descriptions of mental process, the emphasis on quantity distracted men's minds from the perception that contrast and ratio and shape are the base of mentality. Pythagoras and Plato knew that pattern was fundamental to all mind and ideation. But this wisdom was thrust away and lost in the mists of the supposedly indescribable mystery called "mind." This was sufficient to end systematic investigation. By the middle of the nineteenth century any reference to mind in biological circles was viewed as obscurantism or simple heresy. Notably it was the Lamarckians such as Samuel Butler and Lamarck himself who carried the tradition of mental explanation through that period of quantitative materialism. I do not accept their central thesis about heredity, but they must be given credit for maintaining an all-important philosophic tradition.

Already by the nineteenth century, the biological philosophers, like the engineers and tradesmen, were soaked with the nonsense of quantitative science. Then in 1859, with the publication of Darwin's *On the Origin of Species,* they were given that theory of biological evolution that precisely matched the philosophy of the industrial revolution. It fell into place atop the Cartesian split between mind and matter, neatly fitting into a philosophy of secular reason which had been developing since the Reformation. Inquiry into mental processes was then rigidly excluded—tabooed—in biological circles.

In addition to his coordinates and his dualism of mind and matter, Descartes is even better known for his famous sentence, *cogito, ergo sum*: "I think, therefore I am." We may wonder today exactly what his sentence meant to him, but it is clear that, in building a whole philosophy upon the premise of thought, he did not intend that the dichotomy between mind and matter should lead to an atrophy of all thinking about thought.

I regard the conventional views of mind, matter, thought, and materialism, the natural and the supernatural, as totally unacceptable. I repudiate contemporary materialism as strongly as I repudiate the fashionable hankering after the supernatural. However, the dilemma between materialism and the supernatural becomes less cogent when you discover that neither of these two modes, materialism and supernaturalism, is epistemologically valid.

Before you jump from the frying pan of materialism into the fire of supernaturalism, it is a good idea to take a long look at the "stuff" of which "material science" is made. This stuff is certainly not material, and there is no particular reason to call it supernatural. For lack of a better word let me call it "mental."

Let me start as close to the material as possible and state categorically (and what is a category?) that there is no such *thing* as, for instance, chlorine. Chlorine is a name for a class and there is no such *thing* as a class. It is in a sense true, of course, that if you put chlorine and sodium together, you will see a reaction of some violence and the formation of common salt. It is not the truth of that statement that is at issue. What is at issue is whether the *statement* is chemistry—whether the statement is material. Are there in nature such things as *classes*? And I submit that there are none until we get to the world of living things. But in the world of living things, the Creatura of Jung and of the Gnostics, there are really classes. Insofar as living things contain communication, insofar as they are, as we say, "organized," they must contain something of the nature of *message*, events that travel within the living thing or between one living thing and others. And in the world of communication, there must necessarily be categories and classes and similar devices. But these devices do not correspond to the physical causes by which the materialist accounts for events. There are no messages or classes in the prebiological universe.

Materialism is a set of descriptive propositions referring to a universe in which there are no descriptive propositions. Its vocabulary and syntax, its epistemology, is suitable only for the description of such a universe. We cannot even use its language to describe our activity in description.

We have then to ask, what is a descriptive proposition? And to resolve this question it is reasonable to return to the scientific laboratory and look at what the scientist does in order to make descriptive propositions. His procedure is not too complicated:

He devises or buys an instrument to be the interface between his mind and the presumably material world. This instrument is the analog of a sense organ, an extension of his senses. We therefore may expect that the nature of mental process, the nature of perception, will be latent in the instrument used. This is trivially the case with the microscope. It is less obvious in the case of a balance. If we ask him, the scientist will probably tell us that the balance is a device for measuring weight, but here I believe is his first error. An ordinary beam balance with a fulcrum in the middle of a beam and pans at each end is not primarily a device for measuring weight. It is a device that *compares* weights—a very different matter. The balance will only become a device for measuring weights when one of the items to be compared has itself an already known (or defined) weight. In other words, it is not the balance but a further addition to the balance that enables the scientist to speak of measuring weight.

When the scientist makes this addition, he departs from the nature of the balance in a very profound way. He changes the basic epistemology of his tool. The balance itself is not a device for measuring weights, it is a device for comparing forces exerted by weights through levers. The beam is a lever and if the lengths of the beam on each side of the fulcrum are equal and if the weights are equal in the pans, then it is possible to say there is no difference between the weights in the pans. A more exact translation of what the balance tells us would be: "The ratio between the weights in the pans is unity." What I am getting at is that the balance is primarily a device for measuring ratios; that it is only secondarily a device for detecting subtractive difference; and that these are very different concepts. Our entire epistemology will take different shape as we look for subtractive or ratio differences.

A subtractive difference has certain of the characteristics of material. In the language of applied mathematics a subtractive difference between two weights is of the dimensions of weight (measured in ounces or grams). It is one degree closer to materialism than the ratio between two weights which is of zero dimensions.

In this sense, then, the ordinary chemical balance in the laboratory, functioning between a man and an unknown quantity of "material," contains within itself the whole paradox of the boundary between the mental and the physical. On the one hand it is a sense organ responsive to the nonmaterial concepts of ratio and contrast, and on the other hand it comes to be used by the scientist to perceive something he thinks is closer to being material, namely a quantity with real dimensions. In sum, the weighing scale does to (shall I say) truth exactly what the scientist does to the truth of psychological process. It is a device for constructing a science that ignores the true nature of sense organs of any organism including the scientist.

·

The negative purpose of this book is to brush away some of the more ludicrous and dangerous epistemological fallacies fashionable in our civilization today. But this is not my only purpose, nor indeed my principal purpose. I believe that when some of the nonsense is cleared away, it will be possible to look at many matters which at present are deemed to be as fuzzy as "mind" and therefore outside the ken of science.

Aesthetics, for example, will become accessible to serious thought. The beautiful and the ugly, the literal and the metaphoric, the sane and the insane, the humorous and the serious . . . all these and even love and hate are matters that science presently avoids. But in a few years, when the split between problems of mind and problems of matter ceases to be a central determinant of what it is impossible to think about, they will become accessible to formal thought. At present most of these matters are simply inaccessible, and scientists—even in anthropology and psychiatry—will step aside, and for good reason. My colleagues and I are still incapable of investigating such delicate matters. We are loaded down with fallacies such as those I have mentioned and—like angels—we should fear to tread such regions, but not forever.

As I write this book, I find myself still between the Scylla of established materialism, with its quantitative thinking, applied science, and "controlled" experiments on one side, and the Charybdis of romantic supernaturalism on the other. My task is to explore whether there is a sane and valid place for religion somewhere between these two nightmares of nonsense. Whether, if neither muddleheadedness nor hypocrisy is necessary to religion, there might be found in knowledge and in art the basis to support an affirmation of the sacred that would celebrate natural unity.

Would such a religion offer a new kind of unity? And could it breed a new and badly needed humility?

VI Metalogue:

Why Placebos? (MCB)

DAUGHTER: Why placebos? I mean, when you were complaining about mechanical views of human beings, why did you pick placebos, of all things, to underline their inadequacy? A placebo is just pretend medicine, isn't it, that you give to patients and maybe they are fooled into feeling better? All that does is show how gullible human beings are.

FATHER: By no means. The efficacy of placebos is a proof that human life, human healing and suffering, belong to the world of mental process, in which differences—ideas, information, even absences— can be causes.

I had a chance recently to talk to a whole group of M.D.'s that the governor had called together, so I gave them a new version, following McCulloch, of the psalmist's riddle: "What is a man that he may know illness and (perhaps) cure it?" and second, "What is illness that a man may know it and (perhaps) cure it?" You can catch 'em on placebos, you know; that's where the inconsistency in their materialism shows up.

You see, physiological medicine is like behavioral psychology and Darwinian evolution. All those boys are trained to exclude mind as an explanatory principle and the training of doctors turns them strongly towards this materialism. As a result, they feel that they should not tell the patient when they prescribe a sugar pill. Only material causes are "real." But then silly patients really believe they have minds and so, in thirty percent of cases, a placebo will work. The doctor believes the placebo to be a lie. So don't tell the patients that it is a placebo—because if you do, their minds will tell them that it won't work. And so on.

What is interesting is that the most conspicuous techniques of healing by visualization now being developed outside established medicine invite the patient to invent his or her own placebo. The placebo cannot be a lie in such a case!

DAUGHTER: Let's turn it around. Is there anything that doctors do that *isn't* a placebo?

FATHER: Hmm. Well, on my last go-round with established medicine, I ended up one rib short—two ribs, as it happens, since they took the first one a few years ago—you should have seen my surgeon's surprise when I told him I was one down already. They do indeed cut and dose with chemicals that have predictable or partly predictable material effects. But the problem still remains of how those sequences of cause and effect fit into and interact with the much more complicated Creatural sequences.

I've come to the conclusion that the only way to make sense of my own hospitalization is to see that it all worked as one gigantic placebo. The surgical boys went in and gave me a diagnosis of inoperable cancer right on top of my superior vena cava, but that was only part of the story, because although "nothing could be done," a great deal happened and I was going strong eighteen months later.

I was, I fear, a rather conspicuous patient—not quite conventional. I created a satisfactory diet: very good port wine and Stilton cheese; soft-boiled eggs and avocado; fruit—I remember some excellent mangos. And all those good things supplemented by the routine hospital meals. When you're terminal, nobody restricts your diet.

And then I was busy giving unofficial bedside seminars to the medical staff, in which subjects I don't now remember—I guess a mixture of life and death, anthropology and cybernetics, and so on.

I was successful—but not "good" in the narrow sense. Sleepwalking. I never did that before. But about four days after the operation, I got out of bed at two o'clock in the morning, fast asleep and full of tubes. . . no, that's not recommended.

DAUGHTER: I remember hearing about that, everyone was very upset.

FATHER: It gave me contact with Cleo, a very large black nurse who was on night duty. Her deep compassionate humor. And there was an

Austrian girl who is an initiate of the Filipino psychic school of surgery. She came breezing in at 11 P.M. "They can't stop me—I'm a reverend." She sniffed me and patted me and listened and finally said, "Well, Gregory, you're a fake." I asked what that meant and she said, "You do not have a degenerative condition with your chest. If you had, I would know it."

I said, "But they were in there three days ago with knives and they saw it."

"I know that," she said. "What they saw was a *dying* cancer. They were too late." And she grinned.

So, Cap, was the grin a part of my treatment?

DAUGHTER: You had to be defined as "terminal," and Rosita had to be a "reverend" or none of the treatment would have worked? Okay, but if a grin could be part of your treatment, then the idea of an inoperable cancer could maybe kill you too.

FATHER: Indeed. Although it might also have the opposite effect. One of the problems about human beings, you know, is that if we think of men and women as logs of wood, they will come to resemble logs of wood. If we think of them as rascals, they will approximate rascality—even presidents will attempt this. If we think of them as artists . . . and so on.

DAUGHTER: Thinking of them as artists . . . I'd like to try that.

FATHER: But be careful. Whether we teach men to be logs of wood or to be rascals, if later we regret what we have done—we wish we had a population of responsible businessmen or angels or whatever, of which to make a nation or a world—we cannot gratify our new wish at all fast. The habits of thought become, as they say, "hard programmed."

DAUGHTER: Then what?

FATHER: It will take a long time and intense experience to undo what we have implanted. If we have taught men to be rascals, we cannot immediately set up a system appropriate to saints because the rascals will take advantage of the change.

DAUGHTER: Right. Like me trying to be honest with college professors when some of them were already addicted to dishonesty.

FATHER: In all human affairs there is a lag, a stickiness or viscosity. And our errors will, I think, take longer to correct than to commit.

DAUGHTER: So you told all this to a large number of people right out of Establishment medicine. They must have loved you.

FATHER: Well, nowadays in any group like that most of them are involved in some kinds of treatment that see the human being in cybernetic terms: self-regulating, responsive to difference, and so on. But even while they are indeed learning, I continue to be distrustful—they are, after all, the *sangha*.

DAUGHTER: The what?

FATHER: The *sangha*. What Buddhists call the clergy. Any information is altered when it is incorporated in an establishment.

DAUGHTER: I know. You would like to see them part of the development of a new religious view as they change their views of the body-mind relationship—but you get uneasy when you think of that view getting institutionalized or established.

FATHER: Mmm. We have to have in mind a floating devotion. Devotion to a floating creed.

DAUGHTER: And try to find some way of combining consistency with a kind of pluralism—at least pluralism is what I thought you meant when you spoke of the medley of beliefs at Esalen, most of which you thoroughly disagree with, as somehow protecting the species from obsolescence. As if the prevalent mechanistic ideas were a sort of monocrop, like genetically uniform fields of wheat, and even super-stition could provide a degree of resilience, like the diversity in a wild population. You want to be careful you don't get misunderstood when you talk about heresy, which reminds people of the Inquisition.

FATHER: The issue of consistency is the issue of how things *fit together*, not of whether they are the same. Our ideas about medicine and about the patient have to fit together with the patient's own experience. A certain consistency is necessary to integration, but uniformity is surely one of those things that becomes toxic beyond a certain level.

DAUGHTER: Still, Daddy, it must be hard to find a way through the different kinds of nonsense.

FATHER: Well, yes. But the game is worth the candle.

VII *Let Not Thy*

Left Hand Know (GB)

> Let not thy left hand know what thy right hand doeth.
> —Matt. 6:3

IN THE PROCESSES we call perceiving, knowing, and acting, a certain decorum must be followed, and when these quite obscure rules are not observed, the validity of our mental processes is jeopardized. Above all, these rules concern the preservation of the fine lines dividing the sacred from the secular, the aesthetic from the appetitive, the deliberate from the unconscious, and thought from feeling.

I do not know whether abstract philosophy will support the necessity of these dividing lines, but I am sure that these divisions are a usual feature of human epistemologies and that they are component in the natural history of human knowledge and action. Similar dividing lines are surely to be found in all human cultures, though surely each culture will have its unique ways of handling the resulting paradoxes. I introduce the fact of these divisions, then, as evidence that the domain of Epistemology—of mental explanation—is ordered, real, and must be examined.

In the present chapter I shall illustrate, with a series of narratives, what happens when these lines are breached or threatened.

Back in 1960, I was acting as a guinea pig for a psychologist, Joe Adams, who was studying psychedelic phenomena. He gave me a hundred grams of LSD, and as the drug began to take effect, I started to tell him what I wanted to get from the experience—that I wanted insight into the aesthetic organization of behavior. Joe said, "Wait a minute! Wait while I get the tape recorder going." When he finally got the machine going, he asked me to repeat what I had been saying.

Anybody who has had LSD will know that the flow of ideas is such that to "repeat" any piece is almost impossible. I did the best I could but this clumsiness on Joe's part established a certain struggle between us. Interestingly enough, our roles in that struggle were reversed, so that later on he was scolding me for thinking too much instead of being spontaneous when it was my spontaneity that he had attacked with his machine. In reply, I defended the intellectual position.

At a certain point, he said, "Gregory, you think too much."

"Thinking is my job in life," I said. Later he went off and brought back a rosebud from the garden. A beautiful and fresh bud, which he gave me, saying, "Stop thinking. Take a look at that."

I held the bud and looked at it, and it was complex and beautiful. So, equating the process of evolution with the process of thought, I said, "Gee, Joe, think of all the thought that went into that!"

Evidently there is a problem, not simply to avoid thought and the use of the intellect because it is sometimes bad for spontaneity of feeling, but to map out what *sorts* of thought are bad for spontaneity, and what sorts of thought are the very stuff of which spontaneity is made.

Later in the same LSD session I remarked to Joe, "This stuff is all very well. It's very pretty but it's trivial."

Joe said, "What do you mean, trivial?"

I had been watching endless shapes and colors collapsing and breaking and reforming, and I said, "Yes, it's trivial. It's like the patterns of breaking waves or glass. What I see is only the planes of fracture, not the stuff itself. I mean that Prospero was wrong when he said, 'We are such stuff as dreams are made on.' What he should have said is, 'Dreams are bits and pieces of the stuff of which we are made,' and *what that stuff is*, Joe, is quite another question."

Even though we can discuss the ideas which we "have" and what we perceive through our senses, and so on, the enveloping question, the question of the nature of the envelope in which all that "experience" is contained, is a very different and much more profound question, which approaches matters that are part of religion.

I come with two sorts of questions posed by these stories: What is the nature of the continuum or matrix of which or in which "ideas" are made? And what sorts of ideas create distraction or confusion in the operation of that matrix so that creativity is destroyed?

In 1974, I received a phone call from Governor Brown's office, asking me to give the speech at the Governor's Prayer Breakfast. It seems that every state governor—and the president—has an annual "prayer breakfast." This institution was originally started by some members of the national Senate. They felt it would be a good thing.

I was a little hesitant and pointed out that I am after all only an unbaptized anthropologist. Was that really what the governor wanted for his prayer breakfast? Well, yes, that was what he wanted. So I consented to give the speech.

The speech was to be in January, so there was plenty of time—about five months. But quite soon I received a fat envelope from the office of Judge MacBride, the principal federal judge in Sacramento. He would be master of ceremonies at the breakfast and was clearly worried. He told me at some length that this was a valued religious and traditional occasion and indicated that I should respect its traditions and, to help me, he even sent samples of other speeches delivered by other persons at other prayer breakfasts.

So I wrote out my speech. The judge had instructed me that it should last eighteen and a half minutes, so I wrote it out—a thing I rarely do— and I sent a copy to his office to relieve his anxiety.

Here is what I wrote and later read to the assembly:

.

I am an anthropologist. And the task of an anthropologist causes him to land himself in strange places. That is, places that are strange to him but, of course, not strange to the people who belong in those places. So, here I am at the governor's breakfast in what is for me a strange place but what is for many of you a place where you belong and have your natural being. I am here to relate this strange place to other strange places in the world where men gather together perhaps in prayer, perhaps in celebration, perhaps simply to affirm that there is something bigger in the world than money and pocketknives and automobiles.

One of the things children have to learn about prayer is that you do not pray for pocketknives. Some learn it and some don't.

If we're going to talk about such matters as prayer and religion, we need an example, a specimen, about which to talk. The trouble, you see, is that words like "religion" and "prayer" get used in many different senses in different times and in different parts of the world. And what I would ask you is for a moment's agreement that at least while I'm speaking, you understand that what I'm talking about is that which is illustrated by the following example.

A well-known anthropologist, Sol Tax, was working with a group of American Indians outside Iowa City some twenty or more years ago. They invited him to the National Convention of the Native American Church, which was to be held quite close to Iowa City within a very few days. This is the church whose central sacrament is peyote—the little psychedelic cactus button which helps to determine the religious state. Now, the church was under attack for using what would be called a drug; and it occurred to Sol Tax, the anthropologist, that he would be helping these people if he made a film of the convention and of the very impressive rituals which would go with it. Such a film might serve as evidence that this worship is in fact religious and therefore entitled to the freedom that constitutionally this country grants to religion. He therefore dashed back to Chicago (his home base) and was able to get a movie truck and some technicians and a stock of film and cameras. He told his people to wait in Iowa City while he went and talked to the Indians to get their approval of the project. In the discussion that ensued between the anthropologist and the Indians, it gradually became clear to Tax that

They could not picture themselves engaged in the very personal matter of prayer in front of a camera. As one after another expressed his views, pro and con, the tension heightened. To defile a single ritual to save the church became the stated issue, and none tried to avoid it. Not a person argued that perhaps the church was not in as great danger as they thought. . . . They seemed to accept the dilemma as posed as though they were acting out a Greek tragedy. As he [Sol Tax] sat in front of the room, together with the president of the church, and as he listened with fascination to the speeches, gradually the realization came that they were choosing their integrity over their existence. Although these were the more politically oriented members of the church, they could not sacrifice a longed-for and a sacred night of prayer. When everyone had spoken, the president rose and said that if the others wished to have the movie made, he had no objections; but then he begged to be excused from the ceremony. Of course, this ended any possibility for making the movie; the sense of the meeting was clear. *

*This account comes from *Man's Role in Changing the Face of the Earth*, Symposium of the Wenner-Gren Foundation, ed. W. L. Thomas, Jr. (Chicago: U of Chicago P, 1956), 953.

The curious paradox in this story is that the truly religious nature of the peyote sacrament was proven by the leaders' refusal to accept the pragmatic compromise of having their church validated by a method alien to the reverence in which they held it.

This example, however, does not define the word "religion." It only defines the hedging necessary to preserve religion from that changing of its context—that reframing—which will turn it into the temporal and the secular, and perhaps only too easily into entertainment.

Let me give you another example to come a little closer to what I mean by religion. To show what is to be protected from various kinds of defilement. The following poem by Coleridge is probably well known to many of you. It is part of the story of a ship in terrible straits. The decks are littered with corpses who have died of thirst, and one sailor, the "Ancient Mariner," survives to tell the tale. [His killing of the Albatross was the event that began the ship's misfortunes, and the body of the dead bird has been hung around his neck.] This piece is the central fulcrum—the turning point—of the whole poem. I've always found it singularly moving.

> Beyond the shadow of the ship,
> I watched the water snakes:
> They moved in tracks of shining white,
> And when they reared, the elfish light
> Fell off in hoary flakes.
>
> Within the shadow of the ship
> I watched their rich attire:
> Blue, glossy green, and velvet black,
> They coiled and swam; and every track
> Was a flash of golden fire.
>
> O happy living things! no tongue
> Their beauty might declare:
> A spring of love gushed from my heart,
> And I blessed them unaware:
> Sure my kind saint took pity on me,
> And I blessed them unaware.
>
> The selfsame moment I could pray;
> And from my neck so free
> The Albatross fell off, and sank
> Like lead into the sea.*

*Samuel Taylor Coleridge, "The Rime of the Ancient Mariner," lines 272–91.

Of course, I am not suggesting that blessing the water snakes caused the rain that then came. That would be another logic in another, more secular, language. What I am suggesting is that the nature of matters such as prayer, religion, and the like is most evident at moments of *change*—at moments of what the Buddhists call Enlightenment. And while Enlightenment may involve many sorts of experience, I think it important here to notice how often Enlightenment is a sudden realization of the biological nature of the world in which we live. It is a sudden discovery or realization of *life*.

The water snakes give us a hint of that. Another example, even more vivid but perhaps less familiar, alas, is the case of Job.

Job, you will remember, is like Little Jack Horner. He sticks his finger in the pie and gives to the poor, and says, "What a good boy am I." He has a God who is exactly like himself and who therefore boasts to Satan about Job's virtue. Satan is perhaps the most real part of Job's person, deeply hidden and repressed within him. He sets to work to demonstrate that Job's pietism is really no good. Finally, after infinite sufferings, a God who is much less pious and pedantic speaks out of the whirlwind and gives Job three chapters of the most extraordinary sermon ever written, which consists in telling him that he does not know any natural history.

Knowest thou the time when the wild goats of the rock bring forth? or canst thou mark when the hinds do calve?

Canst thou number the months that they fulfill? or knowest thou the time when they bring forth?

They bow themselves, they bring forth their young ones, they cast out their sorrows.

Their young ones are in good liking. . . .

—Job 39:1–4

Well, that is what I told the assembled politicians and officials at the prayer breakfast. I concluded by saying that I would be much happier about the world in which I live, and about how my civilization is going to treat the world—the sorts of pollution and exploitation it is going to engage in and all the rest of that—if I felt really sure that my governors and my representatives knew how many months the hinds fulfill and how they bring forth their young.

·

We met in due course for breakfast in an enormous exhibition hall—thirteen hundred people at hundreds of little tables laid out with fruit and cheese. I remember that there was a good deal of comment about this frugal but healthy meal. The press was there in force—perhaps twenty men with still cameras and a few with movie cameras going around like stage horses—one man carrying camera and searchlight while another followed with thirty or forty pounds of battery.

When we had all selected our tables, Judge MacBride went up to the podium to welcome us. He pointed out that this was a sacred and not a secular occasion and therefore there would be no photographing of the participants! The faces of the pressmen fell and the batteries suddenly seemed extra heavy. So, to comfort the press, MacBride threw in a last remark: "Of course, it's all right to photograph the Sufi choir!"

They later sang like angels. I, after all, was there to talk about religion but they exhibited a little of it.

My family and I and the choir had arrived the night before, and Brown had taken us all to dinner at a Chinese restaurant. Somebody at dinner mentioned the dome of the capitol, and one of the choir wondered how it would be to sing under it. So at eleven o'clock at night we all tramped down to the capitol, which Brown opened with his key. And, under the dome, the choir gathered itself and opened its mouth. Out of it came the most beautiful sounds—some Sufi chants, some Gregorian, some secular Elizabethan, and so on.

But the story of Sol Tax and the Indians in Iowa is a heavy story and I was perhaps a cad to throw it at MacBride. After all he had not, I suppose, intended to commit the party to so religious an occasion and was only afraid I might breach the decorum, the patina in which such rituals get covered and made safe.

I had used that same story in 1969 on the first day of a Wenner-Gren Conference at Burg Wartenstein in Austria. I was chairman and had gathered about twenty thinkers, biologists and anthropologists and others, to try to discuss aesthetic determination in human and animal behavior, the same general question that had led me to try LSD: Do aesthetic factors play a role in changing what animals and people do in their relationships? It was a good group, but in the opening of the conference, I told the Sol Tax story in order to lay on them a standard of integrity.

In the story, the Indians perceive that it is nonsense to sacrifice integrity in order to save a religion whose only validity—whose point and purpose—is the cultivation of integrity. The Indians declined to save their religion on those terms.

My gathering of scientists took a look at the story and panicked. They thought that the Indians were perhaps being unreasonable or overzealous. Perhaps "holier than thou." And so on. They took a worldly view of the whole story. So I lost my conference that first morning and after that for eight days we were trying to find our way back to an integration of the group. We never did succeed in doing so.

Something useful—or interesting—can perhaps be said about religion and behavior by combining the Sol Tax story with the story of the Ancient Mariner and the sea snakes . . . when he blessed them *unaware* . . . and then there is the importance of a knowledge of natural history. When I raised these matters at the prayer breakfast, I wanted the point to remain implicit—not to be said in so many words and perhaps killed by the many words—but implicit in the setting of the stories side by side.

Here I will try to spell out the questions: First about cameras and photography. I have to ask how these instruments could invalidate a religious rite. What *is* a religious rite that a camera could invalidate it? And remember that Judge MacBride came to the breakfast from the world of courts of law, where also cameras have usually been forbidden. If we define a religious rite as a sequence of actions whose meaning or validity would be weakened by photography, then the proceedings of a court of law constitute, indeed, a religious rite.

Put it this way: The Ancient Mariner could not have blessed the sea snakes *unaware* if he had been accompanied on his famous voyage by a pressman with camera and flashbulbs.

Insofar as religion is concerned with absolution of guilt (and occidental religion is concerned with this, among many other matters), the rite which is the necessary condition of absolution must be partly (but which part?) unconscious, unaware. If the Ancient Mariner had said to himself, "I know how to get rid of the guilt of killing the Albatross: I will go back to the tropics and find some sea snakes, and I will bless them by moonlight," the Albatross would have stayed hanging on his neck to this day.

But, after all, there never was any Albatross, nor any Ancient Mariner. It is only a story, a poem, a work of art . . . a parable.

·

There is a story, rather well known, of a man who got into a bus with a big cage covered with brown paper. He was quite drunk and quite a nuisance, insisting that the cage be set next to him on the seat. They asked him, "What is in the cage?" and he told them, "A mongoose." They asked him what he wanted a mongoose for and he explained that a drinking man needs a mongoose for the snakes of delirium tremens. They said, "But those are not *real* snakes."

He answered triumphantly in a whisper, "Ah . . . but you see, it's not a *real* mongoose."

Is that the paradigm for all religion and all psychotherapy? Is it all bosh? And what do we mean when we say, "There is no Santa Claus!"?

If it's all bosh, then the sensible man will simply go home and forget it. He might spend the evening fixing the plumbing in his house or filling out his income-tax returns. But such sensible men have never been numerous enough to tidy up the civilization, getting rid of all mythological "junk." Indeed almost every culture of the world has its mythical figures *and* forces the children to look directly at these figures to learn that they do not have the same reality as pots and pans or even persons.

In every initiating culture, the novices must first experience the mystery of the masked figures and then each novice must wear and dance in the mask. He must himself swing the bull-roarer and will do so with glee. (But why so gleeful?)

And what of the Bread and Wine? The communicant "partakes" of these—eats and drinks them—and there could hardly be a more definite demonstration that the Bread is indeed just bread and the Wine of no distinguished vintage. And yet . . .

I once tried to help a patient who combined alcoholism with psychosis. He came from a religious family of fundamentalist Christians. In that family, they were not allowed to mention Santa Claus, because the first believing and the then being disillusioned might make the children into atheists. From "There is no Santa Claus," they might conclude, "There is no Jehovah."

For the present discussion, let me suggest that the sentence "There is no Jehovah" might mean "There is no matrix of mind, no continuity, no *pattern* in the stuff of which we are made."

Why must the Ancient Mariner be "unaware" when he blesses the sea snakes?

Similar questions are posed by the following tale—a story known to every Balinese. Why is it appropriate that Adji Darma, the old folk hero, will lose his knowledge of the language of the animals if he ever tells anybody that he understands that language?

The story is complex and every piece of it fits together with all the other pieces to be a discussion of the questions I am raising.

Here is the story:

.

Adji Darma (literally "Father Patient" or "Father Long Suffering") was walking in the forest one day and there he found two snakes copulating. The male snake was just an ordinary viper but the female was a cobra princess: they were breaking caste rules. So Adji Darma got a stick and beat them. They slithered off into the bushes. The cobra girl went straight to her daddy, the king of all the cobras, and told him: "That old man, he's no good. He tried to rape me in the forest."

The snake king said, "Oh, did he?" and called for Adji Darma. When the old man came before him, the king said, "What *did* happen in the bushes?" and Adji told him.

The king said, "Yes. Just what I thought. You did right to beat them and you shall be rewarded. Henceforth you shall understand the language of the animals. But there is one condition: If you ever tell anybody that you know the language of the animals, this gift will be taken from you."

So Adji went home and in bed that night, as he lay beside his wife, he listened to the gecko lizards up in the thatch. The geckos say "heh! heh!" with a sound like the laughter of people who laugh at dirty stories. Indeed it was dirty stories that they laughed at, and Adji Darma with his new knowledge was able to hear and understand the stories. He laughed too.

His wife said, "Adji, what are you laughing at?"

"Oh . . . oh . . . nothing, dear."

"But you were laughing. You were laughing at something."

"No. It was just a thought I had, dear, it wasn't important."

"Adji, you were laughing at *me*. You don't love me anymore." And so on.

But still he did not tell her what he was laughing at, because he was not willing to lose the language of the animals.

His wife worried at this more and more and finally became sick, went into a decline, and died.

Then the old man began to feel terribly guilty and remorseful. He had killed his wife just because he selfishly wanted to go on knowing the language of the animals.

So he decided to have a suttee which would be the reverse of the ordinary. In the ordinary suttee, the widow jumps into the pyre on which her husband's body is being burned. He would jump into the flames of his wife's cremation.

A great pyre of wood was therefore built and decorated, as was the custom, with flowers and colored leaves; and beside it he had the people build a platform with a ladder up to it so that from this platform he could jump into the flames.

Before the cremation, he went up onto the platform to see that it was as it should be and how it would be to jump. While he was there, two goats came by in the grass below, a billy goat and a pregnant nanny, and they were talking.

Nanny said, "Billy, get me some of those leaves. Those pretty leaves. I must have some to eat."

But Billy said, "Baaaaaa."

Nanny said, "Billy, please. You don't love me, Billy. If you loved me, you would get them. You don't love me anymore." And so on.

But Billy only said, "Baaa. Baaa."

Adji Darma listened to this and suddenly he had an idea. He said to himself, "Ha! That's what I ought to have said to her," and he practiced saying it two or three times, "Baaa! Baaa!" Then he got down off the platform and went home.

He lived happily ever after.

·

I have now lined up a series of pieces of data—hints about how the world is—and all the pieces share the notion of *not communicating* something under some circumstances. It is important that the Ancient Mariner not tell himself that he is blessing the snakes, and especially that he not define a "purpose" of the act of blessing. He must bless them "unaware." Similarly, Adji Darma shall not tell anybody that he understands the language of the animals. The Indians at Iowa City shall not be photographed. The camera shall not point at their ritual actions to make them see themselves and tell the world about these mysteries. I am irritated by Joe's interrupting my psychedelic trip while he sets up a tape recorder, and still more irritated when he asks me to repeat what I had begun to say, which obviously could only be done with extra consciousness. And so on.

I cannot even say clearly how many examples of the same phenomenon—this avoidance of communication—are contained in the stories I have set side by side. After all, Adji must not only conceal the secret of his knowledge of the language of the animals; he must conceal the fact *that there is a secret*, and this is what he failed to do.

We find over and over again in different parts of the world and different epochs of religious thought a recurrent emphasis on the notion that discovery, invention, and knowledge in general must be regarded as dangerous. Many examples are familiar: Prometheus was chained to the rock for inventing the domestication of fire, which he stole from Phoebus Apollo; Adam was punished for eating the forbidden fruit from the tree of knowledge; and so on. Greek mythology proposes the danger of knowledge again and again, especially cross-sex knowledge, which is always fatal. The guilty man is torn to pieces, and the Greeks even had a word for this fate, which we might Anglicize to say that he is *sparagmated*. Examples include Actaeon, who accidentally spied on Artemis bathing and was torn apart by her dogs, and Orpheus, who was torn to pieces by nymphs after his return from Hades, where he went to bring back Eurydice. He looked over his shoulder at her as he was leading her back and therefore lost her forever. There is also Pentheus, the disciplinarian king who was led by Bacchus to spy on the Bacchae in Euripides' play of that name. The god had the king dress up as a woman and climb a tree to watch the women's festivities. They detected him, uprooted the tree, and tore him to pieces. His mother was among the women, and in the final scene of the play she comes back from the mountains carrying her son's head, screaming about the "lion" that they had killed. Her father, Cadmus, then performs an act of psychotherapy. "Who did you marry?" The queen answers. "What son was born?" Again she answers. Finally, Cadmus points to the head of Pentheus: "Who is that?" Then the queen suddenly recognizes her son's head. The mythical outcome of male voyeurism is death by being torn apart.

We laughingly say to children, "Curiosity killed the pussy cat," but to the Greeks it was no laughing matter.

I believe that this is a very important and significant matter, and that *noncommunication* of certain sorts is needed if we are to maintain the "sacred." Communication is undesirable, not because of fear, but because communication would somehow alter the nature of the ideas.

There are, of course, monastic orders whose members are under constraint to avoid all verbal communication. (Why especially the verbal?) These are the so-called silent orders. But if we want to know the precise *contexts* of that noncommunication which is the mark of the sacred, they will not give many clues. By avoiding all speech they tell us very little.

For the moment, let us simply say that there are many matters and many circumstances in which *consciousness* is undesirable and silence is golden, so that secrecy can be used as a *marker* to tell us that we are approaching holy ground. Then if we had enough instances of the unuttered, we could begin to reach for a definition of the "sacred." At a later stage, it will be possible to juxtapose with the stories given here examples of necessary noncommunication from the field of biology, which I believe to be formally comparable.

What is it that men and women hold sacred? Are there perhaps processes in the working of all living systems such that, if news or information of these processes reaches other parts of the system, the working together of the whole will be paralyzed or disrupted? What does it mean to hold something sacred? And why does it matter?

VIII *Metalogue:*

Secrets (MCB)

DAUGHTER: This stuff is a pain to edit.

FATHER: Then leave it alone. I can't think why you want to tinker with it when you are very unlikely to improve it.

DAUGHTER: Oh really? Look, here is what's bothering me. You have stuck into this chapter the whole piece published in CQ about the governor's prayer breakfast, and much of that is a tale within a tale within a tale. For instance, Gregory Bateson (now) telling a story about GB (in 1974), talking about the Ancient Mariner talking about a previous experience with sea snakes. Three "abouts." Or GB (in 1980) talking about GB (in 1974) talking about Sol Tax (in 1956) talking about Indians (at some earlier time) talking about the propriety of a film *about* their ritual. And isn't the ritual *about* something too, something other than pocketknives?

It's (((()))) or even ((((()(((()))). I can just tell you that some well-trained copyeditor over at Macmillan is going to want me to clean that up, knock out some of the intermediate steps, put it in indirect discourse, and so on.

FATHER: Hmm. I might have gotten around to doing that myself.

DAUGHTER: Well, probably the reason you didn't was because you were lazy or never got around to it. *But* I can think of much more interesting reasons why you might have not done it, and that's what holds me back. And they're related.

FATHER: Go on.

DAUGHTER: Someone once told me that an inset story is a standard hypnotic device, a trance induction device . . . at the most obvious level, if we are told that Scheherazade told a tale of fantasy, we are tempted to believe that she, at least, is real. The visions of the Ancient Mariner gain verisimilitude from the confrontation with the wedding guests that frames them, so the Ancient Mariner himself seems real.

FATHER: Well, I am real. Or I was. Whatever any of that may mean.

DAUGHTER: Ah, but if the story is a story about violations of fine distinctions in human communication, you're guilty yourself. That poor judge! Whether purposefully or not, you set him up on that photography business. And you don't for a minute believe that photography at the governor's prayer breakfast would be a sacrilege—for heaven's sake, that's what they put them on for.

FATHER: No, you're right that photography at a prayer breakfast at this moment in our history is not a sacrilege—but the *habit* of photography in such contexts, and the notion of prayer as *for* something, are both symptoms of pathology. We have so largely lost track of the sacred that we are even becoming incapable of committing sacrilege.

DAUGHTER: So what you did was the kind of thing therapists try to do now, forcing the patient into a reframing or redefinition of context?

FATHER: Notice, Cap, that your description fits the Job story as well. God tells Job from the whirlwind that Job cannot complain about what is going wrong in the relationship between him and God unless his sense of himself includes a knowledge of when the wild goats bring forth. That puts his troubles into parentheses.

DAUGHTER: God as psychotherapist? Is religion really about the construction and dismantling of parentheses? And is schizophrenia analyzable as a tale of lost parentheses?

FATHER: Well, it surely cannot be *about* any *thing*.

DAUGHTER: It used to bother me a lot that people go off to church or temple and talk in one kind of way and then they bracket all that and go off to lie and cheat or whatever during the week. It didn't seem to me that religion was any good at all unless it was pervasive.

FATHER: Whereas in fact the shifting of context between Sunday and the rest of the week might be important.

DAUGHTER: Well, but *still* I think you stuck the story in there like that because you're lazy! *And* I don't think the Adji Darma story fits into this chapter at all. You just like telling it.

FATHER: I wonder if you think the story is antiwomen.

DAUGHTER: Of course it is. But I'm not complaining about that, any more than I would feel free to fix your pronouns, writing *he or she* every time you use a "generic" he.

FATHER: I did change that in some of the last things I wrote.

DAUGHTER: Yeah, I know. But now look at Adji: He understands the language of the animals, and he ends up thinking he should have said "Baaa" to his wife who doesn't. . . . And somehow, that makes it okay that she died. I'm sure you're right that the theme of the importance of keeping a secret pervades mythology from all sorts of cultures, but that's a funny example to pick.

FATHER: Well, if you will stop launching red herrings, I'll suggest a few pieces that may be relevant. The story is about the need to limit or control knowledge or communication across species lines and across gender lines—the basic *discontinuities* of natural history. You will remember that Tiresias in Greek mythology also became a seer originally because he had separated two copulating snakes, and in his case that gave him access to cross-sex knowledge, while Adji has been given access to cross-species knowledge. Tiresias lost his vision when he enraged Hera by saying that women have more fun than men in bed. This matter of cross-sex knowledge is certainly something we'll come back to. And then there may be interesting issues having to do with responsibility.

DAUGHTER: So that's something to flag then. Not that you got very far with the issue of responsibility before you died, but it is lurking in the underbrush. But now there is something else bothering me here, and that's this business of *secrecy*. I feel certain that you've just gotten it all wrong. Next thing we know, you'll be writing press releases for the Pentagon.

FATHER: Now, wait, why are you upset? Press releases?!

DAUGHTER: Because I feel about secrecy the way you feel about public relations. Secrecy—more and more of it—is the kind of thing the Pentagon wants.

FATHER: Look, would you stop importing your politics into this discussion? You're expressing a standard liberal political position, but I'm not at all sure the world is better off when everything is known, public, demystified.

DAUGHTER: Well, but let's stay with the politics for a minute. Secrecy is an instrument of power and control. It always horrified me to see my academic colleagues trying to control the flow of information, sanctimoniously claiming it was the responsible thing to do, protecting the rights and privacy of others, etc., but all the time using it to manipulate. Why not work for an open system? And why not have some candor in relations between people?

FATHER: Openness is one of those things that can be overdone. Remember, in biology everything becomes toxic beyond some optimal point.

DAUGHTER: Yeah, but . . . Okay, neither of us is talking about quantity. I don't want more and more information—certainly information overload is a kind of toxicity, and everyone knowing the same thing might be a toxic kind of uniformity. And for all your elitist tendencies, I don't believe you want to block the flow of information in ways that facilitate blackmail and manipulation. So whatever you mean by secrecy, and whatever I mean by openness, we're talking past each other. And I'm not at all sure that all those stories you tell make the same point.

Look, for starters, why not formulate a seventh criterion for mental systems! I stuck the list of your six criteria into chapter 2 (pp. 18–19) for readers who haven't read *Mind and Nature*, since you were sort of laying it out piecemeal. But now I put it to you that those six criteria provide the basis for another one:

7. *In mental process information must be unevenly distributed among the interacting parts.*

This seems to me to be true for all sorts of reasons, some of them trivial and some of them rather interesting. The simplest case would be that of information that will eventually spread throughout the system, but that requires time for receipt and decoding.

FATHER: Hmm. No respectable organism would or could distribute information uniformly.

DAUGHTER: Right, but think of a committee made up of rather similar sorts of parts, even so information moves through it. Or look, it's even more interesting to think of an embryo with the same DNA in every cell, *only* able to develop as the information available to different cells changes. And what if the movement of information gave us a way of describing time?

FATHER: Well, I let you talk me into including logical hierarchy as a criterion, but it may be that both numbers 6 and 7 simply follow from the others.

DAUGHTER: Okay, but now look where we've gotten. If something like secrecy—an uneven distribution of information within a given sys-

tem—is a necessary characteristic of mental systems, then we won't
make the mistake of attaching value to it. You won't be tempted to
make it the hero of the piece, and I won't be tempted to make it the
villain. There's a parallel political issue with hierarchy, too.

As a matter of fact, I can take that a step further. What if certain
kinds of secrecy do in fact function as markers for the sacred, but
that's because "the sacred" is a way of coping with certain epistemological problems—maybe necessary ones?

FATHER: Are sacred secrets perhaps *designed* to be revealed?

DAUGHTER: Yes, of course! The initiate gets whipped by masked dancers,
then the dancers take off their masks, turn out not to be gods, and
the initiates put on the masks themselves—and that whole sequence
is what makes it possible to live with some fact of life. Secrecy is just
a piece of it . . . but it's one of the ways to make revelation possible.

FATHER: I'm reminded of Tolly's whole presentation of *concurrence* at
Burg Wartenstein. You remember, concurrence gave a sort of intellectual bridge between the notions of information and causation, since
one of the ways two events could be linked was by knowledge.*

DAUGHTER: And you couldn't have a god in the system, since omni-
science would destroy flexibility. You need a different word, you know,
maybe *unknowing* or *mystery*, preferably a word that would highlight
the fact that a lack of self-consciousness is right in the center of this
business of noncommunication . . .

FATHER: Secrecy was something I found in common among the various
stories . . .

DAUGHTER: Induction!

FATHER: Hush. It's perfectly reasonable to try to determine what several
different cases have in common . . . and then search for others that
share the same common factor. What isn't so smart is to reify that
common feature you have teased out of your data. It's all right to say
that both opium and barbiturates cause sleep in humans—except that
having said that, you're even more likely to attribute the effect to a
"dormitive principle" than you would be with only one case.

DAUGHTER: The fact of unknowing as a factor of unity and flexibility in
systems . . . When is it important that systems sustain internal boundaries by a sort of profound reflexive ignorance?

FATHER: I have been talking about the *sacred* as related to a knowledge

*Our Own Metaphor, 180–98.

of the whole—but the other side of that coin may be a certain necessary gradient of knowledge. The next step will be to look for analogous kinds of noncommunication that are not artifacts of human cultural systems.

DAUGHTER: Daddy, there's something else in the Adji Darma story. The question "Do you love me?" doesn't work, does it, any more than Joe Adams's instructing you to record spontaneity or photographing prayer or prescribing sea snakes or even getting the violin right one note at a time? They all masquerade as reporting, but they change the context of the interaction.

FATHER: No. No, Cap, asking it doesn't work.

IX *Defenses of*

Faith (GB)

A SECOND GROUP of examples of noncommunication or unknowing will move us somewhat closer to the more clearly biological. These examples are necessarily very different from those I have already offered, but I believe the issues to be formally comparable.

It is seemingly a general truth in biology that the body that is adjusting itself to the stresses and vicissitudes of experience shall not communicate with the DNA, the carrier of genetic instructions for the next generation. No news of the body's adjustments shall be registered in the DNA to affect the offspring. In the old phrase, there shall be *no inheritance of acquired characteristics*.

Similarly, it is apparently necessary that we have no knowledge of the processes by which in our perception images are formed.

Can these two very different prohibitions on the transmission of information be compared to each other? And can they be compared to the kinds of necessary noncommunication discussed in the previous chapter? I maintain that if there were communication across the so-called Weismannian barrier, the whole process of evolution would break down. Similarly, if we were aware of the processes whereby we form mental images, we would no longer be able to trust them as a basis for action. They say the centipede always knew how to walk until somebody asked it which leg it would move first.

In chapter 7 I showed that there are messages in human affairs (descriptions, news, injunctions, premises, and propositions of many sorts) that had better not be communicated to certain parts of certain systems. But this has been indicated in only the most general way. I have not stopped to define the formal characteristics of such messages nor under what circumstances these messages become pathogenic; nor have I explored the application of this notion to other kinds of systems, such as organisms or populations.

If we think of information as traveling in a network of trains of cause and effect, does it then become possible for us to describe in some formal way how any given message is located in the network and thence to identify which (even "true") messages should not—for the sake of the whole system—be located where?

I will focus on cases where the pathogenic process—the blockage or confusion—is not due to a local effect of the message alone, but is a result of relationship between the message and the total system that is its overall context. Thus, I exclude as trivial those cases in which the disaster or pathology induced by successful communication falls only in a part of the system. Often A will not tell B a given truth because the telling will hurt either A or B. We protect our own and each other's feelings, and we may sometimes be wise to do so. There are, of course, people who see it as almost a duty to communicate information that will give pain; and sometimes such people have wisdom on their side. I am not concerned here to judge these cases, except to note that these people form a subspecies of those who rush in where angels fear to tread. I am here concerned only with the formal characteristics of sequences in which damage to the system (A *plus* B) results from the message and/or its communication.

The asking of this question generates a maze of complex considerations. First come the tangles of the relationship between prior state, new information, and outcome within (B), the part of the system that receives the new information, but those tangles are only the beginning of the matter. After that come the complexities of the relationship between the recipient part (B) and the communicator (A). For instance, one might ask of a personal relationship, what was the context of a communication, what was the message conveyed, and what sidelights did the message and its communication throw upon the relationship between the persons? If we ignore the relatively simple problems of tact and protection of the pride or self-image of either person individually, we still face the problems of integration in the relationship.

Suppose that somebody had advised the Ancient Mariner to take a voyage to the South Seas, there to search for sea snakes so that he might bless them (but not "unaware"), surely no Albatross would have fallen from his neck! The possibility of change from his disintegrate state of self-reproach to a state of integration would have been precluded by the conscious knowledge of the injunction to follow a recipe.

•

But to say that consciousness may make impossible some desired sequence of events is only to invoke familiar experience—a common substitute for explanation in the behavioral sciences. Credibility may thereby be established, but mystery remains.

The road to explanation lies first through abduction and thence to mapping the phenomena onto tautology. I have argued elsewhere that individual mind and phylogenetic evolution are a useful abductive pair—are mutually cases under similar tautological rules. If you want to explain a psychological phenomenon, go look at biological evolution; and if you want to explain some phenomenon in evolution, try to find formal psychological analogies, and take a look at your own experience of what it is to have—or be—a mind. Epistemology, the pattern which connects, is, after all, one, not many.

I therefore shall analyze the flaw in the Lamarckian hypothesis and compare it with the problem of the Ancient Mariner. Is it so that "inheritance of acquired characteristics" would induce into biological evolution the same sort of confusion and blockage that sending the Ancient Mariner to the South Seas to find sea snakes would introduce into the process of his escape from guilt? If the comparison be valid, it will surely throw light on both the evolutionary and the human mental process.

I am interested, at this moment, only in the formal objections to the Lamarckian hypothesis. It is no doubt correct to say that (a) there is no experimental evidence for such inheritance and (b) no connection can be imagined by which news of an acquired characteristic (say a strengthened right biceps brought about by exercise) could be transmitted to the ova or spermatozoa of the individual organism. But these otherwise very important considerations are not relevant to the problem of the Ancient Mariner and his self-consciousness. In these respects there is no analogy between the Ancient Mariner and the hypothetical Lamarckian organism. There is plenty of evidence for the assertion that conscious purpose may distort spontaneity and, alas, plenty of pathways of internal communication by which such messages and injunctions may travel. I ask instead, what would the whole of biology look like if the inheritance of acquired characteristics were general? What would be the effect on biological evolution of such a hypothetical process?

Darwin was driven to the Lamarckian fallacy by *time*. He believed that the age of the earth was insufficient to provide time for the vast sweep of evolutionary process and, in order to speed up his model of evolution, he introduced into that model the Lamarckian hypothesis. To rely only on random genetic change combined with natural selection seemed insufficient, and Lamarckian inheritance would provide a *shortcut*, speeding things up by introducing something like *purpose* into the system. And, notably, our hypothetical procedure for the cure of the Ancient Mariner's guilt was likewise an introduction of purpose into that system. Should the Ancient Mariner go purposeless on his voyage, or should he deliberately search for sea snakes with the purpose of blessing them and so escaping from his guilt? Purpose will save *time*. If he knows what he is looking for, he will waste no time in scanning arctic seas.

What then is a shortcut? What is wrong with the proposed shortcuts in evolution and in the resolution of guilt? What is wrong, in principle, with shortcuts?

In a large variety of cases—perhaps in all cases in which the shortcut generates trouble—the root of the matter is an error in logical typing. Somewhere in the sequence of actions and ideas, we can expect to find a class treated as though it were one of its members; or a member treated as though it were identical with the class; a uniqueness treated as a generality or a generality treated as a uniqueness. It is legitimate (and usual) to think of a process or change as an ordered class of states, but a mistake to think of any one of these states as if it were the class of which it is only a member. According to the Lamarckian hypothesis, an individual parent organism is to pass on to its offspring through the digital machinery of genetics some somatic characteristic acquired in response to environmental stress. The hypothesis asserts that "the acquired characteristic is inherited" and there the matter is left as though these words could be meaningful.

It is characteristic of the individual creature that, under environmental conditions of use and disuse, etc., it will change. All right. But this is not the characteristic that is supposedly passed on; not the *potentiality for change* but the *state achieved by the change* is what is to be inherited, and that characteristic is not inherent in the parent. According to hypothesis the offspring should differ from the parent in that they will show the supposedly inherited characteristic even when the environmental conditions do not demand it.

But to assert that the man-made hypothesis of the inheritance of acquired characteristics is semantic nonsense is not the same as to assert that if the hypothesis were true, the whole process of evolution would be bogged down. What is crucial is that the individual creature would be inflicting upon its offspring a rigidity from which the parent itself did not suffer. It is this *loss of flexibility* that would be lethal to the total process.

So—if there be formal analogy between the case of Lamarckian "inheritance" and the conscious purpose that might block the release of the Ancient Mariner from his guilt, we should look in the latter case for an error in classification that would prevent the desired change—error in which a process is treated as a state. It is precisely the conscious reification of his guilt in the Albatross that makes it impossible for the Ancient Mariner to get rid of his guilt. Guilt is not a thing. The matter must be handed over to more unconscious mental processes whose epistemology is less grotesque. [And if the Mariner is to solve his problem, he must not know he is doing so.

[Consciousness is necessarily very limited.] That it is so limited is perhaps best demonstrated by an example from a set of experiments on perception that were pioneered by an ophthalmologist, Adelbert Ames, Jr., now, alas, deceased. He showed that in the act of vision you rely on a whole mass of presuppositions, which you cannot inspect or state in words—such abstract rules as those of parallax and perspective. Using them, you construct your mental image.

It is epistemologically inaccurate to say that "you see me." What you see is an *image* of me made by processes of which you are quite unconscious.

It would be nonsense, of course, to say that "you" make these images. You have almost no control over the making of them. (And if you had that sort of control, your trust in the images that perception displays before your inner eye would be much reduced.)

So we all make—my mental processes make for me—this beautiful quilt. Patches of green and brown, black and white as I walk through the woods. But I cannot by introspection investigate that creative process. I know which way I aim my eyes and I am conscious of the *product* of perception, but I know nothing of the middle process by which the images are formed.

That middle process is governed by presuppositions. What Adelbert Ames discovered was a method of investigating those presuppositions, and an account of his experiments is a good way of arriving at a recognition of the importance of these presuppositions of which we are normally unaware.

If I am traveling in a moving train, the cows on the embankment seem to get left behind while the distant mountains seem to travel with me. On the basis of this difference in appearances, an image is created in which the mountains are depicted as farther from me than the cows. The underlying premise is that that which gets left behind is closer to me than that which seems to go along with me or which is more slowly left behind.

One of Ames' experiments demonstrates that the mechanisms of unconscious process in the brain in every normal human being deal with and rely on the mathematical regularities of such parallax.

A pack of Lucky Strike cigarettes is set up halfway along a narrow table. At the far end of the table, about five feet from the subject, is a book of paper matches. These objects are raised above the table on spikes about six inches high. The experimenter has the subject note the size and position of these objects from above and then stoop to see them through a round hole in a plank which stands up from the edge of the table at the subject's end. The subject now has only monocular vision, but the two objects still appear to be in their places and to be of their familiar size.

Ames then tells the subject to slide the plank sideways while still looking through the holes. Instantly the appearance, the *image*, changes. The Lucky Strike pack is now seen to be at the far end of the table and is magnified to twice its normal size. It looks like a dummy pack in some shop window. The book of matches seems to have come close, to be where the Lucky Strikes were, but it is only half its known size and looks as if it belonged in a dollhouse.

This illusion is created by levers under the table. When the subject moves the peephole sideways, the objects are also moved: the cigarettes were moved in tandem to appear stationary, as the distant mountains do from the train. This made them appear distant. The matches were moved in the reverse direction so as to be left behind by the subject's motion, and this made them appear nearby. Parallax was reversed and the subject then made the size of the images appropriate to the reversal. In a word, your machinery of perception, *how* you perceive, is governed by a system of presuppositions I call your epistemology: a whole philosophy deep in your mind but beyond your consciousness.

Of course, you do not have to move your head every time you need to know about depth. You have other presuppositions you can rely on for this purpose. First, the contrast between what you see with one eye and what you see with the other will be available to compare with the contrast you get by moving your head. After that you can cross-check with a whole series of presuppositions not quite so firmly held as those of parallax—that if things appear to overlap, the thing that is partly concealed is further from you than the thing that conceals it; that if similar things appear to be of different sizes, the one that appears bigger is the closer; and so on.

.

[The Ames experiments can be used to demonstrate two important notions, first that the images we experience are not "out there," and second that we are, perhaps necessarily, unaware of what is going on in our own minds. We think we see, but actually we create images, all unconsciously. What then is one to make of Descartes' famous conclusion, *cogito, ergo sum?*]

The *cogito* is ambiguous. At what level are we to interpret it? What does it mean? What is it to *think*? What is it to *be*? Does it mean "I think that I think, and therefore I think I am"? Can I in fact know that I think? And are we, in reaching such a conclusion, relying on presuppositions of which we are unaware?

There is a discrepancy of logical type between "think" and "be." Descartes is trying to jump from the frying pan of *thought, ideas, images, opinions, arguments,* etc., into the fire of existence and action. But that jump is itself unmapped. Between two such contrasting universes there can be no *ergo*—no totally self-evident link. There is no looking before the leap from *cogito* to *sum*.

Parallel to the *cogito* is another deep epistemological generalization: *I see, therefore it is.* Seeing is believing. We might roughly Latinize this to include the other senses, even though sight carries the greatest conviction for most people, as *percipio, ergo est.* The two halves of Descartes' *cogito* refer to a single subject, a first person singular, but in the *percipio* there are two subjects: I and it. These two subjects are separated by the circumstances of imagery. The "it" which I perceive is ambiguous: is it my image which I make? Or is it some object outside of myself—the

Ding an sich of which I make an image? Or perhaps there is no "it." In English the separation is forced upon us by the structure of our language, but the Latin makes no explicit cleavage between the event of thinking and the thinker. It does not separate the pronoun from the verb. That separation could come later, much later, and raises another set of epistemological problems. The first miracle is the event of thinking, which can (also later) be named. The problems multiply as we explore further. Warren McCulloch long ago pointed out that every message is both command and report. In the simplest case, a sequence of three neurons— A, B, and C—the firing of B is a report that "A recently fired" and a command: "C must quickly fire." In one aspect the neural impulse refers to the past, in the other aspect it determines a future. B's report is, in the nature of the case, *never* totally reliable, for the firing of A can never be the only possible cause of B's later firing: Neurons sometimes fire "spontaneously." In principle, no causal network is to be read backwards. Similarly, C may fail to obey B's injunction.

There are *gaps* in this process, which make the sequential firing of neurons unsure; and there are multiple such gaps on the way to propositions like the *cogito* that are at first glance "self-evident." In the aggregates of propositions that are called "faiths," or religious creeds, it is ultimately not the propositions that assert indubitable and self-evident truth but the links between them. It is these links that we dare not doubt— and indeed doubt is comfortingly excluded by the logical or quasi-logical nature of the links. We are defended from doubt by an *unawareness* of the gaps.

But the jump is always there. If I look through my corporeal eyes and see an image of the rising sun, the propositions "I look" and "I see" have a sort of validity different from that of any conclusion about the world outside my skin. "I see a sun rising" is a proposition that indeed, as Descartes insists, cannot be doubted, but the extrapolation from this to the outside world—*"There is a sun"*—is always unsure and must be supported by faith. Another problem is that all such images are retrospective. The assertion of the image, qua description of the external world, is always in a past tense. Our senses can only tell us at best what *was* so a moment ago. We do in fact read the causal sequence backwards. But this fundamentally unreliable information is delivered to the perceiving self in the most convincing and indubitable form as an *image*. It is this faith—a faith in our own mental process—that must always be defended!

It is commonly thought that faith is necessary for religion—that the supernatural aspects of mythology must not be questioned—so the gap between the observer and the supernatural is covered by faith. But when we recognize the gap between *cogito* and *sum*, and the similar gap between *percipio* and *est*, "faith" comes to have quite a different meaning. Gaps such as these are a necessity of our being, to be covered by "faith" in a very intimate and deep sense of that word. Then what is ordinarily called "religion," the net of ritual, mythology, and mystification, begins to show itself as a sort of cocoon woven to protect that more intimate—and utterly necessary—faith.

By some admirable and mysterious skill, some miracle of neural circuitry, we form images of that which we see. The forming of such images is in fact what we call "seeing." But to base complete belief upon the image is an act of faith. This faith is, in a healthy mind, involuntary and unconscious. You cannot doubt the validity of your images when these are accompanied by that extra tag of information which says that the material for the given image was collected by a sense organ.

How lucky we are, how good is God—that we cannot perceive the processes of our creation of our own images! These miraculous mental processes are simply not accessible to our conscious inspection.

When you are dizzy and the floor seems to heave up towards you, only by the exercise of trained determination can you act upon your "knowledge" that, of course, the floor is remaining stationary, as it should. Indeed, that greater faith accompanied by will, whereby we resist the response to dizziness, is I think always supported by a *conscious* skepticism regarding the visual-kinesthetic imagery. We can say to ourselves, "I know that this swirling of the floor and walls is a misleading product of my processes of image formation." But even so, there is no consciousness of the processes by which the swirling images were made—only a consciousness that they are indeed artifact. We can know about the processes of perception, but we cannot be directly aware of them. [Even at this level, however, consciousness opens the door to tinkering.]

If we had continual awareness of our image-making processes, our images would cease to be credible. It is indeed a merciful dispensation that we know not the processes of our own creativity—which sometimes are the processes of self-deceit.

To be unconscious of these processes is the first line of our defense against loss of faith. A little faith in perception is vitally necessary, and by packing our data into the form of images, we convince ourselves of the validity of our belief. *Seeing is believing*. But faith is in believing that seeing is believing. As Blake said of the "corporeal," which we believe we know, "It is in Fallacy, and its Existence an Imposture."*

Still, all of this is familiar. It is platitude to assert that every perception and every link between perception and motion is made possible by faith in presuppositions. Hamlet reminds his mother, "Sense sure you have, else you could have no motion." The links between sense and motion are indispensable to living, but the links depend always upon presuppositions that are commonly either absolutely inaccessible to consciousness, or momentarily left unexamined in the immediacy of action. There is no time for more than a little consciousness.

The matter becomes more subtle, more coercive, and somewhat more mysterious when we ask formally analogous questions about larger systems, such as groups of organisms, and particularly about families, communities, and tribes, constellations of organisms who (partially at least) share what anthropologists call "culture." One of the meanings of that overworked word is the local epistemology, the aggregate of presuppositions that underlie all communication and interaction between persons, even in dyads, groups with only two members.

[It is at this point that our discussion of perception links up with the discussion of inheritance, for in each case the fact that many presuppositions are inaccessible to examination or alteration results in a certain conservatism, since that which is outside of awareness is also unquestioned. It may be useful, then, to examine the conservatism characteristic of all such systems of presuppositions and the mechanisms by which such systems are maintained and kept stable.]

Young-men-in-a-hurry may be impatient of such conservatism, and psychiatrists may diagnose conservatism as pathological rigidity, etc., etc. But I am not concerned at the moment to reach judgments of value, only to understand the processes and their necessity.

Of all interactional conservative devices, undoubtedly the most fundamental—most ancient and profound, and most instructive as providing a diagram of what I am talking about—is sex.

We forget so easily—and by forgetting we preserve our presuppositions unexamined—that the prime function of the sexual component in reproduction (literally the production of the similar) is the *maintenance of similarity* among members of the species. And here similarity is the necessary condition for viability of communication and interaction. The

Catalogue for the Year 1810.

mechanism and its goal become identical: that compatibility which is necessary for interaction is maintained by creating a test-tube trial of similarity. If the gametes are not sufficiently similar, a zygote formed from their meeting cannot survive. At the cellular level every living organism is the embodiment of a tested sharing of biological presuppositions.

Tests against the outside world will come later—many of them. At the moment of fertilization—fusion of gametes—each gamete is a validating template for the other. What is surely tested is the chromosomal constitution of each, but no doubt the similarity of the whole cellular structure is also verified. And note that this first test is not of the *meaning* of the chromosomal message, the process of epigenesis and the later outcome in the developed individual or phenotype that will be tested by the need to survive in a given environment. The test is just a proofreader's trick, comparing the format of one text with that of the other, but ignoring the nature and meaning of the message material which is being tested. Other tests will come later and will not be exclusively conservative.

Samuel Butler famously asserted that "the hen is an egg's way of making another egg." We might amplify that to say that the hen is the proof (the test) of the excellence of the egg; and that the moment of fusion between two gametes is the first proof or test of their mutual excellence. Note that excellence is in some sense always *mutual*; the conservatism whose mechanics I am discussing is always interactive.

From these very elementary generalities, it is possible to proceed in several directions, which can only be suggested here. There is the undoubted truth that the relations between presuppositions (in some widest sense of that word) are never simply dyadic. We must go on to consider a greater complexity. It is not a matter of simple dyadic comparison as my reference to sexual fusion might seem to suggest. We can begin by considering a pair of gametal characteristics that meet in fertilization. But always each must exist in the context of many characteristics, and the comparison will not be a simple yes-or-no test of similarity but a complex fitting or wrestling together (in real time) of related but never totally similar *networks of propositions*, which must combine in a coherent set of injunctions for the epigenesis and growth of the organism. There is room for—indeed there is benefit from—a little variation, but only a limited amount.

That's one component of the picture—the increasing complexity as we go on from dyadic to more complex relations between the items of presupposition. (We could use an alternative term that is virtually synonymous and speak of "preconceptions"—in a literal, prezygotic sense!)

The second pathway of increasing complexity we are invited to follow by the infinitely complex and systemic biosphere is a spin-off from the way systems are nested within systems, the fact of hierarchical organizations. For instance, as natural historians of the family we face a more than dyadic constellation of persons. To the nondyadic tangle of related presuppositions, we must add the nondyadic tangle of persons in which the family is the mechanism of cultural transmission. In looking at human beings we deal not simply with genetics, the digital names for settings of the bias of the system, but with another order of change—the facts of learning and teaching. (And do not forget that in what is called "cultural transmission," parents learn from and are as much changed as their children!)

The complexity of the phenomena is beginning to run away with us and whenever that happens, the correct and orthodox procedure is reductionism—to stand off from the data and consider what sort of simplified (always oversimplified) mapping will do least damage to the elegant interconnections of the observed world.

We must take care, however, to preserve in our theories at least the biological nature (cybernetic, hierarchic, holistic, nonlineal, systemic nature—call it what you will) of the world and our relations to it. Let us not pretend that mental phenomena can be mapped onto the characteristics of billiard balls.

X Metalogue:

Are You Creeping Up?

(MCB)

DAUGHTER: Are you creeping up on the subject of consciousness?

FATHER: I suppose I am. People are always after me to discuss consciousness, and I am generally pretty leery of the subject. After all, until we understand more about how information moves within systems, we won't be able to do much with the special case represented by consciousness.

DAUGHTER: So that's what consciousness is? A special case of information transmission within the human person?

FATHER: Surely, but that is really a very inadequate way of saying it. There is also a shift in logical types, because consciousness means that *you know that you know*. That's why the question is so much more complex.

DAUGHTER: No, but look—there's another similarity to the Lamarckian case. Genetic information characterizes an entire organism, recurring in every cell even though it is locally expressed. Change produced by environmental stress has to be local, even though it may be widespread. The shift in logical types is obscured by the fact of succeeding generations, but "nature" is of a higher logical type than "nurture," right? And more conservative, of course.

FATHER: Hmm. It's perhaps a related issue that the value of sexual reproduction seems to outweigh its disadvantages. The species sloughs off a vast number of effective genetic combinations and workable adaptations by reshuffling genetic material. It's a high price for the opportunity of cross-checking.

DAUGHTER: I know. You meet someone and you think, wow, this person is a product of a superb combination of genetics and environment, we ought to be able to keep this one going. It strikes me that both sexual reproduction and death are pretty elegant inventions. The myth that says eating from the tree of knowledge is the origin of death, well, it has a truth to it in this business of preserving and accumulating information. After all, you need a way to eliminate some too. And the standard vulgarization of the myth, that the coming of death has something to do with sexuality, also fits.

FATHER: Not sexuality but self-consciousness. Remember, after eating the apple Adam and Eve became *aware* of their nakedness.

DAUGHTER: If Lamarckian inheritance worked, wouldn't you rapidly get different species, individual organisms too different to be cross-fertile?

FATHER: That's right. With too much discrepancy between the parents, either the embryo dies or the offspring is itself infertile. Either way, the effect is conservative.

DAUGHTER: Snails, Daddy. Remember that business you told me about with the snails in Hawaii? How did that go?

FATHER: Umm. That's a different story, but it fits in here somewhere. As you know, every spiral is either right-handed or left-handed, and right-handed snails cannot mate with left-handed snails. But it turns out that a reversal of the direction of the spiral occurs with some frequency in certain snails—probably no more is involved than a single change of sign in the genome. At any rate, it occurs with sufficient frequency so that the offspring with reversed direction can find reversed mates and so can reproduce. But this then leads to a new and separate breeding population subject to its own selection and genetic drift, and when the sequence eventually occurs in the opposite direction, the new reversed batch will be unable to mate with their distant cousins. You get a proliferation of species.

DAUGHTER: Cutting off interbreeding, which hastens genetic divergence—is that an example of this noncommunication business? Come to think of it, genetic diversity gives one kind of stability within the species and then another at the ecosystem level, with lots of species.

Daddy, you once said that you would derive consciousness from your analysis of the similarity between learning and evolution. Maybe that would help me see the relationship between the epistemological material and the cybernetic diagrams on the one hand, and the anecdotes and myths and questions of how we act in the world on the other.

FATHER: "How we act in the world." Hmm. Well, I remain skeptical about both knowledge and action for very similar reasons. There is a double set of illusions—mirror images perhaps.

It is clear—as you know—that we do not *see* external objects and persons: "we" "see" *images* of those (therefore hypothetical) external entities. It is *we* who *make* the images. It is less clear—but must also be true—that we similarly do not have direct knowledge of our own actions.

We know (in part) what we intended.

We perceive (in part) what we are doing—we hear images of the sound of our own voices; we see or feel images of the motions of our limbs. We know not *how* we move our arms and legs.

In principle, our *output* is as indirectly known to us as our *input*. Ha!

DAUGHTER: So is it the same mistake, when we think we can decide on some action, as it is when we think we really see something?

FATHER: It strikes me that just as the Ames experiments demonstrate to you the general fact that indeed you do not see external objects but only images of those "objects," it should be possible to devise analogous experiments to demonstrate to you or anyone that you have no direct knowledge of your own actions.

DAUGHTER: I'm not sure I'd like that very much. But what would such an experiment look like?

FATHER: Well, let's see. If we follow the model of the experiments on depth perception, we would do well to devise experiments to study some particular characteristic that perception lends to the experience of one's own action.

DAUGHTER: Hmm. That sounds right.

FATHER: For instance, you could try unity or beginning-and-end, or intensity dimensions like duration or violence. We could make a list and then ask which ones are more accessible to experiment. Let's see: balance; irreversibility; precision; consciousness; effect; efficiency. . . .

DAUGHTER: You know, some of these characteristics pull us right into questions of aesthetics. Your old friend "grace is going to turn up.

FATHER: But wait, Cap. First I want to ask, why or how does it happen that this matter is even more difficult to think about than is the matter demonstrated in the Ames experiments? Do we then *desire* to be responsible for our own activities (even though somehow and somewhere we recognize that of course "free will" is nonsense)?

What does it mean to *lend* to our own actions the characteristic which we call "free will"? And what then is the contrast between "voluntary" actions mediated by striped muscles and "involuntary" actions mediated by unstriped muscle and autonomic nervous system?

Either these questions are nonsense—or they propose a lifetime of work . . .

DAUGHTER: Daddy, you're going too fast. And you're declaiming at me.

FATHER: Look. The doctrine of "free will" is to action as the notion of "direct vision" is to perception—but "direct vision" makes perception into a *passive* business. "Free will" makes action *more* active.

In other words, we subtract or repress our awareness that perception is active and repress our awareness that action is passive—? This it is to be *conscious*?

DAUGHTER: I like the idea of a sort of pincers maneuver on consciousness from the two directions of action and perception. But I know you were also working on giving the word a meaning in terms of the systemic model we've been using of the relationship between structure and flux.

For instance, Daddy, I found a diagram in a copy of a letter you sent to John Todd. It's an awful mess, but—

FATHER: Nonsense. It's not final, but it should be perfectly clear.

DAUGHTER: Well, anyway, what I want to pull out of it and explore is the notion that it might tell us how to apply the ideas in "Defenses of Faith" to the model in chapter 4.

FATHER: Good. That, of course, is exactly what a model is for—you see certain formal possibilities and look back to see whether they in fact illuminate something that occurs in the world.

DAUGHTER: Let's have a look at this, then, and see what we can get out of it.

STRUCTURE
(i.e. Thresholds, Settings,
States, etc.)

FUNCTION
(i.e. events, actions,
etc.)

Upper Boundary of Niche

Residents Threshold for hot or cold

Resident sets bias.

State of Bias or Threshold for ON/OFF

Snitch turns to ON (or to OFF)

sub-sub-system "thermostat"

ON + OFF state of Switch

Boundary of Sub-system "house"

Temperature rises / falls.

Temperature is N°.

etc.

Shapes of arrows: ↙ denotes: events change a setting.

" : a setting determines an event

↑ an aggregate of events (sub-system) determines events in a larger system —

↑ Events determine a crucial event.

↖ Lamarckian causation— (lethal).

↗ — Consciousness (?)

It's not final but good enough to play with it.

DAUGHTER: What interests me is your experiment of finding possible interpretations for the arrows in your diagrams if they are reversed. I guess this zigzag is easiest to read in comparison with Figure 1B on page 41, but that's just because the zigzag format includes time. The arrow downward from structure to flux, which represents a setting determining an event, say genotype setting the parameters for phenotype ($\searrow$), you remember? If that direction were reversed ($\nwarrow$), you said, it would be Lamarckian inheritance—and lethal. Then you seemed to suggest that the arrow whereby events change a setting ($\swarrow$), read in reverse ($\nearrow$), might—maybe—correspond to consciousness? Are they both short circuits of some kind?

FATHER: Well, that was very tentative. I still need to play with it some more. Another possibility for a definition of consciousness would be in the way subsystems are hooked into a larger whole.

DAUGHTER: Ah, but look. Lamarckian inheritance does make sense and is not lethal in populations—at the next level up—and consciousness is by definition a next-level-up phenomenon. Obviously, if you try to model a phenomenon of higher logical type at too low a level, you will get something that looks like pathology. My guess is that only the very best consciousness will do, whatever that is. Daddy, do *you* think consciousness is lethal?

FATHER: Mmm. Empirically it seems on its way to being so. Human consciousness linked with purpose might turn out to be rather like the tail of the argus pheasant, an extreme elaboration of a particular trait that sends a species into an evolutionary cul-de-sac. But that's happened before. What is frightening is the possibility that the presence of a creature like us anywhere in the system may eventually be lethal to the entire system.

DAUGHTER: If . . . let's suppose . . . consciousness has to do with relationship between subsystems . . . then secrecy or unawareness would mean that the system would both know and not know. There would be knowledge that was okay at one level, but would be toxic at another. In spite of what you say about the Ancient Mariner, people do go in search of psychological or spiritual experiences all the time, both knowing and not knowing what they are looking for. And hopefully containing the information with which to recognize the experience when they meet it.

FATHER: "And recognize the place for the first time?" Part of any spiritual discipline, however, is discovering—repeatedly—that one had it all wrong. You both knew and did not know.

DAUGHTER: Look—I just saw it. Reversing that arrow is more like *projection* or wishful thinking than consciousness.

FATHER: Mmm. Well, it was an experiment.

DAUGHTER: But I'm interested in projection in just this context, because projection is what most people say religion is. A sort of compensation. And yet from time to time over the years, you have suggested that religion—or something like religion—might be a necessary sort of control mechanism in a given culture, the only way it maintains its equilibrium vis-à-vis its ecosystem.

FATHER: Both could be true. Both could be true either trivially or at a more complex level.

DAUGHTER: Or maybe what a religion supplies could be something like perspective, broader and longer, to give the kind of context that makes it seem worthwhile to plant trees.

FATHER: This is certainly a matter that comes up in many religious traditions. There are in fact a set of complicated relationships between time, purpose, and consciousness. T. S. Eliot talks about this, and so does Screwtape.

DAUGHTER: Screwtape?

FATHER: Yes—the senior devil in C. S. Lewis's *Screwtape Letters*, writing to his nephew advising him on how to corrupt the human being who is in his especial charge. The advice is: Keep him always thinking of the past and the future. Never let him live in the present. The past and the future are in time. The present is *timeless* and *eternal*.

DAUGHTER: Timeless?

FATHER: Nonappetitive. Without *purpose* and without *desire*. "Unattached," as the Buddhists say. Did I ever tell you about *tempo* and *perlu*? It seems that in the last hundred years and perhaps quite recently, these two words, meaning time and purpose, were added through borrowing to the Balinese language. And yet the Balinese were fascinated by complex calendrical elaborations, none of which were treated as cumulative.

DAUGHTER: Did they have a word for that "timeless present"?

FATHER: I guess not. They would not need it till they had *perlu* and *tempo*. But wait. There's a distinction we need to make here. You see, there are two sorts of "time."

DAUGHTER: You say "time" as if the word had quotes on it.

FATHER: Oh? Well, yes. I mean two ideas which people have, and both ideas are called "time." More technically, they are called *synchronic* and *diachronic* time. Or should I say two sorts of change?

DAUGHTER: Is every event a change?

FATHER: Oh yes, certainly—if an egg hatches, that's a change. The chick was inside before and now it's outside—that's a change. But if I am talking about the total life of the species of bird, the egg hatching is only a synchronic change. It's not a change in the life of the species. It's just a part of the ongoing total process of life, just as the traditional Balinese calendar used to cycle through its different systems of festivals without getting anywhere.

DAUGHTER: And "diachronic"?

FATHER: That's when the event is seen as foreign to the "total process." If somebody scatters DDT in the woods and the birds die from eating the earthworms that ate the DDT—that's diachronic from the point of view of the bird-watcher, whose focus is on the repetitive processes of the life of—let's say—the woodpeckers.

DAUGHTER: But can an event—a change—can it shift from being synchronic to being diachronic?

FATHER: No—of course not. "It" isn't anything. It (the change) is only something which somebody pulled out of the great flux of events and made a subject of conversation. A subject of explanation, perhaps.

DAUGHTER: So—it's just a matter of how we look at it? I mean—could I see the single swing of a clock's pendulum as either synchronic or diachronic? Can I plant a tree as if its maturation were part of the present? Can I see the extermination of the plankton as either synchronic or diachronic?

FATHER: Surely—but you would have to stretch your imagination. Ordinarily we say, "The clock ticks," and the ticking is part of its ongoing way of being. To see the single swing of the pendulum as diachronic, you must narrow your vision to focus on something smaller than the single oscillation. To see the death of our world's plankton as synchronic, you would have to focus on the whole galaxy perhaps—

DAUGHTER: But is synchronic time only another name for the Eternal Present?

FATHER: I think so—yes. A less poetic way of talking, but very nearly the same. It's like burning the chaparral—the scrub on the California hills. The movie stars who live on the hillsides see the burning of the chaparral as an irreversible event which may destroy their way of life. And the rangers agree with that view. But the Indians who used to live there set fire to the chaparral every few years themselves. For them, it was part of the nature of their chaparral that it burn periodically.

DAUGHTER: They had a wider view?

FATHER: Yes—the movie stars are what the Orientals call *attached*.

DAUGHTER: Is it a good thing to be unattached and to see everything that happens in a bigger, synchronic frame? Always a bigger frame?

FATHER: Personally, I would look after the chaparral, but I would let the galaxy look after itself.

But that's ambiguous. To see myself as part of a system which includes me and the chaparral frames a reason for my action—to preserve the ongoing cycling of *us* (me and the chaparral) by actively burning off the chaparral. I think synchronic action—framed like that—is Taoist—it's a sort of passivity. There is no diachronic action in the Eternal Present. But to rush to preserve the human species against a galactic threat or to get ready for a biblical apocalypse, that would be diachronic.

DAUGHTER: You mean there would be no reason to fuss unless you saw the threatened change as diachronic. Is dying diachronic?

FATHER: Not in the wider frame, no. But there is admittedly a tendency to see it that way.

DAUGHTER: You know, you have to think yourself out of the Eternal Present before you try to *do anything about anything*. That's where we always get into arguments. It's as if you need to have two points of view, from inside and from outside, both at the same time.

Daddy, I remember you used to talk about totemism as perhaps the necessary system of ideas for the Australian aborigines, or the mass as the necessary ritual in medieval European life. . . . If the mass is somehow what keeps me sane, it will be worth defending, and losing it would be thoroughly diachronic.

FATHER: You see, the mass could embody—encapsulate—some complex truth you had no access to in any other form. And it could do that even while proposing a great many propositions of lower logical type that seem like nonsense, as long as these are such as not to create significant contradiction.

DAUGHTER: Or maybe contradictions are avoided by keeping different kinds of propositions separate? Is that part of the differential distribution of information? But do you mean that I might not even be able to state those most important truths?

FATHER: It would be a different kind of knowing, the kind of knowledge we call *character*, built in at a very pervasive and abstract level. And, alas, the destruction of totemism or the secularization of the mass can also affect people at a very deep level. They can learn such premises as "nothing is sacred," or "nothing has to be seen as part of a larger whole," or "all that matters is the bottom line." The whole range of potentialities that go with the human capacity to learn has its shadow side—a creature without consciousness has no possibility of becoming schizophrenic.

XI   The Messages of

Nature and Nurture (GB)

I AM continually surprised at the lighthearted way in which scientists assert that some characteristic of an organism is to be explained by invoking *either* the environment *or* the genotype. Let me make clear, therefore, what I believe to be the relation between these two explanatory systems. It is precisely in the *relation* between the two systems that the tangles occur which make me hesitate to assign any given characteristic to one or the other.

In the description of an organism, consider any component that is subject to change under environmental impact—for example, the color of the skin. In those human beings who are not albinos the color of the skin is subject to darkening or tanning when the skin is exposed to sunshine. Now, imagine that we are asking about a particular human being, to what is the particular degree of brown in his skin to be assigned? Is it genotypically or phenotypically determined?

The answer, of course, will involve both genotype and phenotype. Some persons are born browner than others, and all, so far as I know (with the exception of albinos), are capable of becoming more brown under sunshine. We may, therefore, say immediately that genotype is involved in two ways: in determining the starting point of tanning and in determining an ability to tan. On the other hand, the environment is involved in exploiting the ability to tan, to produce the phenotypic color of the given individual.

The next question is whether there is not only a tanning under the influence of sunshine but also, possibly, an *increase in ability* to tan under sunshine. Could we, by tanning and bleaching and tanning and bleaching an individual successively a number of times, increase his "skill" in turning brown under sunshine? If so, then the genotype and the phenotype are both involved at the next level of abstraction, the genotype in providing the individual with not only an ability to tan but with an ability to learn to tan and the environment correspondingly taking up this ability.

But, then again, there is the question of whether the genotype conceivably provides an ability *to learn to change the ability* to tan. This would seem exceedingly unlikely, but the question must be asked when we are dealing with a creature subject to learning, to environmental impact. Insofar as the creature is subject to such impact, it is always made so by the characteristics of its genotypic determination.

In the end, if we want to ask about tanning or about any other phenomenon of environmental change or learning, the question we have to ask is the logical type of the specification provided by the genotype. Does it define skin color? Does it define ability to change skin color? Does it define the ability to change the ability to change skin color? And so on. For every descriptive proposition we may utter about a phenotype, there is a background of explanation which, at successive logical type levels, will always peel off into the genotype. The particular environment, of course, is still always relevant for explanation.

I believe that something of this sort is necessarily so, and from this it follows that a major question or set of questions we have to be aware of concerns the logical typing of the genotypic message.

The case of blood sugar is interesting. The actual concentration of sugar in the blood varies from minute to minute with intake of carbohydrates, liver action, exercise, and the length of time between meals, etc. But these changes must be kept within tolerance. There is an upper threshold and a lower threshold and the organism *must* keep the blood sugar level within these limits, on pain of extreme discomfort and/or death. But these limits are changeable under environmental pressure, such as chronic starvation, training, and acclimation. Finally, the abstract component in the trait—that indeed blood sugar has an upper limit that is modifiable by experience—must be referred to genetic control.

It is said that in the 1920s when Germany was restricted by the Treaty of Versailles to a parade-ground army of ten thousand men, very strict tests were applied to the men who volunteered for this army. They were to be the cream of the rising generation not only in physique but also in physiology and dedication. A blood sample was taken from each volunteer at the beginning of the test. He was then asked to climb over a simple barrier in the recruiting office, and then to climb back, and then to go on climbing until he could not climb anymore. When *he* decided that he "could not," his blood was again sampled. Those were accepted into the army who were most able to reduce their blood sugar, overcoming exhaustion by determination. No doubt the trait *"able to reduce blood sugar"* would be subject to quantitative change through training or practice, but also, no doubt, some individuals would (probably for genetic reasons) respond more and more rapidly to such training.

It is no simple matter to identify the trait that is specified by the genotype. Let us consider some cases at a rather naive level. There used to be, in the American Museum of Natural History in New York, an exhibit designed to show the bell-shaped curve of random distribution of a variable. This curve was made from a bucket of clams randomly collected on the Long Island shore. The clams in question have a variable number of ridges going from the hinge radially towards the periphery of the shell. The number of ridges varied, as I remember, from about nine or ten to about twenty. A curve was made by piling up one shell on top of the other—all the nine-ridged shells to make one vertical column and then next to it all the ten-ridged shells—and then drawing a curve on the wall behind them at the height of the different piles. It appeared then that somewhere in the middle range one column was higher than all the other columns and that the height of the columns fell off both towards the shells with fewer ridges and towards those with more ridges. But curiously, interestingly, the curve so produced was actually not a clean Gaussian curve. It was skewed. And it was in fact skewed so that the norm was closer to the end having fewer ridges.

I looked at this curve and wondered why it was skewed, and it occurred to me that perhaps the coordinates were wrongly chosen. That perhaps what affected the growth of the clam was not the number of ridges but how closely packed the ridges might be. That is, there might be more difference from the growing clam's point of view between having nine ridges and having ten ridges than there is between having eighteen ridges and having nineteen. How much space is there for more ridges? What angle does each ridge occupy? It therefore followed that perhaps the curve should have been plotted not against the number of ridges but against the reciprocal of this number. Against, that is, the average angle between ridges. If these increments had been used, the curve would have undergone a change, because in fact the curve of the reciprocal $(x = \frac{1}{y})$ is not a straight line. It is a parabola. Therefore, a skewing of the curve might be neutralized. It was clear in any case that if the curve plotted against the number of ridges were in fact a normal curve, then the curve plotted against the angles between ridges could not possibly be one. Conversely, if the curve plotted against the angle should be normal, then the other, plotted against the number of ridges, would have to be skewed. It therefore seemed a reasonable question to ask whether one curve might perhaps give in some sense a *truer* picture of the state of affairs than the other— "truer" in the sense that one curve rather than the other might more accurately reflect the genotypic message.

A very little arithmetic and some graph paper showed that the curve was immediately much less skewed and, in a sense, would have been a better museum exhibit had it been plotted against the angle rather than the number of ridges.

Thinking about this very simple example will illustrate what I mean by inquiring about the logical type of the genotypic message. Is it conceivable that in the case of these clams the genotypic message contains somehow a direct reference to a *number* of ridges? Or is it more probable that in fact the message contains no substantive of that order at all— probably contains no analog of a substantive? There might indeed be no "word" for an angle, so that the whole message would be somehow carried as a name of an operation, if you please, in some sort of group-theoretic definition of the pattern of ridges and angles. In this case, estimating by angles (that is, by the *relation* between ridges) will certainly be a more appropriate way to describe the organism than stating the number of ridges.

We, after all, can look at the whole clam and count the ridges, but in the process of growth the message of the DNA must be locally read. A reference to number cannot be *locally* useful, but a reference to *relation* between the local patch of tissue and the neighboring regions could conceivably be significant. The larger patterns must always be carried in the form of detailed instructions to the component parts.

The essence of the matter is that if we are concerned with environment and with genotypic determination, what we ultimately most desire is that our description of the individual phenotype shall be in a language appropriate to the genotypic messages and to the environmental impacts that have shaped that phenotype.

If we look at, say, a crab, we note that it has two chelae and eight walking appendages on the thorax, i.e. two claws and four pairs of legs. But it is not a trivial matter to decide whether we will say this animal has "ten appendages on the thorax" or "five pairs of appendages on the thorax" or "one pair of claws and four pairs of walking legs on the thorax." No doubt there are other ways of stating the matter, but the point I want to make is merely that one of these ways can be better than others in applying to the phenotype a syntax of description that will reflect the messages from the genotype that have determined that phenotype. And note that the description of phenotype that best reflects the injunctions of genotype will also, necessarily, bring to the fore whatever components of the phenotype have been determined by environmental impact. The two sorts of determinism will, in fact, be sorted out and their relations clearly indicated in the ultimate perfect description, which will reflect both.

But note further that the notion of number represented in our description of the clams is a totally different concept—a different logical type, if you please—from number as represented by the number of appendages on the thorax of the crab. In the one case, that of the clam, number would seem to refer to a quantity. The very fact that it varies on something like a normal curve indicates immediately that this is a matter of more-or-less. On the other hand, the appendages of the crab are strictly limited and are not a quantity but essentially a pattern. And this difference between quantity and pattern is important right through the biological world and no doubt right through the behavior of the entities in the biological world. We may expect it to be not only anatomical but also behavioral. (I presume that the theoretical approaches for anatomy, physiology, and behavior are a single set of approaches.)

In the relation between genetics and morphogenesis, we face over and over again problems that are really double problems. This double character of almost every problem in communication was summarized by Warren McCulloch in the title of his famous paper "What is a number, that a man may know it, and a man, that he may know a number?"* In our case the problems become: "What is the message of the DNA that the embryo may receive it, and what is an embryo, that it may receive the DNA's message?" The problem becomes sharply compelling when

*Repr. in his *Embodiments of Mind* (Cambridge, Mass.: MIT P, 1965), 1–18.

we deal with such matters as symmetry, metamerism (segmentation), and multiple organs.

I suggested above that we might say either that the crab has "ten" appendages or "five pairs" of appendages on its thorax. But this evidently won't do at all. Imagine that a particular locality—a small region—of the developing embryo must receive some version of the instructions governing these multiple limbs. The version that specifies "five" or "ten" can be of no use to the specific restricted locality. How shall this spot— this bunch of cells in this particular region of the developing embryo— know about a number that is in fact embodied in the larger aggregate of tissues developing those appendages? The restricted locality of the single cell needs to have information not only that there should be five appendages but that there are already elsewhere four or three or two or whatever the situation at a given moment may be. The situation is left obscure even when we change from saying "five" or "ten" to saying a *pattern* of five, a quincunx, say, or whatever may be appropriate.

What the particular patch of growing cells or the single cell needs is *both* information about the total pattern *and* information about what the particular patch is to become in this gestalt. (Alternatively the whole embryology must be what is called mosaic. In the smaller nematodes, it is claimed that the outcome of every cell division is literally pre-scribed.)

The relation between pattern and quantity becomes especially important when we look at the relations between environmental impact and genotypic determinants. Another way of looking at the difference between these two sorts of explanation is that genotypic explanation commonly invokes the digital and the patterned, whereas the impacts of environment are likely to take the form of quantities, stresses, and the like. We may think, perhaps, of the soma—the developing body—of the individual as the arena where quantity meets pattern. And precisely because environmental determination tends to be quantitative, while genotypic determination tends to be a matter of patterns, people—scientists—exhibit strong preferences and are ready to guess lightheartedly at which explanation shall be applied in which case. It would seem that some people prefer quantitative explanations, while others prefer explanations by the invoking of pattern.

These two states of mind, which are almost different enough to be regarded as different epistemologies, have become embodied in political doctrines. Specifically, Marxist dialectic has concerned itself with the relation between quantity and quality or, as I would say, between quantity and pattern. The orthodox notion is, as I understand it, that all important social change is brought on or precipitated by quantitative "pressures," "tensions," and the like. These quantities supposedly build up to some sort of breaking point, at which point a discontinuous step occurs in the social evolution leading to a new gestalt. The essence of the matter is that it is quantity that determines this step and, by corollary, it is assumed that the necessary ingredients for the next change will always and necessarily be present when the quantity becomes sufficiently stressful.

A model commonly cited from the physical world for this phenomenon is that of a chain which under tension will always, in the end, break at its weakest link. In case the links are equal and virtually non-discriminable, the chain may go beyond its ordinary breaking point but, in the end, a weakest link will be discovered and this will be the point of fracture. Another model is the crystallization of a slowly cooling liquid. The crystallization process will always start from some particular point— some minute inequality or fragment of dirt—and once started will proceed to completion. Very pure and clean substances in very smooth containers may be supercooled by a few degrees, but in the end the change will occur and, if there was supercooling, it is likely to be rapid.

Another example of relationship between quantitative and qualitative change is the relation between jamming of traffic on the roads and the population of automobiles on which such jamming depends. The population of automobiles in a given region grows slowly through the years, but the velocity at which automobiles can travel remains constant until a certain threshold value of automobile population is reached. The curve of the population of automobiles is a slowly increasing, smooth curve accelerating slightly as time passes. In contrast, the curve of time spent by each automobile on each mile of the road runs along at a horizontal constant value to a certain point. Then quite suddenly, when the number of automobiles passes that threshold, there is jamming on the roads and the curve representing time spent per mile on the road skyrockets steeply.

We may say that an increase in number of automobiles was in some sense "good"—had a positive value up to a certain point—but beyond that point the number of automobiles in the area has become toxic.

The dialectical view of history is comparable. It assumes that at a given point in history, say the middle of the nineteenth century, social differentiation and pressures were such that a theory of evolution of a particular kind would be generated to reflect that social system. To the Marxist it is, as I understand it, irrelevant whether that theory was produced by Darwin, or Wallace, or Chambers, or by any other of the half-dozen leading biologists who were then on the point of creating an evolutionary theory of that general kind. The Marxist assumption is that when the time is ripe the man will always be present. There will always be someone who will form the crystallization point for the new gestalt. And, indeed, the theory of evolution and its history would seem to confirm this. There were several men in the 1850s who were ready to create a theory of evolution, and this theory, or something like it, was more or less inevitable, give or take ten years before or after the actual date of publication of *The Origin of Species*. It was also, no doubt, politically inevitable that Lamarckian evolution should disappear from the scene at that time and that the cybernetic philosophy of evolution, though actually proposed by Wallace, should not become a dominant theme.

For the Marxists the essence of the matter is that quantity will determine what happens and that pattern will be generated in response to quantitative change.

My own view of the matter, as it has developed in the last few years, is almost the precise contrary of this or, should we say, the precise complement of this. Namely, I have argued that quantity can never under any circumstances explain pattern. That the informational content of quantity, as such, is zero.

It has seemed increasingly clear to me that the vulgar use of "energy" as an explanatory device is fallacious precisely because quantity does *not* determine pattern. I would argue that quantity of tension applied to the chain will not break it *except* by the discovery of the weakest link—that, in fact, the pattern is latent in the chain before the application of the tension and is, as the photographers might say, "developed" under tension.

I am thus temperamentally and intellectually one of those who prefer explanation by pattern to explanation by quantity.

Recently, however, I have begun to see how these two sorts of explanation may fit together. I have for a long time felt an uneasiness about what is meant by the concept of "a question," about whether it was possible for something like a question to be embodied in the prelinguistic biological world.

Let me be clear that I don't now mean a question that a perceiving organism might put to an environment. We might say that the rat exploring in a box is in some sense asking if that box is safe or dangerous, but that is not what concerns us here.

Instead, I am asking whether, at a deeper level, there can be something like a *question* expressed in the language of the injunctions, etc., that are at the base of genetics, morphogenesis, adaptation, and the like. What would the word "question" mean at this deep biological level?

The paradigm I have been carrying in my mind for some time to represent what I mean by a "question" at the morphogenetic level is the sequence of events that follows fertilization of the vertebrate egg, as demonstrated with the eggs of the frog. The unfertilized frog egg, as is well known, is a radially symmetrical system in which the two poles (the upper or "animal" and the lower or "vegetal") are differentiated in that the animal pole has more protoplasm and indeed is the region of the nucleus, while the vegetal pole is more heavily endowed with yolk. But the egg is, it seems, similar all around its equator. There is no differentiation of the plane that will be the future plane of bilateral symmetry of the tadpole. This plane is then determined by the entry of a spermatozoon, usually somewhat below the equator, so that a line drawn through the point of entry and connecting the two poles defines the future midventral line of bilateral symmetry. The environment thus provides the *answer* to the question: Where? which seems to be latent all around the unfertilized egg.

In other words, the egg does not contain the needed information, and neither is this information embodied in any complex way in the DNA of the spermatozoon. Indeed, with a frog's egg, a spermatozoon is not even necessary. The effect can be achieved by pricking the egg with the fiber of a camel's-hair brush. Such an unfertilized egg will then develop into a fully grown frog, albeit haploid (having only a half number of chromosomes).

It was this figure that I carried in mind as a paradigm for thinking about the nature of a question. It seemed to me that we might think of the state of the egg immediately before fertilization as a state of question, a state of *readiness to receive a certain piece of information*, information that is then provided by the entry of the spermatozoon.

Combining this model with what I have said about quantity and quality in the Marxist dialectic and relating all this to the battles that have been fought to and fro over the problem of environmental determinism versus genetic determinism and to the Lamarckian battles, which have also had their political angles, it occurred to me that perhaps *the question is quantitative while the answer is qualitative*. It seemed to me that the state of the egg at the moment of fertilization could probably be described in terms of some quantity of "tension," tension that is in some sense resolved by the essentially digital or qualitative answer provided by the spermatozoon. The question: Where? is a distributed quantity. The answer "there" is a precise digital answer—a digital patterned resolution.

To go back to the chain and the weakest link, it seemed to me that both in the chain and in the case of the frog's egg, the particular digital answer is provided out of the random. The question, however, comes in from the quantitative, represented by increasing tension.

Let us return to the problem of describing an organism and of what is going to happen to the parts of that description as the creature undergoes the processes of growth, environmental impact, or evolution. We may conveniently follow Ashby in regarding the description of an organism as a list of propositional variables, running perhaps to some millions of propositions. Each of these propositions or values has the characteristic that above a certain level it will become lethal. In other words, the organism has the task of maintaining every variable within limits of tolerance—upper and lower. The organism is enabled to do this by the fact of homeostatic circuits. The variables of which we have a list are very densely and complexly interconnected in circuits having homeostatic or metahomeostatic characteristics. In such systems there are two types of pathology, or should we say pathways to disaster. In the first place, any monotone change—i.e. any continuous increase or decrease in the value of any variable—must inevitably lead to destruction of the system or to such deep (or "radical") disturbance that it is almost impossible to say that we are now dealing with the "same" system. That is one pathway to disaster, death, or radical change.

On the other hand, it is equally disastrous to peg or fix the value of any variable, because fixing the value of any variable will in the end disrupt the homeostatic processes. If the variable is one that normally changes rather easily and quickly, the fixing of it will tend to disturb those slow-moving variables which are at the core of the whole organism. The acrobat, for example, is unable to maintain his position on the high wire if the position of his balancing pole relative to himself is fixed. He must vary the one in order to maintain the truth of the ongoing propositional variable: "I am on the wire."

The picture we get is that a qualitative change in any variable is going to have a discontinuous effect upon the homeostatic structure. What was said earlier about quantity and quality becomes an alternative version of what Ashby has said in describing the system as a series of homeostatic circuits. These are partly synonymous descriptions. Ashby has added a new facet in pointing out that to *prevent* change in the superficial variables is to *promote* change in the more profound. (This is the process that is exploited in the strategy of the "obedience strike," when protesting workers achieve a slowdown simply by conforming strictly to regulations.)

The matter becomes much more complex when we are talking not about evolution, with changes that occur once and for all, but about embryology. In the process of development, a lot of crises are going to occur having this Ashbian form. Perhaps merely growth in size would be enough to disrupt a whole series of homeostases. The embryology is then going to have step functions built into it because of this curious relation between quantity and pattern. Furthermore, the embryo usually cannot trust to the random to provide the specification of the fracture planes of the system where it will break under the stress of some continuous change. In evolution, the random must be trusted to provide the planes of fracture, but in embryology these patterns of breaking must themselves be reliably determined by DNA message or by some other circumstance within the carefully protected embryo. As a crab automatically breaks off its own legs, or a lizard its tail, so there must be a place, a fracture plane, ready to define the break in embryological process and the new gestalt following the break.

The whole matter becomes still more complicated when we start to think of response or learning mediated by the central nervous system. A neuron, after all, is an almost precise analog of the frog's egg discussed earlier. A neuron is a component in the fabric of the organism that builds up a defined state of readiness—a quantity of "tension"—to be triggered by some external event, or by some external condition that can be made into an event. That state of tension is a "question" in the same sense that the tension of the frog's egg, previous to the arrival of the spermatozoon, is a question. The neuron, however, must go through the cycle over and over again and is, in fact, a specially designed piece of the organism that can do this over and over again. The neuron builds up a state, is triggered, and then builds up the state again. Both neurons and muscle fibers have this general characteristic. Upon this the whole organization of the creature depends.

This "relaxation-oscillation" characteristic of the neuron can be seen, if you will, as a repetitive, patterned sequence of "revolutionary" changes. (I understand that something of the sort occurs in parts of South America.)

Up to this point, I have focused upon *discontinuity* in the relation between input and response and have suggested that there are deep necessities lying behind the empirical facts of threshold and discontinuity. It is not only that the signal is improved by a high signal/noise ratio, it is also a necessity of complex cybernetic organization that many changes shall have flip-flop characteristics. Homeostatic control, however quantitative and "analogic" it may be, must always depend upon thresholds, and there will always be discontinuity between quantitative control and the breakdown of control that occurs when quantities become too great. [In chapter 4 it was suggested that thresholds, which define the limit of fluctuation, should be recognized as the *structure* of a given system.]

Let me now indicate another necessity—namely, that where discontinuity is lacking or is blurred by statistical response of smaller units (e.g. populations of neurons), regularities like those described by the Weber-Fechner laws shall operate. If there be cybernetic systems on other planets so complex that we might be willing to call them "organisms," then, surely, those systems must be characterized by a Weber-Fechner relationship whenever the relation across an interface is continuously variable on both sides.

What is asserted by the Weber-Fechner laws can be said in two ways:

1. Wherever a sense organ is used to compare two values of the same perceivable quantity (weight, brightness, etc.), there will be a threshold of perceivable difference below which the sense organ cannot discriminate between the quantities. This threshold of difference will be a *ratio*, and this ratio will be constant over a wide range of values. For example, if the experimental subject can just discriminate between the perceived weight of thirty grams and the perceived weight of forty grams (a ratio of 3 : 4), then he will also just discriminate between three pounds and four pounds.
2. This is another way of saying that there will be a relation between input and sensation such that the quantity or intensity of sensation will vary as the logarithm of the intensity of the input.

This relation seems to characterize the interfaces between environment and nerve wherever the interface is mediated by a sense organ. It is especially precise in the case of the retina, as shown long ago by Selig Hecht.

Interestingly, the same relation that characterizes afferent, or incoming, impulses was encountered by Norbert Wiener at the interface between efferent nerve and muscle:* The isometric tension of the muscle is proportional to the logarithm of the frequency of neural impulses in the nerve serving that muscle.

So far as I know, there is no quantitative knowledge yet available of the relation between the response of an individual cell and the intensity of hormonal or other chemical messages impacting upon it. We do not know whether hormonal communication is Weber-Fechnerian.

As to the necessity of this Weber-Fechner relation in biological communication, the following considerations can be urged:

1. All digital information is concerned with *difference*. In map-territory relations (of whatever kind, in the widest sense) that which gets from the territory to the map is always and necessarily *news of difference*. If the territory is homogeneous, there is no mark upon the map. A succinct definition of information is "a difference which makes a difference at a distance."

2. The concept of difference enters *twice* into understanding the process of perception: first, there must be a difference latent or implicit in the territory, and secondly, that difference must be converted into an *event* within the perceiving system—i.e. the difference must overcome a threshold, must be different from a threshold value.

3. The sense organs are like the lining of the stomach in functioning as filters to protect the organism from the violence or toxicity of the environment. They must both admit the "news" and keep out the excessive impact. This is done by varying the response of the organ according to the intensity of the input. The logarithmic scale achieves precisely this: that the effect of inputs shall not increase according to their magnitude, but only according to the logarithm of their magnitude. The difference in effect between one hundred and one thousand units of input shall only equal the difference in effect between one and ten units.

4. The information the organism requires (which will confer survival value) matches the logarithmic scale. The organism benefits by very great sensitivity to very small impacts and does not need such precision in evaluating the gross. To hear a mouse in the grass or a dog bark

---

*Personal communication. I think that Wiener never published the details of this finding. He refers to it, however, in the introduction to his *Cybernetics*.

a mile away—and still not be deafened by one's own voice shouting—
that is the problem.

5. It seems that in all perception (not only in the biological) and in all
measurement, there is something like a Weber-Fechner regularity.
Even in man-made mechanical devices, the arithmetic sensitivity of
the device falls off with the magnitude of the variable to be measured.
A laboratory balance is only accurate in measuring comparatively
small quantities, and error is usually computed as a percentage, i.e.
as a *ratio*.

(Interestingly, the *Encyclopaedia Britannica* carries a skewed
curve of the variable product of two hundred repetitions of a chemical
process.* Here the skewing is probably a result of the Weber-Fechner
law operating in the measurement of the various ingredients. Human
eyes (and possibly some balances) are affected equally by equal *ratios*.
They are therefore more sensitive to difference on the subtractive side
of any norm, and less sensitive to difference on the additive side.)

6. It seems that the interface between nerve and environment is characterized by a deep difference in *kind*, i.e. in logical typing, between
what is on one side of the interface and what is on the other. What
is quantitative on the input side becomes qualitative and discontinuous
on the perception side. Neurons obey an "all-or-nothing" rule, and,
to make them report continuous variation in a *quantity*, it is necessary
to employ a statistical device—either the statistics of a population of
neurons or the frequency of response of the single neuron.

All of these considerations work together to set the *mind* in special
relation to the *body*. My arms and legs obey one set of laws and equations
in terms of their purely physical characteristics—weight, length, temperature, etc. But, chiefly owing to the transformations of quantity im-
posed by the Weber-Fechner relation, my arms and legs obey quite
different laws in their controlled motions within the communication
systems I call "mind." We are dealing here with the interface between
Creatura and Pleroma.

Fechner was surely a very remarkable man, at least a hundred years
ahead of his time. He seems to have seen even then that the mind-body
problem could not be settled by denying the reality of the mind. It was
not good enough to assert that all biological causation was simply a
materialistic impact of billiard balls. Nor was it good enough to assert

*In a footnote to the 1965 edition, under "Error, theory of . . ."

that mind was a separate transcendent agent, a supernatural which could be divorced from body.

Fechner avoided both these forms of nonsense by asserting the logarithmic relation between message as carried in the communication systems of the body and the material quantities characterizing the impacts of the external "corporeal" universe.

Arguably it was Fechner who took the first steps, but much remains to be done. Our task over the next twenty years is to build up an Epistemology and a body of fact which shall unite the fields of genetics, morphogenesis, and learning. These three subjects are already clearly one field in which the concepts of a more abstract natural history or Epistemology will be explanatory themes. The Epistemology we shall construct will be both tautology—an abstract system making sense within its own terms—*and* natural history. It shall be that tautology onto which the empirical facts can be mapped. The metazoan cell, of course, already embodies just such an Epistemology. The relations between quantity and quality, the necessities of self-correction and homeostasis, and so on— all of this is determinant and component in the interaction between the cell and the environment it inhabits. But alas, the epistemologies of different human communities, notably those of the modern West, which govern interaction with the environment, are very far from providing what is needed.

XII   *Metalogue:*

Addiction (MCB & GB)

FATHER: Where are you going to put addiction?

DAUGHTER: I'm not really sure it fits.

FATHER: It's a nice problem, Cap, about which we know almost nothing—almost nothing formally. It's one of the big ones, on which civilizations rise and fall. I used to give it to the Esalen work scholars because I haven't thought it through yet, as a way of showing them how one goes about thinking about something like this.

DAUGHTER: Hmm. Well, you've got quite a few of the pieces, some from working on alcoholism and then some other bits that come from thinking of the arms race as an addiction. Where did you start?

FATHER: Addiction being a systemic phenomenon, it should be possible to model it. I gave them the old story of Norbert Wiener and the schizophrenic machine. In Palo Alto we had gotten to the point of understanding that schizophrenia had something to do with metaphor—not knowing that metaphors are metaphors, or taking literal things and handling them as if they were metaphors, or something screwy in that region. And Wiener said to me, suppose that I am an engineer and I would like you as my customer to specify to me what characteristics you will want built into a machine to agree that that machine is schizophrenic.

DAUGHTER: Difficult.

FATHER: But useful because it forces you to decide whether you really mean something by the word *schizophrenia* or is it just a nice cultural myth for locking troublesome people away in lunatic asylums. So we played around with it and came up with an imaginary, voice-activated machine, sort of like a telephone exchange: you would say to the machine, connect me to subscriber number 348, and in the course of talking to subscriber number 348 you would ask him to send you 247 pigs FOB Detroit, and the machine would disconnect you from the first subscriber and connect you to 247. It falsifies the use of the number—the logical type of the number. And if it does that not a hundred percent regularly but irregularly, I would be willing to call it a schizophrenic machine.

DAUGHTER: How did you get from there to the double bind in explaining the etiology of schizophrenia?

FATHER: I wrote to Wiener a bit later, asking whether there might be any place we could go for research money on the engineering side of the world. So in my letter I started exploring the question: If you had a machine that was capable of learning, how would you teach it to show this symptom? You would punish it sporadically for being *right* in its logical typing of numerals. This would put it in a very uncomfortable position in which the commonsense thing for it to do would be to be unpredictably wrong. And from there we got to the double bind.

DAUGHTER: You're usually a bit dubious about comparing people to machines . . . if you want to think through a machine that's prone to addiction, you're going to have to translate all sorts of things like fear or loneliness or insecurity. You have to have a need or a problem of some sort, and something that looks like a solution but actually makes the need greater.

FATHER: It's fairly obviously a mistake to use an anesthetic to try to dull the pain of a chronic maladjustment.

DAUGHTER: That goes with a lot of stuff you've been talking about over the years about the immorality of palliatives, like food shipments to Africa without solutions to the problems of population growth and environmental degradation.

FATHER: And then there's Samuel Butler's wisecrack that if the headache preceded the joys of intoxication instead of following them, then alcoholism would be a virtue, and highly disciplined mystics would cultivate it and so on.

DAUGHTER: Is this where the connection comes, for *Angels*? Certainly there are people for whom religion is a palliative and lots of New Age religion is really a way of getting high? Or did you just plan to put addiction in on spec that the different trains of thought do tend to hook up? Or—I know, it's because it's a form of learning.

Do you remember a paper I wrote a few years ago about the way in which religion can be converted into entertainment, and the way in which people in our society are *trained* in the capacity to be bored? We think of ritual as boring unless it's dressed up with new and interesting music or vestments, because we've been trained to be subject to boredom.

FATHER: Collingwood talks about the difference between art and entertainment: that the real thing leaves you richer at the end and feeling good but requires a certain discipline at the beginning to attend to it, whereas entertainment requires no discipline to enjoy it at the beginning and leaves you sort of dead at the end. Education has become increasingly a matter of trying to seduce children into paying attention by sugaring the pill at the beginning, keeping them entertained.

DAUGHTER: The other day you said that a shortcut is an error in logical typing, which is kind of a gnomic saying that's been nagging at me. I have a feeling that it doesn't apply to all classes of shortcuts, but a palliative may be a kind of shortcut? Maybe there is a connection between the feedback issue, where negative feedback is replaced by positive feedback, leading to an increase in the addiction, and some kind of logical typing problem.

FATHER: Cap, do you know the endorphin story? It is now known that under pain, the brain itself secretes substances called endorphins. It doesn't know what they are called but that's what the chemists call them. And these substances have a good deal of the effect of morphine in annulling pain, so that you have an alternative, to use your own endorphins or to use an artificial painkiller. If you use the artificial painkiller, then you diminish the production of your own. You get the general phenomenon of Faustian adjustment, getting some kind of magical control in your own life in exchange for ending up where the fire burns. The shortcut control always lands you in trouble . . . you get caught.

DAUGHTER: Mmm. Acknowledging that you are caught does seem to be critical to getting out of an addiction.

FATHER: We've even got one or two University of California regents who feel caught in the arms race, but that's not enough for getting out.

The other thing you probably need is a disaster, what Alcoholics Anonymous calls "hitting bottom"—you have to wake up in the gutter one morning, or lose your job. And if, in general, a given disaster is insufficient, then the level of disaster you need is increased. But confronting and fighting the addiction is not a useful thing to do, increasing division between mind and body and trying to make a fight between them. I regard that as a terrible trap.

DAUGHTER: Don't you have to believe in God to be AA?

FATHER: The two first steps are admitting that you are an alcoholic and life has become unbearable, and admitting that there is a principle in the universe, God perhaps, which is stronger than you are. So you transcend by some sort of double surrender. There is a sort of equation between the alcohol and God, which are both more powerful than you are, and God is identified with your unconscious, so he becomes an immanent God, not a God on top of the hill or up in the clouds, that you can shake your fist at and wail. Bill W., who started AA, was a very clever man, very clever. It turns out he had been talking to an ex-patient of Jung's.

DAUGHTER: There's a very famous prayer too, isn't there? Asking for "the serenity to accept the things I cannot change, the courage to change the things that I can, and the wisdom to know the difference."

FATHER: It's double-sidedly open. You get the same picture from Percival, the nineteenth-century psychotic whose journal I edited. At the first stage of his psychosis, his voices double-bind him: "I was tormented by the commands of what I imagined [to be] the Holy Spirit to say other things which as often as I attempted, I was fearfully rebuked for beginning in my own voice and not in a voice given me by spirits."*
At the next stage, though, his voices change their tune: "At another time, my spirits began singing to me in this strain. You are in a lunatic asylum if you will, if not you are in, etc., etc., that is Samuel Hobbs if you will, if not it is Hermanent Herbert." (That was one of his fancy psychotic names for one of the warders.) So you see his voices become therapists. I'm sure it must happen all the time and the damn therapists don't notice it.

Now, next to that we'll put something Oppie said—Robert Oppenheimer—that the world was going in the direction of hell with a

---

*Percival's Narrative: A Patient's Account of His Psychosis, 1830–32, by John Percival, ed. and with an introduction by Gregory Bateson (Stanford, Calif.: Stanford UP, 1961).

high velocity, a positive acceleration, and probably a positive rate of change of acceleration, and will perhaps not reach its destination *"only on that condition* that we and the Russians be willing to let it." Right now, every move that we make in trying to make ourselves safer speeds the thing on its way to hell.

DAUGHTER: So there's a problem of transcendence. Two sides, and you have to deal with both. It reminds me of that dolphin you wrote about in Hawaii. The show was about dolphin training and the trainer would wait to see a *new* piece of behavior, and then reinforce it by blowing the whistle or giving a fish or whatever. This meant that whatever was right and rewarded in the previous session was now wrong and not rewarded, because it was no longer "new." So then after—how many? a dozen sessions?—one day the dolphin got all excited in the holding tank, splashing around, and when it came out it immediately did a whole series of new behaviors that no one had ever seen in the species before. It got the idea.

FATHER: It must have been very frustrating, very painful for the porpoise. One of the interesting things about it is that when we repeated the sequence as an experiment, we could never quite get the trainer to obey the rules. The wretched trainer would always throw an occasional fish to the porpoise because she said she would "lose" the porpoise if she didn't. Well, if a therapist is going to force a patient into a new order of insight, it may be necessary to throw him a few unearned fish to mitigate the pain. But notice that this pain is of the general type which Samuel Butler said would be virtuous, pain that precedes the solving of the problem. And this is what happens if you successfully cold turkey an addiction to a drug. You have adapted to the drug, and now the disruption of the second-order adaptation is going to be painful.

DAUGHTER: Daddy, I never know when you are talking about schizophrenia and transcending double binds and when you are talking about addiction. Are they really that similar or is it just habit?

FATHER: Hmm. Well, they have in common the need to get beyond talking as if there were a something that existed inside the single individual, schizophrenia or addiction. The similarity derives from the fact that mental characteristics are relational—between two persons, say, or between a person and the environment. You have to have an A and a B. A could be a person and B could be a person, or A could be a liver and B a colon. In order to get an adaptation in the colon, you have to change the liver, but every time you change the liver, you've thrown the colon out of kilter again. There's first-level learning to do the right thing in a particular context, but then you need a wider learning at the next level to deal with the fact of the changing context, which you create by your own response. I mean, life is hell, and only actors onstage are allowed to go on behaving in a uniform manner.

DAUGHTER: Can *growth* become addictive? It can certainly create problems.

FATHER: Yes, well, growth always presents the problem of how you can grow without altering proportions, perhaps fatally. A palm tree, for instance, has no cambium surrounding the trunk, no way of depositing additional layers of wood and becoming thicker as it grows taller. A palm tree just grows at the top and eventually it falls over. Continuous first-order change is fatal. So, does the pain of growth come out of the need for second-order change? And is addiction somehow the reciprocal or opposite of growth?

DAUGHTER: So we've got addiction and schizophrenia and growth and adaptation . . . I think this conversation is getting out of hand.

FATHER: And the work scholars wanted to add "attachment" too. With a civilization changing technologically at a rapid rate, the relationship of these words begins to be a sort of pincers that keeps catching us. The University of California has a relationship with two very large labs devoted to investigating atomic weaponry, Livermore and Los Alamos, where we employ some thirteen thousand people. It's a very elaborate organic attachment, not just a parasite we could shake off tomorrow and feel relief, but a symbiont whose tissues have grown together with our tissues. And the withdrawal symptoms would be pretty remarkable if we started to drop it.

DAUGHTER: I'm always amazed that people think one could simply eliminate atomic weaponry or cold turkey the arms race.

FATHER: The regents don't even seem willing, in the middle of the whole seven-hundred-million-dollar business of physics and nuclear research, to put up the two or three million it would take to crack the formal characteristics of addiction-adaptation-attachment, as these concern the entire nation.

DAUGHTER: Yes, well, don't grumble. We've got a hypothetical engineer all ready to build us a machine but we haven't even worked out the specifications.

FATHER: Okay. So what have we got. Learning is to occur at two levels and to involve two interlocking parts or entities or something of that kind. And there's another problem. If you describe an organism, it will take a great number of descriptive statements—how many eyes it has and the position of its eyes relative to its nose and the mouth somewhat south of that . . . and body temperature and blood-sugar levels and so on. Now these descriptive statements aren't separate, they are all interlocked in loops of various kinds, with all sorts of escalations and self-corrections. If you change any of them beyond a certain point, your creature is sort of tied by the leg, hampered by its changes. You get stress and if you go too far, then death. And a nation is like that too.

DAUGHTER: How about the binge alcoholic? Does he fit in here?

FATHER: Indeed. He holds the opinion that life depends upon a particular sort of change, not upon having a certain amount of alcohol in the blood but upon having a rising gradient. There are binge alcoholics who are very skillful at maintaining a just-positive gradient of alcohol in the blood, keeping it going for four or five days maybe. But you know, in these systems of interlocking variables, you cannot take one variable and change it continuously in one direction. Something will break and the alcoholic will find himself at four o'clock one morning in the gutter. Not good. He spoiled that binge. He had been so careful, you know. And of course nations become addicted to having a continuously increasing gross national product, which is exactly the same sort of problem as the palm tree. You cannot take a variable in an interlocking system and have it change continuously in the same direction.

DAUGHTER: Cycles of boom and bust. Wars. Rather drastic solutions. And in between we try and be more and more careful without changing the basic distortion.

Daddy, that fish you were talking about, that the trainer gives to the porpoise even though it hasn't earned it, to maintain the relationship? It would be easy to become addicted to that.

FATHER: Ah, the pleasure of intoxication without the preliminary headache.

DAUGHTER: Well, and that takes us back to entertainment. However much I enjoy learning something new or writing or even arguing with you, there's still a cost in doing it that keeps it from getting out of hand. Because the conversation also supplies the headache.

FATHER: Well, yes. And in art, as opposed to entertainment, it is always uphill in a certain sense, so the effort precedes the reward rather than the reward being spooned out. One of the things that is important in depression is not to get caught in the notion that entertainment will relieve it. It will, you know, briefly, but it will not banish it. As reassurance is the food of anxiety, so entertainment is the food of depression. I wonder about this around Esalen—all the various techniques that we devise doing this and that to our bodies and our spirits— which of them are really in the nature of climbing and which are really in the nature of going downhill? But then, maybe anything that is therapeutic is also addictive.

DAUGHTER: You . . . I wish you wouldn't keep letting the ideas spread out. I wish we could get to a concept of addiction that would explain the damage that gets done, the way people get hurt.

FATHER: Yes, well, that's why we need to think in terms of a machine. So we can talk about formal questions without moralizing or sentimentalizing. In any case, the shift of attention from individual to interactive process moves us away from questions of value. Instead of good or bad we can think in terms of "reversible" or "irreversible," "self-limiting" or "self-maximizing." We need to think in terms of two parts of a system, with some kind of interface between them.

DAUGHTER: The alcoholic and demon rum?

FATHER: Indeed, for often one of the parts is nonliving. The planet Pluto may be nonliving when it is considered as a separate entity. But if there is interaction between Pluto and "me," it is legitimate to examine the characteristics of a larger whole of which Pluto and "I" are parts. This larger whole will have "life" because a component part, "me," is living, just as the whole that I call "me" has nonliving components, like teeth or blood serum. And if the loss of some part of the system (B) will diminish or destroy the life of the other (A), we could say that A is addicted to B.

DAUGHTER: Help! Whoa! You just put everything into this grab bag, and addiction stopped being a useful concept and instead became an alternative term for any systemic interdependency. You might as well say that I'm addicted to oxygen!

FATHER: Quite.

DAUGHTER: But . . . but no. I think you want to distinguish three levels. Level one would be systemic *dependency*, and would include my relationship to air, protein, gravity, the fish's relationship to water, and so on. All those things without which I cannot function, so that they have to be included in any picture of how functioning is possible. That's the unit of survival, isn't it? It reminds us to think of the interdependent parts as part of a whole, not just liver and colon but also organism and environment.

And then level two would involve the process of *acquiring* such a dependency, which implies a systemic change, especially when it's irreversible or only reversible at some kind of cost. Here is where our model has to match up with a model of such things as learning, adaptation, acclimation, and so on. At this point you may have some real solutions. Like taking a steady dosage of medication for high blood pressure—sure you're dependent: the medicine has become part of the system that is you, your survival. Then level three would be what you often get with drugs or alcohol or armaments races or GNPs, where there is an *escalation*. I have a stable sort of dependency on the heating system of my house, but when I start changing the bias through the course of the winter, so that I have it set in the seventies by February, that's what you would want to reserve the term *addiction* for . . .

FATHER: As long as you use the terms in a way that focuses on the system: you and the thermostat and the fossil fuels that have become a part of your life. And usually with the term *addiction* we do refer not only to an escalating process, but also to one in which the addictive step is believed to be adaptive or therapeutic or perhaps just enhancing, but in fact leaves the need unmet. I'd be quite happy to be addicted to a working disarmament treaty, but the armaments boys are addicted to feeling not just strong but stronger—stronger than yesterday and stronger than the Russians. The arms race both leaves us vulnerable to war and tends to escalate.

DAUGHTER: Not just a treaty to limit arms, right? But a treaty to *dis*arm, in which each step created a need for the next step. Imagine a world in which the political process became so *addicted to disarming* that after all the real weapons were gone, we had an annual ritual of burning cardboard mock-ups to bring back the good feeling!

FATHER: A change of sign in fact.

DAUGHTER: Daddy, before we move on from this, I want to try out an idea. It seems to me that my level one—an ordinary sustained organic dependency—fits your zero learning, and matches up with the diagrams of a heating system or shooting with a rifle in chapter 4. I have a certain need for drinking water, and when my thirst passes a certain threshold it triggers a switch that makes me get up from my typing and take a drink. Something like that. And the system keeps going around the same homeostatic cycle. But with addiction, the hit of whatever it is *resets the bias*, changes the structure, as you call it, so next time I'll need more. Is it like calibration, changing the system every time?

FATHER: Instead of meeting a need, you're creating one.

DAUGHTER: And look, Daddy, it matches with what you said about Lamarckian evolution being fatal, doesn't it!?

FATHER: So now it's your turn to do some thinking. As I said, the question could hardly be more important.

XIII The Unmocked

God (GB)

> Be not deceived; God is not mocked.
> —Gal. 6:7

WHAT has been said so far can be read as argument or evidence for the reality of very large mental systems, systems of ecological size and larger, within which the mentality of the single human being is a subsystem. These large mental systems are characterized by, among other things, constraints on the transmission of information between their parts. Indeed, we can argue from the circumstance that some information should not reach some locations in large, organized systems to assert the *real* nature of these systems—to assert the existence of that whole whose integrity would be threatened by inappropriate communication. By the word "real" in this context, I mean simply that it is *necessary for explanation* to think in terms of organizations of this size, attributing to these systems the characteristics of mental process (as defined by the criteria listed in chapter 2).

But it is one thing to claim that this is necessary and not surprising and quite another to go on to say, however vaguely, what sort of mind such a vast organization might be. What characteristics would such minds expectably show? Are they, perhaps, the sort of thing that men have called gods?

The great theistic religions of the world have ascribed many sorts of mentality to the highest gods, but almost invariably their characteristics have been derived from human models. Gods have been variously imagined as loving, vengeful, capricious, long-suffering, patient, impatient, cunning, incorruptible, bribable, childish, elderly, masculine, feminine, sexy, sexless, and so on.

What mental characteristics are to be expected in any large mental system or mind, the basic premises of whose character shall coincide with what we claim to know of cybernetics and systems theory? Starting from these premises, we surely cannot arrive at a lineal, billiard-ball materialism. But what sort of religion we shall develop is not clear. Will the vast organized system have free will? Is this "God" capable of humor? Deceit? Error? Mental pathology? Can such a God perceive beauty? Or ugliness? What events or circumstances can impinge upon this God's sense organs? Are there indeed organs of sense in such a system? And limitations of threshold? And attention? Is such a God capable of failure? Frustration? And, finally, consciousness?

The great historical religions of the world have either answered such questions without pausing to note that these are questions that permit more than one answer, or they have obscured the matter under a mass of dogma and devotion. To ask such questions may indeed disturb faith, so that the questions themselves might seem to define a region where angels would appropriately fear to tread.

Two things, however, are clear about any religion that might derive from cybernetics and systems theory, ecology and natural history. First, that in the asking of questions, there will be no limit to our hubris; and second, that there shall always be humility in our acceptance of answers. In these two characteristics we shall be in sharp contrast with most of the religions of the world. They show little humility in their espousal of answers but great fear about what questions they will ask.

If we can show that a recognition of a certain unity in the total fabric is a recurrent characteristic, it is possible that some of the most disparate epistemologies that human culture has generated may give clues as to how we should proceed.

I. Tragedy

It seems that the dramatists of classical Greece and possibly their audiences and the philosophers who throve in that culture believed that an action occurring in one generation could set a context or set a process going which would determine the shape of personal history for a long time to come.

The story of the House of Atreus in myth and drama is a case in point. The initial murder of Chrysippus by his stepbrother Atreus starts a sequence in which the wife of Atreus is seduced by Atreus' brother Thyestes, and in the ensuing feud between the brothers, Atreus kills and cooks his brother's son, serving him to his father in a monstrous meal. These events led in the next generation to the sacrifice of Iphigenia by her father, Agamemnon, another son of Thyestes, and so on to the murder of Agamemnon by his wife, Clytemnestra, and her paramour, Aegisthus, brother of Agamemnon and son of Thyestes.

In the next generation, Orestes and Electra, the son and daughter of Agamemnon, avenge their father's murder by killing Clytemnestra, an act of matricide for which the Furies chase and haunt Orestes until Athena intervenes, establishing the court of the Areopagus and trying Orestes before that court, finally dismissing the case. It required the intervention of a goddess to conclude the sequence of *anangke*, or necessity, whereby each killing led irresistibly to the next.

The Greek idea of necessary sequence was, of course, not unique. What is interesting is that the Greeks seem to have thought of *anangke* as a totally impersonal theme in the structure of the human world. It was as if, from the initial act onwards, dice were loaded against the participants. The theme, as it worked itself out, used human emotions and motives as its means, but the theme itself (we would vulgarly call it a "force") was thought to be impersonal, beyond and greater than gods and persons, a bias or warp in the structure of the universe.

Such ideas occur at other times and in other cultures. The Hindu idea of *karma* is similar and differs from *anangke* only in the characteristically Hindu elaboration which includes both "good" and "bad" *karma* and carries recipes for the "burning up" of bad *karma*.

I myself encountered a similar belief among the Iatmul of New Guinea.* The Iatmul shamans claimed that they could see a person's *ngglambi* as a black cloud or aura surrounding him or her. The Iatmul are a sorcery-ridden people and it was quite clear that *ngglambi* followed the pathway of sorcery. A might sin against B, thus incurring the black cloud: B might pay a sorcerer to avenge the first sin, and *ngglambi* would then surround

Naven (Stanford UP ed.), 54ff.

both *B* and the sorcerer. In any case, it was expected that the person with black *ngglambi* would encounter tragedy—perhaps his own death, perhaps that of a relative, for *ngglambi* is contagious—and the tragedy would probably be brought about by sorcery. *Ngglambi*, like *anangke*, worked through human agencies.

The present question, however, does not concern the detailed nature of *anangke, ngglambi, karma,* and other similar conceptions that human individuals attribute to the larger system. The question is simply: What are the characteristics of those mental subsystems called individuals, arising from their aggregation in larger systems also having mental characteristics, that are likely to be expressed by generating such mythologies (true or false) as those of *anangke,* etc.? This is a question of a different order, not to be answered by reification of the larger mental system nor by simply evoking motives of the participant individuals.

A piece of an answer can be tentatively offered, if only to show the reader the direction of our inquiry.

Anangke, karma, and *ngglambi* are reified abstractions, the last being the most concretely imagined, so that shamans even "see" it. The others are less reified and are perceptible only in their supposed effects, above all in the myths—the quasi-miraculous tales that exemplify the workings of the principle.

Now, it is well known in human interaction that individual beliefs become self-validating, both directly, by "suggestion," so that the believer tends to see or hear or taste that which he believes; or indirectly, so that the belief may validate itself by shaping the actions of the believers in a way which brings to pass that which they believe, hope, or fear may be the case. Then let me chalk up as a characteristic of human individuals a potential for pathology arising out of the fact that they are of a flexible and viscous nature. They clot together to create aggregates which become the embodiment of themes of which the individuals themselves are or may be unconscious.

In terms of such a hypothesis, *anangke* and *karma* are particular epiphenomena brought about by the clustering of flexible subsystems.

II. CONTRADICTORY AND CONFLICTING THEMES

Another mental characteristic of larger systems can be exemplified from themes of Greek drama. In that complex corpus of shared ideas, there existed side by side with the Oresteia a second cross-generational sequence of myths bound together by the concept of *anangke* and starting from a specific act. Cadmus incurred the wrath of Ares by killing a sacred serpent, and this set the stage for repeated episodes of trouble in the royal house of Thebes. Eventually, the oracle at Delphi predicted that Laius, king of Thebes, would have a son who would kill him and marry his own mother, Jocasta, the wife of Laius.

Laius then tried to thwart the oracle and thus, in spite of himself, precisely brought on himself the working out of the tragic necessity. First he refused sexual contact with Jocasta to avoid the begetting of the son who would kill him. But she made him drunk and the child was begotten. When the baby was born, Laius commanded that he be bound and abandoned on the mountainside. But again Laius' plan failed. The baby was found by a shepherd and adopted by Polybus, king of Corinth. The boy was named Oedipus, or Swollen Footed, because the baby's feet were swollen from being tied together when he was exposed on the mountain.

As Oedipus grew up, he was taunted by the other boys, who said he did not resemble his father. He therefore went to Delphi for an explanation and was condemned by the oracle as the boy fated to kill his father and marry his mother. Oedipus, not knowing that he was an adopted child and believing that Polybus was his true father, then fled. He would not return to Corinth lest he should kill.

Fleeing thus, he met with an unknown man in a chariot who rudely refused him right of way. He killed that unknown man, who was in fact Laius, his true father. Proceeding on his way, he encountered a Sphinx outside Thebes and answered her riddle, "What is it that walks first on four legs, then on two, and finally on three?" The Sphinx then destroyed herself, and Oedipus found himself suddenly a hero who had conferred a great benefit upon the city of Thebes. He became king of that city by marrying Jocasta. By her he had four children. Finally, plague struck the city and the oracle attributed the cause of the plague to one man's horrible action. Oedipus insisted on investigating this matter, although the blind sage Tiresias had advised him to let sleeping dogs lie. The truth was finally exposed. Oedipus, the king of Thebes, was himself the man who had killed his father and married his mother. Jocasta then hanged herself in horror and Oedipus blinded himself with a pin from her scarf.

Oedipus was exiled from Thebes and wandered the world, accompanied by his daughter Antigone. Finally, old and blind, he arrived at Colonos, outside Athens. There he mysteriously vanished in the groves sacred to the Furies, presumably accepted by them into their afterlife.

It is immediately interesting to note a formal contrast between this tale and the Orestes sequence, for Oedipus went spontaneously to the grove of the Furies, whereas Orestes was chased by them. This contrast is explained in the finale of Aeschylus' Orestes trilogy, where Athena lays down the law that Athens is a patriarchal society in which wives are not fully kin to their offspring, who remain in the gens, or clan, of the father. The mother is a "stranger" and matricide is therefore no crime. (After all, Athena never had a mother; she sprang fully armed from the head of her father, Zeus.) The Furies, on the other hand, matriarchal goddesses, will forgive Oedipus, the boy who kills his father and has four children by his mother, but will not pardon Orestes the matricide.

In fact, the culture of classical Athens carried two utterly contrasting mythological sequences, the Oedipus sequence, which is the nightmare of crime against the father, and the Orestes nightmare of crime against the mother.

I personally am dissatisfied with Athena's explanation, in which she dismisses the Furies as a bunch of old hags, obsolete survivors of a more primitive matriarchy. As an anthropologist, I do not believe that there ever existed any society that was one hundred percent matriarchal nor any that was one hundred percent patriarchal. In many societies, kinship is asymmetrical, so that a different *kind* of relationship is developed on each side of the genealogy. The child has different obligations and privileges vis-à-vis his maternal uncles from those implicit in his relationship with paternal uncles. But always there are benefits and duties on both sides. The whole play, Aeschylus' *Eumenides*, is very strange, as also is the *Oedipus at Colonos* of Sophocles. I can only read the *Eumenides* as either extremely jingoistic Athenian patriotism or, more probably, a caricature of that patriotism. The *Colonos*, on the other hand, is surely a very serious piece, no less patriotic than the *Eumenides*, since it, too, deals with the ancient history of the city of Athens. Strangely, the members of the audience are expected to understand that old, blind Oedipus is now a sacred figure and there is almost a war brewing between Oedipus' descendants in Thebes and Theseus, the founder of the new city of Athens. Both parties want Oedipus to die on their national territory and to become somehow a guardian spirit of that land.

My suspicion—and it is to illustrate this that I have introduced the tales—is that each myth owes something to the other, and they are a balancing pair that is a product jointly of a culture divided in its emphasis on matriarchy or patriarchy. I would ask whether this double expression of the conflicting views is not somehow typical of the divided larger mind.

The syncretic dualism of Christian mythology provides a similar but more astonishing example. Jehovah is clearly a transcendent god of Babylonian times whose location is on top of an artificial mountain, or *ziggurat*. Jesus, in clear contrast, is a deity whose location is in the human breast. He is an incarnate deity, like Pharoah and like every ancient Egyptian who was addressed in mortuary ceremonies as Osiris.

It is not that one or the other of these double phrasings is right, or that it is wrong to have such double myths. What seems to be true is that it is characteristic of large cultural systems that they carry such double myths and opinions, not only with no serious trouble, but perhaps even reflecting in the latent contradictions some fundamental characteristic of the larger mentality.

In this connection, Greek mythology is especially interesting because its stories did not draw the line between the more secular and human gestalten and the larger themes of fate and destiny in the same way as these lines are drawn among us today. The Greek classification was different from ours. Greek gods are like humans, they are puppets of fate just like people, and the interaction between the forces of what seems a larger mind and mere gods and humans is continually being pointed out by the chorus. They see that the gods and heroes and themselves are alike puppets of fate. The gods and heroes in themselves are as secular as our superman, whom indeed they somewhat resemble.

In mythology and especially drama, the eerie and the mysterious— the truly religious overtones—are contained in such abstractions as *anangke* or *nemesis*. We are told rather unconvincingly that Nemesis is a goddess and that the gods will punish the arrogance of power which is called *hubris*. But in truth these are the names of themes or principles, which give an underlying religious flavor to life and drama; the gods are at most the outward, though not visible, symbols of these more mysterious principles. A similar state of affairs exists in Balinese religion, where, however, the gods are almost totally drained of all personal characteristics. They (except for Rangda, the Witch, and the Barong, or dragon) have only names, directions, colors, calendric days, and so on. In dealing with each of them it is the appropriate etiquette that is important.

.

At the beginning of this chapter, I said that the focus would be upon validating the existence of very large systems. This goal may now be made more specific by asking what features of human religions, ancient and modern, become intelligible in the light of cybernetic theory and similar advances in epistemology. It is time to reverse the trend which since Copernicus has been in the direction of debunking mythology, to begin to pick up the many epistemological components of religion that have been brushed aside. In doing so, we may come upon important notions partly displaced by trash (particularly the kind of trash produced by religious people pretending to scientific authority, which is not their business) or partly lost by the failure to understand what religion was about, that has characterized most of the scientific debunking. The battle over the Book of Genesis is a piece of history of which neither the evolutionists nor the fundamentalists should be proud. But I have discussed that matter elsewhere and intend here to pick up what can be picked up after the battles are over—would that they were!

Religion does not consist in recognizing little bits of miracles (*miracula*, "little marvels"), such as every religious leader tries to avoid providing but which his followers will always insist upon, but vast aggregates of organization having immanent mental characteristics. I suggest that the Greeks were close to religion in concepts such as *anangke*, *nemesis*, and *hubris*, and diverged from religion when their oracles claimed supernatural authority, or when their mythologists embroidered the tales of the various gods in the pantheon.

Can we on our part recognize among the scientific findings enough of the basic principles of traditional religion to give a base for some rapprochement? In the thinking that has led to my present position, I've used a combination of approaches—logical, epistemological, and traditional—going from one to another as the circumstances of my life provided the opportunity and as the form of the argument suggested. I am trying to investigate the communicational regularities in the biosphere, assuming that in doing so, I shall also be investigating interwoven regularities in a system so pervasive and so determinant that we may even apply the word "god" to it. The regularities we discover—including regularities and necessities of communication and logic—form a unity in which we make our home. They might be seen as the peculiarities of the god whom we might call Eco.

There is a parable which says that when the ecological god looks down and sees the human species sinning against its ecology—by greed or by taking shortcuts or taking steps in the wrong order—he sighs and *involuntarily* sends the pollution and the radioactive fallout. It is of no avail to tell him that the offense was only a small one, that you are sorry and that you will not do it again. It is no use to make sacrifices and offer bribes. The ecological God is incorruptible and therefore is not mocked.

If we look among the necessities of communication and logic to find what might appropriately be recognized as sacred, we must note that these matters have been investigated long and ponderously by a very great many people, most of whom do not at all think of themselves as students of natural history. One class of those people call themselves *logicians*. They do not draw distinctions between the phenomena of communication and those of physics and chemistry; they do not assert, as I do, that different rules of logic apply in the explanation of living, recursive systems. But they have laid down a large number of rules about what steps shall be acceptable in joining together the propositions to make the theorems of any tautology. Furthermore, they have classified the various kinds of steps and kinds of sequences of steps and have given names to the different species of sequences, such as the different types of syllogism discussed in chapter 2. [Their taxonomies are not unlike the taxonomies constructed of insect or butterfly species, and indeed these different species of syllogism live in different niches and have different needs for their survival.] We might well adopt this classification as a first step towards a natural history of the world of communication. The steps that the logicians have identified would then be candidates for the role of examples in our search for eternal verities that characterize that world, more abstract than the propositions of Augustine.

But, alas, logic is blemished, particularly when it attempts to deal with circular causal systems, in which the analogs of logical relations are causal sequences that proceed in a circle, like the paradox of Epimenides the Cretan, who declared, "All Cretans are liars." This paradox the logician dismisses as trivial, but the observer of "things"—even things that can hardly claim to be alive—knows that the Epimenides argument is a paradigm for the relations in any self-correcting circuit, such as that of the simple buzzer or house doorbell.

I have taken the presence of such circuits to be one of the criteria by which I define a mind, along with coding, hierarchical organization, and collateral energy supply. Such circuits can be found in many mechanical and electrical forms, such as the house thermostat described in chapter 4 or the device that controls water level in the tank of a toilet, but more significantly they arise in the physiology of organisms that must correct for variations in temperature, blood sugar, etc., and in ecosystems where different populations (say snowshoe rabbits and lynxes) vary in interconnected ways, keeping the whole in balance. Logic tends to be lineal, moving from A to B or from a premise to a conclusion; logic frowns on arguments that move in circles. [Similarly, formal logic rejects as invalid the metaphorical connections that are so pervasive in the natural world.]

I am therefore unwilling in the description of life to trust to logic or logicians as a source of verities. It is, however, interesting to consider the properties of the self-corrective circuit itself as an example of profound abstract verity, and this is the subject matter of cybernetics and the first step in using cybernetics in moving towards new ways of thinking about nature. Perhaps we may be driven later to some still more profound and abstract set of descriptions of relations—but the relations of circuits will do for a starter, always remembering the verity that there are inevitable limitations on any act of description, which we have yet to spell out in detail.

XIV Metalogue:

It's Not Here (MCB)

DAUGHTER: Daddy, it's just *not here*.

FATHER: What's not?

DAUGHTER: You just don't spell out what, finally, you mean by "the sacred," and you don't tell us beans about Eco. We need more before we'll be ready to go off on a new discussion of epistemology in the biological world and your particular notion of "structure." It's not easy for people to equate the "pattern which connects" with the sacred or see your kind of description, which sounds so dry, as proposing a sort of epiphany. At least that's how I interpret the link between the section that deals with unifying ideas like *anangke* or *karma* or *ngglambi* and what you then go on to say about the problems of thinking about the biological world, which I've set up as the next chapter. You get all involved in talking about your favorite Greek tragedies and then you go off on a discussion of epistemology, but you don't really draw the connections. I can see what some of the connections have to be, but I can't know that I see it the way you do.

You know, it struck me when I was working on this part of the manuscript that what you had done was to whack out a huge hunk of draft for your editor, putting everything that's now in chapter 13 and everything that's now in chapter 15 together, so it came out as a sort of model of the whole book, groping and all. Daddy, do you remember the story of McCulloch's mother?

FATHER: Which was that?

DAUGHTER: It was one of your favorite stories for a while. I guess you were having a discussion with some of the cybernetics people at Warren McCulloch's house about information retrieval. He went into the kitchen to get coffee, and there he found his mother, who must have been a very old lady by that time, and she was in a rage. "You talk about information retrieval," she said, "but you cheat. I know what the problem is because I don't have any memory anymore. The only way I can find anything is to keep *a little bit of everything everywhere*."

FATHER: Well, that really is the problem of the book. But the first step away from false analytical distinctions such as that represented by Cartesian dualism towards some sort of monism is to get matters that had been separated in the past into the same conversation, and then to establish some formal rules for working with them—what I had planned to call a "syntax of consciousness."

DAUGHTER: If this were a conference I was trying to make sense of, I would keep the chunks of different kinds of material beside each other, to supply something like what you call "double description," and then sneak in little connecting remarks so the reader would make a synthesis at some level.

FATHER: Well, which are some of the connections you would want to make?

DAUGHTER: Well, for example, it seems to me that part of what you keep implying about religion is that it *necessarily* has contradictions embedded in it—paradoxes—and these contradictions are protected from certain kinds of rationalizing knowledge to preserve them in tension, because that tension is what makes religious systems able to function as models of the Creatura. One thing that has always struck me about Islam is that it lies flat on the page, while Christianity is just writhing with contradictions, and maybe that is an important kind of difference. Anyhow, I'd want to take your business about matriarchal and patriarchal elements in Greek religion and put that together with the taboo on transsexual knowledge and put *that* together with bisexual reproduction as a way of both producing and limiting uncertainty. And then I'd want to go off from there to notions of transcending paradox and stir in a good dose of Zen . . .

Do you remember saying once that Nature is a double-binding bitch?

FATHER: One of the ways that the concept of the double bind has been vulgarized, Cap, is to apply it to any no-win situation. If you quote that remark, people will simply think of famines and other natural disasters. The relevance here has to be through the logical types.

DAUGHTER: Yes, especially in the business of thought breaking down when we try to discuss relations between relations between relations— the infinite regress you used to talk about. It must be the case that just as our thinking is limited in how far we can go in such a regress, so too biological systems are limited and the levels collapse into each other. If you wanted to take the analogy between thought and evolution as far as it can go, you should have explored the occurrence of all possible types of cognitive error in evolution.

FATHER: Well, but as I say, "God is not mocked." When something goes wrong in epigenesis, you are likely to get a nonviable organism or one that cannot reproduce. And the effect of certain kinds of evolutionary error is extinction. That which survives is what survives. When tautology is played out in the physical world, error rapidly becomes obvious.

DAUGHTER: Maybe, given a few million years. This has always bothered me in anthropology: a culture is an adaptive system, so if a society survives, we say its culture must be adaptive, and we plunge ahead into the whole argument of functionalism. But the society may in fact be working its way to extinction. If we blow up this planet or plunge it into nuclear winter, you will have a problem there in Hades defining the moment of the error—and I don't think you will locate it at the instant of pushing the button. Versailles maybe? Descartes? The Roman Empire? Or the Garden of Eden?

FATHER: Certainly one way of interpreting the notion of original sin is as a propensity to make certain kinds of epistemological error. The Roman Empire? Protofascism. In fact, Latin seems to me to be a lousy militaristic language and I wish the schools would give it up and return to Greek. Descartes? Certainly.

DAUGHTER: I keep having to explain that in your writing Descartes *stands for* a set of ideas that probably had a more complicated history— Descartes is "emblematic," as they say in lit. crit. A sort of nickname, or a pronoun that stands for "all that rot." And as you know, schools in this country have long since given up both Greek and Latin.

FATHER: They've also given up teaching most proofs in geometry, and given up natural history as well. You see, you cannot learn to care about consistency until you deal with *total systems* and get a feeling for their integration. But you can learn about integration in several ways, and probably need all of them: looking at an ancient ecosystem at climax or looking at a work of art; or looking at a very tightly integrated logical system. My best students have often been either Roman Catholics or Marxists, because both learn something that most of the kids now are never taught, that consistency is important. Most don't even learn to spell. And incidentally, I wish they learned their way around some system of religious belief, with some complex weave of logic and poetry, so they would be familiar with metaphor. Kids!

DAUGHTER: All right. What else?

FATHER: Well, you mentioned Versailles. That's an important one because when punitive peace terms replaced Wilson's Fourteen Points as the basis for ending World War I, it made trust virtually impossible. You can lie as a tactic *in* war but when the falsehood is pushed up the logical type ladder and you lie *about* war and peace, there is no way back. The world is still suffering for the Treaty of Versailles.

DAUGHTER: Hmm. That's a different way of defining the moment of error, but maybe they are connected. Remember Skip Rappaport talking about his New Guinea people?* There was a series of links in the integration of that culture between their subsistence and their mythology, and there were certain ideas that were sacred—unquestioned and unquestionable—that held it together. There seem to be two meanings of "sacred" for you: one is "that with which thou shalt not tinker," and the other is a sense of the whole, which can only be met with awe—and not tinkered with.

FATHER: And which inspires humility.

DAUGHTER: Once at Burg Wartenstein we had a conversation about whether one could design an ecological religion that would become the sacred and unquestioned vehicle for an understanding of the interconnections of Creatura. About whether there would be a way to build in a sense of monism and "the pattern which connects" as a premise of thought and character?

FATHER: Hmm. And what did I say to that?

DAUGHTER: Well, you said no. For one thing you said the idea of insider and outsider, the damned and the saved, is too much a part of the notion *religion* for it to be usable. Even if you converted half the

*Roy A. Rappaport, *Ecology, Meaning, and Religion* (Richmond, Calif.: North Atlantic Books, 1979).

world, you would create the line between the converted and the unconverted, the boundary between what Muslims call the realm of war and the realm of peace (or salvation). Then that boundary would become the focus of conflict and mistrust.

FATHER: You cannot *construct* something and designate it as sacred.

DAUGHTER: So Eco really isn't meant to be a god that people might believe in?

FATHER: Certainly not. No, that's wrongly said, because "believe in" has several layers of meaning. It means "believe to exist" and "believe to represent an accurate idea" and "rely on or trust in." I suppose you could say I believe in Eco in the second sense.

DAUGHTER: You know, I think it's possible to believe in something like the Judeo-Christian God, in terms of what He represents and also in terms of trust, without believing in any kind of separate existence for Him.

FATHER: Jehovah? Maybe. But no, the idea of transcendence is pretty basic to Jehovah. The dualism of what you call "separate existence" is too closely knit into the system. And also the dualism of good and evil. "Eco" is not concerned with good or bad in any simple way and is not provided with free will. Indeed, he symbolizes the fact that, say, addiction or even pathology is the other face of adaptation.

DAUGHTER: But still you go on talking about the "sacred." How about Gaia? Did you ever run into the "Gaia hypothesis," as a name for the notion that this planet is a living organism?

FATHER: Just very shortly before I died. Someone showed me some of James Lovelock's writings.

DAUGHTER: Hmm. I'm glad to hear you were reading something current.

FATHER: He is surely right that the condition of the planet can only be explained by the processes of life.

DAUGHTER: Yes, but . . . but it's different. Every time I lecture about the Gaia hypothesis I find myself warning against the danger of thinking of Gaia as a vis-à-vis. You can't say, "Me and Gaia," or "I love Gaia," or "Gaia loves me." And you can't say, "I love Eco," either, can you?

FATHER: They are not the same. The notion Gaia is based in the physical reality of the planet—it's Pleromatic, thingish. When I ask people to think about a god who might be called Eco, I'm trying to make them think about Creatura, about mental process.

DAUGHTER: The word "process" is important there, isn't it?

150 · *Angels Fear*

FATHER: And also the fact that the interconnections are not entirely tight, and that all knowledge has *gaps*, and mental process includes the capacity to form new connections, to act as what I have called self-healing tautologies.

DAUGHTER: So . . . tragedy and opposites and the total fabric? And Eco as a nickname for the logic of mental process, the connectedness that holds all life and evolution together? And It can be violated but cannot be mocked? Perhaps It really is beautiful rather than lovable.

FATHER: Beautiful and terrible. Shiva and Abraxas.

XV   *The Structure in the Fabric* (GB)

I. MAP AND TERRITORY

[When we study the biological world, what we are doing is studying multiple events of communication. In this communicating about communication, we are particularly interested in describing injunctions or commands—messages that might be said to have causal effect in the functioning of the biological world—and in the system of premises that underlies all messages and makes them coherent. In the model on which this book is based, the term "structure" has been used to refer to constraints which characterize systems and define their functioning, such as, for instance, the setting of a thermostat. These are the landmarks in the world of flux. You might say that notions such as *anangke* or *karma* are affirmations of structure. Having noted that the communicative fabric of the living world is ordered, pervasive, and determinant even to the point where one might say of it, that is what men have meant by God, we move ahead in the effort to describe its regularities with some trepidation, looking both for patterns and for gaps in the weave.

[Biologists looking at the natural world *create* their descriptions, for even their most objective recorded data are artifacts of human perception and selection.] A description can never resemble the thing described— above all, the description can never *be* the thing described. The only truth that will approach the absolute level is the truth which the thing itself might provide if we could come that close to it, which, alas, we never can do, as Immanuel Kant pointed out long ago. We can get from the thing itself, the *Ding an sich*, only such information as a few of its immanent differentiations will allow our sense organs and scientific instruments to pick up.

We therefore must look first at the systematic discrepancies which *necessarily* exist between what we can say and what we are trying to describe. Before we begin to draw any map, we must be clear about the difference between "map" and "territory." In description we frequently refer to "structure," not to specify what must be but to attempt to describe the infinite detail of what we have observed. To say that a plant or a leaf has a "structure" means that we can make general descriptive statements about it. We claim, by calling something "structure," that we can do better than concentrate upon single details one at a time. If I say that the spine of an animal is a repetitive structure, uniting the parts into a "column," I am already asserting some sort of regularity or organization among parts. I am making a statement that applies not to any single vertebra but to an aggregate of vertebrae. The very notion of structure always gets away from the infinite detail of the particular. Underlying the very word *structure* is the notion of some sort of generality.

The philosopher Whitehead once remarked that while arithmetic is the science of particular numbers and their handling, algebra is the science that arises when the word "particular" is replaced by the word "any." In this sense, structure is the algebra of that which is to be described; it is always at least one degree more abstract. Structure presumes a gathering and sorting of some of the infinite details, which can then be thrown away and summary statements offered in their place.

It is important to distinguish between classes and groups in this context. The members of a "class," as I here use the word, are gathered together in terms of some *common* characteristic that they share; the members of a "group" are gathered together because each member is somehow a *modulation* of some other member or members. There is some process or, as the mathematicians say, some "operation" by which members of the group are transformed one into another. Indeed, the theory of biological evolution would be much improved if biologists would model their thought and language upon the available mathematics for describing groups. This would force them to develop some theory of structural relatedness more sophisticated than the mere use of "homology" as evidence of phylogenetic history. There is surely a great deal more to be read off from the phenomena of homology than the biologists have yet dreamed of.

In terms of this discrimination between class and group, the aggregate of vertebrae in the spinal cord is a class, inasmuch as every vertebra shares certain features with every other. We may say that every vertebra is built upon the same ground plan. But the aggregate is also a group in the sense that each vertebra is a modulation of the vertebra preceding it in the fore-and-aft sequence. There are, however, interesting discontinuities of modulation between the thoracic and the lumbar. In addition, the vertebrae are interrelated in a third way so that all fit together and work together as part of a single whole.

What was said above about three ways in which the vertebrae are related is a small piece of that larger mystery, the organization of the biosphere. Thus, when we look behind the word "structure," we encounter fragments of paradigm, of how the larger fabric is put together.

There is, however, a more problematic aspect of our notion of "structure," which must be stressed. As we scientists use the word, it promotes in us a false notion that the more concrete details subsumed under a given named structure are somehow *really* components in that structure. That is, we easily come to believe that the way we dissected the real world in order to make our description was the best and most correct way to dissect it.

Chemists may say that all halogens (that genus of elements that includes fluorine and chlorine and so on) share certain formal characteristics in modulated degree, and therefore constitute a "group" and, further, that such groups of elements can be set together to make the periodic table of elements. We may object that this is quite unreal—that these are but formal resemblances and the classification of the items is an artifact, an act of the chemist and not an act of nature.

But criticism of this kind is often inappropriate in biology. If we as biologists think we are using the word "structure" as a physicist or chemist might, we run the risk of *overcorrecting* for that error. [And yet we may also make the opposite error of asking too little of our biological descriptions, believing that if they seem to fit that is all that must be asked.] It is true, of course, that there are no names in a purely physical universe, and the stars have names only because men have named them. Even the constellations exist only as men have seen constellations into the heavens. Similarly, the structural statements of physicists and chemists refer only to structure immanent in their theories, not in the physical world. But that is not so in the biological world. In that world, in the world of communication and organization, the exchange of news and messages is an essential component of what goes on. The anatomy of the spinal cord is determined in embryology by genetic processes and messages from DNA and from other growing organs, and these messages are necessarily summative. They depend upon—they are—structure. Still, the messages *in* biology, like the messages that we make *about* biology, are necessarily different from their referents.

In the biologist's description, structure will always be invoked, and this invocation has several possibilities for truth and error:

1. The biologist's structure may be simply wrong. He may classify a porpoise with the fish. A physicist might equally blunder in, say, the classification of an element.

2. The biologist may attribute structure in a way that is successful as a base for prediction but is not appropriately related to the system of communication within or among the organisms. In this case he is right in the sense that a good physicist is right. His description tallies with the appearances, the phenotypic description of the creatures or population. But he can be wrong in attributing to the system he is describing messages corresponding to those he uses in the description of it. He may assert that a man has two hands, but he should hesitate to attribute a numeral to the language of DNA.

3. The biologist's structure may follow the classification of parts and relations which the DNA and/or other biological systems of control themselves use. It is legitimate to think of structure as causing or shaping the course of events, provided always that we are sure that indeed our statements of structure coincide with and are formally identical with message systems within the plant or animal. It is all right to speak of, say, "apical dominance" in the growth patterns of flowering plants if we are sure that controlling messages indeed travel from the apex downwards and have effect on the growth of more proximal parts. If a biologist invokes relationship or pattern rather than number, he will probably be more exact than the biologist who says that humans have two hands or five fingers. In any case, he has the possibility of being right in a sense the physicist can never achieve.

On the other hand, he has the possibility of being more profoundly wrong than the physicist can ever be.

There is no communication in the material that concerns the physicist, no names and no structure as I have used the word here. That which the physicist must describe is, for example, the fall of a body that cannot witness its own fall. When Bishop Berkeley asks about the tree falling in the forest when he is not there to see and describe it, he is being a physicist. In biology, the developing embryo is always there to witness and critique its own development, to give the orders and control the pathways of change and response.

Within the physical world, strangely enough, there can be no "error" and no "pathology." The sequences of events in which physical entities engage are *un*organized and therefore cannot be *dis*organized. But in biology "error" and even "pathology" are possible— continually possible—because biological entities are organized, as opposed to merely orderly. They contain their own descriptions of themselves and their own recipes for growth.

[4. To say that a description made by a biologist corresponds to the organism's own description is still not to claim direct truth.] All biological descriptions are necessarily structural and, to this extent, all must falsify and simplify or generalize their referent. Even the reports and injunctions that occur and travel inside living creatures are derivative—always it is difference or contrast that triggers the emission of the message, and change rather than state is always the subject matter of morphogenesis or the control of behavior. If to be so limited is necessarily to distort, if an aggregate of messages that mention change and ignore state is thereby a distortive aggregate, then all biological aggregates of messages are to this extent always in error.

[5. Above all, the description made by the biologist is not identical with what he describes, even if he displays a specimen in a museum.] Information is only *about* the things it mentions, even when the things are themselves used to encode the message. Even when a restaurant exhibits a roast of beef turning on a spit to tell customers that here they can eat beef roasted on a spit—even in such ostensive communication, the roasting beef qua carrier of message is, in a sense, not just itself. And when we look at more complex processes of interaction, such as the internal organization of living things, we find that while the ongoing business is indeed immanent in pieces of "matter," the process has regularity because it is itself about its own regularities.

.

"Structure" is a structuring word, and life is normative. To this extent, life resembles many religions. It is, however, not always so that the norms that life seeks are the same as those religion would prefer.

.

II. THE NECESSARY WEFT

Let us now look again at the regularities called by Saint Augustine the Eternal Verities so very long ago, and compare them to the concept of structure we have been using. Modern ears are offended by the notion that any proposition might claim to be true enough to be called an "eternal verity" or might endure forward and back from before the big bang to beyond the black hole, but Saint Augustine certainly would have claimed that span for his "eternity." These Eternal Verities, which were discussed briefly in chapter 2, were such propositions as "three and seven are ten." Today, as I said, our minds rush to repudiate the very mention of eternal truth and, just as quickly, to repudiate the idea that any proposition might be self-evident. It is fashionable today to distrust all propositions that claim to be eternal or self-evident. In this habitual skepticism we forget what was said about the nature of description. No description is true, as we have already remarked, but on the other hand, it is perhaps true eternally that description must always be at a certain remove from the things described. [Indeed, we notice, as we look at the processes of communication in the natural world, that this communication depends throughout on premises and connections that need not be stated. Even the DNA seems to take certain matters as self-evident.]

The verities are very close to being self-evident truths, but the modern critic would say that these propositions are only details, subsidiary propositions even, in larger tautological systems. It will be argued that "$7 + 3 = 10$" is one of an infinite number of similar small pieces which together are generated by the man-made system of interlocking propositions called arithmetic. This system is a tautology, a network of propositions following logically from certain axioms whose truth is not asserted by the mathematician. The mathematicians claim that they assert only that if the axioms be granted, then the other propositions will follow. From the axioms and definitions of arithmetic, it will follow that "$7 + 3 = 10$," but since the mathematicians have not claimed truth for the axioms, they will not claim truth for the propositions. They do not even claim that the axioms refer to anything in the real world. If the applied mathematician wants to map numbers of, for example, oranges onto the mathematical tautology, he must do so at his own risk.

But, in fact, the problem of the eternal and the self-evident has not been entirely avoided by the mathematician's disclaimer in regard to axioms and definitions. I grant that the axioms and definitions are man-made and refer to nothing in particular in the material world. Indeed, I would insist that we do not know enough about the corporeal things of the world to guess even that the axioms might contain truths about things. But, after all, this book is not much concerned with truths about things— only with truths about truths, with the natural history of descriptive propositions, information, injunctions, abstract premises and the aggregate networks of such ideas. Above all, I am trying to build a natural history of the relations between ideas. It is irrelevant when mathematicians assert that their tautologies assert no truths about things, but explosively relevant when they assert that the steps and even the sequences of steps from the axioms to the detailed propositions are self-evident and, perhaps, eternal and true.

As to the referents of all this ratiocination and argument—the "things"— while I can know nothing about any individual thing by itself, I *can* know something about *relations between things*. As an observer, I am in a position resembling that of the mathematician. I, too, can say nothing about a single thing—I cannot even assert from experience that such exists. I can know only something about relations between things. If I say the table is "hard," I am going beyond what my experience would testify. What I know is that the interaction or relationship between the table and some sense organ or instrument has a special character of differential hardness for which I have no ordinary vocabulary, alas, but which I distort by referring the special character of the relationship entirely to one of the components in it. In so doing, I distort what I *could* know about the relationship into a statement about a "thing" which I *cannot* know. It is always relationship between things that is the referent of all valid propositions. It is a man-made notion that "hardness" is immanent in one end of a binary relationship.

It is suggestive that the mathematicians are content to accept the idea that relationships *between* propositions can be self-evident, while they are unwilling to grant this status to the propositions themselves. It is as if they were claiming to know how to talk, but not to know what they are talking about. And that position is precisely parallel to my own. I have great difficulty in discussing the vast mental organization of the world and great difficulty in discussing the parts of it, but it seems to me that we can, with care, talk about how that vast organization thinks. We can explore the kind of links it uses between its propositions, while we can never know what it thinks about.

These links and patterns of relationship which I want to discuss are necessarily regular and form a part of the Eternal Verities, including the rules for joining together items of discourse, together with the natural history of what happens when items are joined together in inappropriate ways. I include in my field of investigation what the DNA says to the growing embryo and to the physiological body. I include what the structure of the brain says to the processes of thought. I include all discourse which bonds together the phenomena of any ecosystem.

The rules of relationship between items of mental or ideational life are not unbreakable "laws" of nature nor even absolute recipes of logic. They may be and often are breached.

But again I say, God is not mocked.

III. Between the Lines

In spite of the limitations of logic, we can borrow from it the notion that the results of computation or abstract reasoning are not what is "eternal" and self-evident, nor, it seems, are the explicit steps leading to those results. What is self-evident is precisely what is *between the lines* of computation. Mathematicians call the underlying pattern of a given computation an algorithm. Out of this we shall attempt to tease the sorts of proposition of which the algorithm is made.

First, there are the definitions, which we agree are only suppositions—protases—if-clauses. Then there follow definitions of process. Finally, there are the given particular items or data. If numbers are such and such and if addition is defined as so and so, we can take "5" and "7," and add them together according to the definitions already given. But there is something else behind all this. The process requires more than has been given, hidden in the arrangements of the lines. It requires injunctions to the human or mechanical calculator to tell him *in what order* the steps shall be performed.

In the textbooks, a part of those instructions are actually dissected out. For instance, most adults must remember from elementary school those abstract statements about the order in which steps of computation shall be performed, which are formally known as the distributive and commutative laws. In equational form, the mathematicians tell us that

$$a + b = b + a,$$

and that

$$a \times b = b \times a.$$

Thus, within the operations of addition and multiplication, the order of items is irrelevant. But when addition steps are to be combined with multiplication steps, the ordering of items is of first importance:

$$(a + b) \times c \text{ is not equal to } a + (b \times c).$$

Observe first that these rules are really not limited to mathematics at all. If you are a cook, you will know that the order of procedures in the kitchen is an essential component in every recipe; if you are a developing embryo, all the component steps of development must be in proper sequence and proper synchrony.

In other words, we cannot object to the commutative and distributive laws as mere spin-off from man-made tautologies. Wherever there is purpose and/or growth and/or evolution, something like the "laws" of sequence will obtain. And these will not be like the "laws" of physics, where no exceptions occur, nor will they be like the "laws" of lawyers, where breach of law is followed by inflicted penalty. The "laws" of the sequence of propositional steps in argument (or injunctional steps in cooking and embryology) can be, and often are, broken, and their breach is not followed by inflicted penalty or vengeance by man or God. Nonetheless, the outcome of the sequence will depend upon the sequence of steps, and if the sequence is in wrong order or some steps are omitted, the outcome will be changed and may be disastrous.

There is a story of Socrates setting out to prove that all education is only a matter of drawing out from the uneducated mind that which it already knows. To demonstrate this, Socrates called in an unfortunate small boy from the street and asked him a long sequence of questions in such a way that the sequence of the boy's answers is the proof of Pythagoras' famous theorem that the area of the square of the hypotenuse is equal to the sum of the areas of the squares of the other two sides of a right-angled triangle. Having gone through this long ritual and obtained the boy's final assent to that which was to be proved, Socrates says, "Look, you see, he knew it all the time."

But that is all nonsense; what the boy did not know and what Socrates provided was the answer at each point to the question: What question should I answer next? Faced with the bare challenge to prove Pythagoras' theorem, the boy would have been speechless, not knowing the order of steps which would build the theorem.

Similarly, the embryo must, above all, know the order of steps for epigenesis. In addition to the instructions in the DNA, it must carry injunctions as to the sequence in which the steps of its development are to be taken. It needs to know the *algorithm* of its development. There is a species of information here different from either the axioms or the operations in each line. Between the lines of a computation is concealed the order of the steps.

·

At this point, I will summarize what has so far been said in this chapter and in chapter 13 about the concept "structure," approached from various angles. I have suggested here that "structure" be thought of as something like the Eternal Verities of Saint Augustine or the commutative and distributive laws of mathematical logic, or like the algorithms that are the recipes for sequence in computation. These should be compared to the notions of order in natural and human events such as the notion of *anangke* that was believed to govern the interwoven lives of men and gods and city-states. Each of these approaches was a groping towards a description of the largest mentally or ecologically organized systems that we can either perceive or imagine—towards, in fact, a definition of something recognizable as sharing many of the attributes of what men call God. There has, however, been nothing said about personification either of God *or of the human individual*. Of individuals, I propose here only that we remember that these are subsystems of the larger whole, each meeting the criteria of what can be called "mental."

In summary, the following points have now been made:

1. "Structure" is an *informational* idea and therefore has its place throughout the whole of biology in the widest sense, from the organization within the virus particle to the phenomena studied by cultural anthropologists.

2. In biology, many regularities are part of—contribute to—their own determination. This *recursiveness* is close to the root of the notion "structure." The news of its regularity is (I assume) not fed back into the atom to control its action at the next instant.

3. The information or injunction which I call "structure" is always *at one remove from its referent.* It is the name, for example, of some characteristic immanent in the referent or, more precisely, it is the name or description of some relation ideally immanent in the referent.

4. Human languages—especially perhaps those of the West—are peculiar in giving undue emphasis to Separable Things. The emphasis is not upon "relations between" but upon the ends of relationship, the relata. This emphasis makes it difficult to keep clearly in mind that the word "structure" is reserved for discussion of *relations* (especially to be avoided is the plural use, "structures").

5. Insofar as the name is never the thing named and the map is never the territory, *"structure" is never "true."*

      (The story is told of Picasso that a stranger in a railway carriage accosted him with the challenge, "Why don't you paint things as they really are?" Picasso demurred, saying that he did not quite understand what the gentleman meant, and the stranger then produced from his wallet a photograph of his wife. "I mean," he said, "like that. That's how she *is.*" Picasso coughed hesitantly and said, "She is rather small, isn't she? And somewhat flat?")

      "Structure" is always a somewhat flattened, abstracted version of "truth"—but structure is all that we can know. The map is never the territory, but it is sometimes useful to discuss how map differs from hypothetical territory. That is as near as we can get to the ineffable, the unsayable. In the cadence of Lewis Carroll: always territory tomorrow, never territory today.

6. It is clear that structure is a *determining* factor. Indeed, structure has repeatedly been regarded as a sort of God—identifying Jehovah with his commandments—or Blake's Urizen with his chains. But to do this will always propose a dualism—a split between the structure and that larger reality in which the structure is immanent. The structure has no separate existence. The tendency to imagine a dualistic uni-

verse is easily corrected by remembering that it is often only we that create the notion of structure in our synthesis of descriptions from data which reach us through the filter of our sense organs. We can, in such cases, remind ourselves that this structure we project upon the "outside" world is only a spin-off from our own perceptions and thought. It is more difficult to achieve this correction of epistemological dualism when we are looking at biological entities, for these— the birds and fishes and people and developing embryos—create their own premises and guidelines and abide by these premises in their development of physiology and systems of action.

It is hard to keep clearly before the scientific mind the general epistemological verity: that the Ten Commandments, the rules of morphogenesis and embryology, and the premises of grammar in animal and human communication are all part of the vast mental process which is immanent in our world and all as real, *and as unreal*, as syllogistic logic.

IV. The Gaps in the Fabric

Now that we have pulled out "structure" from the ongoing organized flux of the universe, it is appropriate to attempt a synthesis—to put it back again. Let us see how our fabric of descriptions and reports and injunctions fits a world fleshed out with life and happenings.

First, it is conspicuously full of holes. If we try to cover life with our descriptions of it—or if we try to think of the totality of an organism as somehow fully covered by its own message systems—we at once see that more description is needed. But, however much structure is added, however minutely detailed our specifications, there are always gaps.

Even without looking at the living subject matter of our structural report, and listening only to what can be said, we feel the jump between each clause of description and each other clause, between the coverage of every sentence of our description and every next sentence. The poem "The Battle of Blenheim" by Robert Southey, describes a child looking at an object he has discovered:

> . . . so large, and smooth, and round . . .
> says Wilhelmine

Later we discover that he is talking about the skull of a soldier killed in battle (" 'twas a famous victory"), but that knowledge is made up of the results of jumping from one statement to another. We must know what "large" means to a "little grandchild" playing in a field. As hearers we must be willing to jump from size to texture, and from texture to shape, to obey a mental recipe which the poet offers us. But compared with the reality, the description is a miserable gathering of outlines. We really have a very incomplete knowledge either of the skull or of little Wilhelmine, and this is not the fault of the poet, who has given us so little to go on. It is an inevitable result of the nature of the communicative process. The data given will never meet each other to cover the subject of description.

Art is the cunning use of what the hearer already knows—what is already in his skull—to make the hearer fill in details. Of course, Wilhelmine was blond! Of course, the skull was rotted clean!

This preinstructed state of the recipient of every message is a necessary condition for all communication. This book can tell you nothing unless you know nine-tenths of it already.

Be that as it may, what is true of tales and words between persons is also true of the internal organization of living things. What can conceivably be said by DNA or by hormones and growth-controlling substances is a quite incomplete coverage of the infinite detail of the events of embryology and the final anatomy and physiology of the creature. The developing tissues must know the apodoses (the then-clauses), the appropriate responses of obedience to the protases provided by DNA (and environment). And seen so, the coverage is going to be sparse. It is, of course, for this reason that plants and animals are patterned and repetitive in their shapes and responses. Redundancy is the economical way to make a limited supply of structural information cover a complex subject.

Everybody knows (or should know) that you cannot learn to dance by merely reading a book. You must also have the actual experience of dancing, which the book necessarily leaves undescribed. It is practice that enables you to put the pieces of instruction together to form patterns.

In sum, all description, all information, is such as to touch upon only a few points in the matter to be described. The rest is left uncovered—hinted at perhaps by extrapolation from what is actually communicated but in principle undetermined and uncontrolled by the message system. The U.S. Constitution, for instance, leaves almost everything unsaid. What lawyers have spun out in addition still defines only a few details and here and there a basic principle of human interaction. Most is left undefined or is left to be worked out after the first formative hint is given.

Similarly, a combination of momentary readiness, determined probably by genetic factors, plus the momentary difference provided by the entry point of the spermatozoon, establish the plane of bilateral symmetry of the embryo frog. After that the matter is left so far as message is concerned. The gross difference immediately established at the critical moment will be sufficient guide for the remainder of the life of the frog. Each generation of cells follows in the now already existing mold.

All of this, however, only brings home to us more vividly the necessary incompleteness of all description, all injunction, and all structure.

Try to describe a leaf or, still better, try to define the difference between two leaves of the same plant, or between the second and third walking appendages (the "legs") of a single, particular crab. You will discover that that which you must specify is *everywhere* in the leaf or in the crab's leg. It will be, in fact, impossible to decide upon any general statement that will be a premise to all the details, and utterly impossible to deal with the details one by one.

"Structure" and "description" will never cover actuality. The *Ding an sich*, the very thing itself, will always comprise an infinitude of details. For the crab's leg or the leaf, only a certain small fraction of the details will have been controlled by genetics or by the specificities of growth. But if you attempt the task proposed above with two leaves or with two legs of the crab, you will discover something about the relation between structure (or description) and actuality. It will quickly appear that there are several sorts of gaps always and necessarily left uncovered by description:

1. There are gaps of detail between details. However fine the mesh of our net of description, smaller details will always escape description. This is not because we are careless or lazy but because in principle the machinery of description—whether it be a language or a halftone block—is digital and discontinuous, whereas the variables immanent in the thing to be described are analogic and continuous. If, on the other hand, the method of description is analogic, we shall encounter the circumstance that no quantity can accurately represent any other quantity—always and inevitably every measurement is approximate.

2. There are gaps between kinds of description, which are not necessarily present in the thing described. "Large" and "smooth" and "round" are separate statements which never meet. The continuum of nature

is constantly broken down into a discontinuum of "variables" in the act of description or specification.

3. A similar discontinuity appears in the hierarchy of descriptive statements. For economy's sake, the describer (or the DNA) must inevitably deal with details in batches. A curved outline will be summarized by its approximation to some mathematical form. The infinitesimals of some shape will be condensed with an equation. Then, having had some success in describing a given batch of details, we will inevitably take a next step in generalization, summarizing the relations between batches. In order to assert the differences between the leaves or the crab's legs (or, for that matter, the nucleic acids), we shall need to specify the formal resemblances which are shared between the pairs of items. And so on. That which will remain unspecified will be the jump from detail to batch of details, and again the next jump between the batch and the batch of batches. These jumps will remain unspecified and uncovered by any description for many reasons. We do not know how to describe such abstract discontinuities. The formulations of mathematics are still rudimentary. But even with more powerful math, we would quickly find ourselves in an infinite regress. Having set up descriptive propositions of two hierarchically related logical types, a higher and a lower, if we then step aside to describe the relation between these two types, this latter description will be of a third type and we shall be bound to describe the relation between the third type and the others, thus embarking on a fourth type, and so on ad infinitum.

This whole argument continues to give a sort of topological picture of the problems of describing any living thing. The argument has its own "structure" and the organism we are trying to describe also has its "structure"—referring in both cases to an interrelated aggregate of messages. But these messages (like all structure and description) can never cover the total detail of that which is to be determined or described. In other words, there are gaps of the various sorts described above. Our diagram of the whole working system must therefore (and this is the topological aspect of the matter) be such that if we travel across it, we shall cross alternately points of formulation and structure, and regions of gap. This will be true regardless of the fineness of the mesh of the network of structure.

[These various kinds of gaps are a characteristic of Creatura, of biological organization and description, about which we have been speaking. The problems of description are, of course, very different in Pleroma, where we may use the informational concept "structure" only to indicate the informational nature of *our* description. The world of flux does not have gaps in the sense used here. Similarly, the temperature in the house described in chapter 4 varies continuously, without the discontinuities marked out on a thermometer or the more important discontinuities of threshold defining the "structure" of the system on the thermostat.]

The whole long groping and argument of this chapter give us then a model, similar to the one sketched in at the end of my *Mind and Nature*,* and elaborating on the model in chapter 4, of the relationship between "form" (or structure) and "process" or (flux).

Before moving on, I want to warn those who will come after and the many who are currently wrestling with similar problems: The difficulty and obscurity of this whole matter arises out of the following circumstances:

1. The "data" of the scientist studying biological phenomena are created by him. They are descriptions of descriptions, forms of forms.
2. At the same time, message material, descriptions, injunctions, and forms (call them what you will) are already immanent in the biological phenomena. This it is to be internally organized, alive.
3. All forms, descriptions, etc.—including those immanent in the organisms—are like language. They are discontinuous and distortive.
4. The forms are totally necessary if we are to understand both the freedoms and the rigidities of living systems. They are to the total process as the axle is to the wheel. By restricting the motion and preventing its movement in other planes, the axle gives the wheel a smoothness in moving in the chosen plane.

---

*There is one fundamental difference between that model and this which I now propose, in that I then saw the "process" side of that model (see Fig. 10, p. 194) as composed of discontinuous steps. This was a serious error which arose because I approached the process side of the model from the "form" side. I needed the process side to fill the gaps in the surely discontinuous formal component and this need was discontinuous. It was surely correct to see the form or structure side as discontinuous and hierarchical, but incorrect to project that discontinuity onto the process side.

XVI Innocence and

Experience (GB & MCB)

THIS CHAPTER will examine those characteristics of the mental ambience or web that appear at *interfaces* between mental subsystems. To begin with, I shall use as a principal example the interface between the old and the young. This interface will be compared with others, especially with the sometimes tragic interface that anthropologists call culture contact and with that interface, often equally tragic, that occurs where human communities encounter natural ecosystems.

Let us start from two well-known limericks which illustrate a phenomenon of mental contact with diagrammatic terseness:

> There was a young man who said, "Damn.
> I begin to perceive that I am
> A creature that moves
> In determinate grooves.
> I'm not even a bus, I'm a *tram*."

To this there is a reply:

> There was an old man who said, "Cuss.
> I must choose between better and wuss.
> By rulings of Fate,
> I must keep myself straight.
> I'm not even a tram; I'm a *bus*."

This pair of verses was no doubt written to underline the illusory nature of free will. I have made a small change to suggest that the bus is older—perhaps more experienced—than the tram.

As you move from a narrower to a slightly wider determinism, you remain within the seemingly determined universe, but you can now stand off from the context in which you live and *see* that context. At this point you have to choose between better and worse. Not everything is so narrowly fixed for you. You become more like a bus than a tram. But you still have the illusion that if only you could reach the next order of freedom, if only you could stand off in another dimension, you would have true free will. Freedom is always imagined to be round the next corner or over the next crest of the mental landscape. We go on doing research and thinking about all sorts of problems, as if we could one day reach the thought that would set us free.

The point of the limericks is not in either but in their juxtaposition. The naiveté of the tram, who thinks he would be free but for those constraining grooves, is demonstrated by the disillusion of the bus, who discovers the constraints and responsibilities of the next order of control. "Freedom" and "responsibility" are a complementary pair, such that an increase in the former will always bring with it an increase in the latter.

The superficial contrast between bus and tram and the fundamental determinism that both must face combine to provide a parable of the relation between youth and age and an instance of a very widespread and basic characteristic of many interfaces between mental systems.

In youth, we are more narrowly grooved, more cramped by social restraints and by limited knowledge of how to do things. As we approach old age, the grooves become wider. This might seem to give us greater freedom, but in fact it makes us more responsible for choice—for *our* choices. [When the "we" of this sentence refers to contemporary human beings in relation to the biosphere, with all the apparent control offered by technology, choice and the need for responsibility are increased.]

I am discussing not an abstract philosophical world of "free will" and "determinism" but a necessary component in the living natural history of every organism. This it is to be a mental creature, and this paradox is an essential component of human life—a component of the mental ambience whenever a certain level of complexity is reached.

We see each other always with distorted eyes. To the eyes of the tram, the bus appears "free." But to the eyes of the bus, the innocence of the tram appears blessed with freedom.

The same contrast obtains in almost all hierarchies and pyramids of authority in which a number of subsystems combine. I was named a regent of the University of California, one of twenty-five persons who constitute the general board of that very large financial and educational concern with one hundred thousand students on nine campuses. Everybody, both inside and outside that institution, thinks that the regents are powerful creatures individually and collectively. Supposedly they can and do really determine what happens in that great university. But, in truth, they are more conscious of lack of power than are the students. I personally had more influence on the processes of education as a senior lecturer than as a regent. In those days I could influence students directly in the classroom. I could put strange ideas into their heads so that they would ask strange questions in other classrooms. They could say to the other teachers, "But Bateson says so and so." As a regent I became frustrated, finding myself more and more limited to decisions about quantity rather than ideas. How many students shall we admit? What fees shall we charge? And how shall we bring the pension system up-to-date? As a regent I largely lost the freedom to shape the questions.

Similarly, I am sure, the president of the United States feels almost totally restricted by the resemblance between himself and a bus. His power to innovate is almost totally negated by his duty to keep things "straight." Most of his decisions must be those which will maintain the status quo. Idealistic and radical presidents must surely weep when they arrive in the White House and discover how little power they have.

And still men strive to be presidents, monarchs, and prime ministers. They strive for what is called "power." Strangely, the illusion of power is a spin-off from—a function of—that distortion of perception that causes the tram to envy the bus. Every lower person is likely to think that every higher person is more free from the "determinate grooves." This it is to be ambitious. Our mental ambience has favored such ambition in a majority of human cultural systems ever since the Neolithic age. Ambition and envy are common by-products of a large class of interfaces between human mental subsystems.

It is the mechanics of illusion that we have to examine—the deluded respect with which innocence views experience and the deluded envy with which experience views innocence.

A not dissimilar state of affairs is characteristic of the relation between the sexes. My old professor of anthropology at Cambridge, Alfred Haddon, used to finish his series of lectures on physical anthropology with the same joke every year. He would bring to the podium a male skull and a female skull and point out the contrast between them. He would point to the heavy brow ridges in the male and the strong roughness of the muscular insertions of the occipital region, and in the female he would point to the general lightness and smoothness of the structure and the unfinished state of the sutures. He would conclude, "You see, the male skull resembles the anthropoid; the female the infantile. Which do you prefer?"

There is, however, an ingenious and merciful dispensation of Providence that causes each sex to envy and perhaps admire the other. May we never be liberated from these illusions . . . .

Is there then no escape from this undercurrent of mental life? Are the particular illusions that characterize the relations between old and young characteristic of all such interfaces, and do these illusions necessarily propose matters of envy and control? What are the mechanics of their occurrence? Can any exceptions be adduced? It is exceptions which would throw light on the nature of the wider mental ambience.

Many sorts of situations exist in which human beings have achieved or preserved some freedom from the illusions which accompany hierarchic superiority.

The first class of exceptions is connected with imminent death. In the Scots language, there is a word, *fey*, which is of the same root as *fate* and *faery* and refers to an elevated state in which many previously unrecognized truths become plain, so that in folklore the fey person is credited with supernatural wisdom and second sight. What we have here is a rather precise term for that state of mind which is induced by the absolute certainty of death. When death is close and utterly sure—and not to be temporized with—then it becomes possible to see with a new clarity and the mind can soar. This state is the result of liberation from appetitive drives and, I suppose, is approximately what the Buddhists call "nonattachment." In William Blake's phrase, it becomes possible to look *through* the eye so that the illusions of success and failure, shame and vanity fall away. If all were at the point of death, envy could be no more.

Returning to the parable of the bus and the tram, we have to remember that both these vehicles (and their human counterparts) have *and cherish* the notion that they are going somewhere. They are totally attached by ego values and it is out of this attachment that they create their illusions of freedom and/or determinism. We may say that the bus is one step nearer to nonattachment but this means nothing. He is either attached or not, and there is no intermediate state (except one of anguish).

It is a necessary characteristic of the ambient mental system—an epistemological necessity—that the premise of purpose will propose the (perhaps unreal) problem of free will and/or determinism. An examination of the relation between ideas of purpose and ideas of freedom brings us closer to what is necessarily true than what little we can say about the separate notions that we call "purpose" and "free will."

On two occasions I have been close to death with surgical interventions, and on both occasions the operation was a failure but the patient lived. I am thankful for both of these experiences, which I have discussed elsewhere. Here I need to say that both experiences were, for me, rich in liberation. Love was closer to the surface and easier to convey, and at the same time there was a feeling of aloneness which was like looking out from some high peak after the exertion of climbing.

This was not a brief exhilaration but lasted for some weeks or months, only slowly giving way to the drabness and multiple worries and attachments of everyday life. My latest experience of this kind was about a year ago, and today I am still not quite returned to normal, to what Eliot calls the "sad time between."

Obviously, the fey state might occur at any age, but old age is, among other things, an approach to death and I think that a difference in degree of feyness is a component in the barrier between age and youth. Not only is age more like the bus and youth more like the tram, but also age begins slowly to discover that the problem of free will is irrelevant.

I have been privileged to see something of another system in which people were partly free of the dilemmas of the bus and the tram. This was on the island of Bali, where I did fieldwork for two years in the company of Margaret Mead, to whom I was then married.*

The occidental notions of purpose and durational time are blurred in Balinese thinking, and even the words for these notions are apparently recently borrowed. In reply to questions of purpose, "Why are you doing so and so?" the Balinese will commonly reply either in terms of patterns of etiquette or in terms of the calendar: "Because it is *Anggara-Kasih.*"

In a word, that frame of mind that caused the tram and the bus to complain of a lack of freedom is absent or poorly developed among the

*See especially Gregory Bateson and Margaret Mead, *Balinese Character: A Photographic Analysis* (New York: The New York Academy of Sciences, 1942).

Balinese. Attachment and purpose must always hinge upon ideas of time.

It is natural, then, to ask whether the Balinese are "fey" in the sense of having a chronic expectation of death. The answer to this question, however, is not simple. Death and the rituals of death are indeed a continual and conspicuous feature of Balinese life. Their cremations are famous. The deceased are carried to the cremation ground in tall towers as much as a hundred feet high, lifted up by a great crowd of men shouting and yelling under the bamboo lattice which supports the tower. They lurch through the village and across the creek, and at the creek there are violent games with the mud, everybody splashing and kicking and laughing. In every such funeral crowd, there will be one or two men who are *sapta*, "free from disgust." These individuals are partly admired as a source of amusement but partly despised for making a show (*adjum-adjuman*) of their strange propensity. They may grab an arm or a leg, wrenching it off the rotting corpse, or one of them may push his face into the abdominal cavity.

This roughhouse play (so-called) is the correct conventional behavior, in marked contrast to the show of grief and "respect for the dead" which convention demands of occidentals. But whether the conventional funeral behavior is an expression of the participants' "feelings," either among the Balinese or among ourselves, may be doubted. In the mountain village of Bajoeng Gede, we witnessed the funeral of the wife of a man who was both deaf and dumb. In this case the bereaved husband wept piteously, and his friends—he had many—excused this shameless grief by saying that, being deaf, he did not know how to conduct himself.

In sum, it is clear that Balinese conventional attitudes towards death are very different from ours and that their attitudes in some ways resemble or simulate nonattachment or the fey state. It appears, however, that the Balinese "happiness" (so-called by them) in the presence of death is not simple. It is possible that they repress the expression of grief just as we repress impulses to ghoulish behavior.

It is, I suspect, not an accident that the Hindu goddess of death has, in Bali, not only her Hindu names, Durga and Kali, and the attributes that go with those names, but she is also Rangda, the Queen of Witches, herself a witch of the Medusa type, with monstrous face and power to paralyze those who approach. In her masked form, she has only to hold out the *anteng* she carries (the sling in which Balinese mothers carry their babies) to freeze any hostile approach.

Witches, perhaps all over the world, resemble the fey and the partially nonattached and exemplify the hostility that this state may incur. The witch traditionally operates on the edge of logic,* making the context appear different from what conventional persons had supposed it to be. She creates contextual puns to make a continual sliding of double binds. Interestingly enough, the traditional European test and/or punishment of witches was by dipping, a grotesque and horrible double bind creating a symmetry between the crime and the punishment. The suspect was tied to the end of a plank to be immersed in water. If he or she sank, this proved innocence but resulted in drowning. To float proved guilt and was followed by burning.

Whether the crime of witchcraft really is especially characteristic of old women I do not know, but that is the stereotype in European folklore and fairy stories. The Balinese in dance or drama are fascinated by pre-adolescent girls who dance the part of Rangda, but Rangda herself is an old hag. In Hinduistic terms, she is Kali-Durga rather than Parvati, but there is a Kali-Durga hidden inside every beautiful little Parvati and, vice versa, a Parvati hidden in every old hag. A prince in every beast and a beast in every prince.

The witch, the *sapta*, the mystic, the schizophrenic, the fool, the prophet, the trickster, and the poet are all variants of the bus. (The witch traditionally has a freedom of three dimensions. He or she is perhaps best symbolized by some flying, lurching, and dizzy vehicle such as a helicopter.) They all share a partial freedom that sets them at odds with the conventional world.

Long ago, in 1949, when psychiatrists still believed in lobotomy, I was a new member of the staff of the Veterans Administration Mental Hospital at Palo Alto. One day one of the residents called me aside to see the blackboard in our largest classroom. A lobotomy meeting had been held there that afternoon and the board was still unerased.

*For examples of such behavior, see: Margaret Murray, *The Witch Cult in Western Europe* (New York: Oxford UP, 1962); Sylvia Townsend Warner, *Lolly Willowes* (Chicago: Academy Chicago, 1979), and Isak Dinesen, *Seven Gothic Tales* (New York: Random House, 1979), etc. These sources are of different kinds. Margaret Murray was an anthropological historian, specializing in medieval Europe. She claimed also to know of two covens of witches still functioning in England before World War II. Sylvia Townsend Warner was a careful and scholarly historical novelist who probably got many ideas from Margaret Murray. Isak Dinesen was a famous Danish novelist whose plot structures have commonly the twisted form of "punning on the context." On at least one occasion, she is reported to have cursed with bell, book, and candle a rival who plagiarized some of her work. It does not seem that the so-called witches of Salem, Massachusetts, at the end of the seventeenth century, were either organized into covens or that they played tricks with context.

This was thirty years ago, of course, and nothing of the sort could happen today, but in those days lobotomy meetings were great social occasions. Everybody who had had anything to do with the case turned up—doctors, nurses, social workers, psychologists, and so on. Perhaps thirty or forty people were there, including the five-man "Lobotomy Committee," under the chairmanship of an outside examiner, a distinguished psychiatrist from another hospital.

When all the tests and reports had been presented, the patient was brought in to be interviewed by the outside examiner.

The examiner gave the patient a piece of chalk and told him, "Draw the figure of a man." The patient went obediently to the blackboard and wrote: DRAW THE FIGURE OF A MAN

The examiner said, "Don't write it. Draw it." And again the patient wrote: DON'T WRITE IT DRAW IT

The examiner said, "Oh, I give up." This time the patient *revised the definition of the context*, which he had already used to assert a kind of freedom, and wrote in large capital letters all across the blackboard:

VICTORY

I believe it to be so that as we climb the ladder of sophistication from youth to age, from innocence to experience, or, in general, from one rung of the ladder of logical typing to another, we necessarily encounter the sorts of complexity exemplified by the mystic, the schizophrenic, and the poet. The network of mind, ugliness, and beauty in which and of which we and all living things are part is so structured that all that I have described *must* occur, given the appropriate conditions.

It's not only so that the bus *must* choose between better and worse, it is also so that vis-à-vis the tram, the bus will envy innocence and conversely the tram will envy experience and the pseudo freedom which experience will give.

.

The mental world is necessarily marked and divided by many interfaces into many subsystems, and therefore to understand the workings of that mental world we can proceed step by step. The mental world is vastly bigger than we are, but we do have various "tricks" that enable us to grasp something of its vastness and its detail. Of these tricks the best known are induction, generalization, and abduction. We gather information about details, we fit the pieces of information together to make pictures or configurations, we summarize them in statements of structure. We then compare our configurations to show how they can be classified as falling under the same or related rules. It is this last step, for which I use the term *abduction*, that is the glue that holds all science (and all religion?) together.

In all of this we are, of course, ourselves exemplifying necessary characteristics of the network of mind of which we are parts, whose branches are immanent in us. It is that network that this book has attempted to study. Specifically, we must bear in mind the barriers that must be maintained if the network of mind is to become richer and more complex, evolving towards something like ecological climax, a semistable system of maximum differentiation, complexity, and elegance. We look for contrasts that develop or differentiate as sophistication increases.

We also look for instances of pathology as partial clues to understanding the conditions for health of the larger network, and for interface phenomena, where the participating subsystems suffer gross reduction, such as the witch and the institutionalized schizophrenic. These are easily recognized as failures of the system and, as such, challenge the individual and the system to do better. More serious are those many cases in which, through the ages, whole long-lived subsystems like societies or ecosystems slowly deteriorate as a result of interaction and interface phenomena.

These are (perhaps always) cases in which *quantity displaces quality*— the tricks by which age, alas, escapes from understanding youth, and the city fathers can choose whether to base their whole system upon buses or upon trams *without understanding either*. A little economics and estimation of costs will do the trick!

Of all imaginary organisms—dragons, protomollusca, missing links, gods, demons, sea monsters, and so on—*economic man is the dullest*. He is dull because his mental processes are all quantitative and his preferences transitive. His evolution can best be comprehended by considering the communicational problems of human cultural contact.

Always at the interface between two civilizations, some degree of mutual understanding must be achieved. In the case of two strongly contrasting systems, sharing a minimum of premises, the establishment of a common ground of communication is not easy and will be the more difficult inasmuch as people, in all cultures, are prone to believe that their values and preconceptions are "true" and "natural." Indeed, this preference for one's own cultural system is probably necessary and universal. However, one preconception which is cross-culturally widespread and perhaps universal is the notion that more is more than not-so-much and that bigger is bigger (and probably better) than not-so-big.

[Thus it is that the dilemmas produced by culture contact are often resolved by focusing on that common premise on which it is easiest to agree, so that the meeting of civilizations is turned into a matter of commerce and an occasion for profit or a jockeying for "power," in which it is assumed that domination of one by the other is the necessary outcome. If we look at the tragedies that occur at the interfaces between two human cultures, it is not surprising that similar tragedies occur at the interface between human societies and ecosystems, leading to gross reduction or slow deterioration. The premises of such encounters have tended to be simplistic, permeating the interpretation of messages, shaping observation, and gradually expressed in the unfolding of events. The premises that led to conflict between settlers and American Indians were the same as those that led to the destruction of the tall grass prairie and that today threaten the rain forests of South America and their inhabitants.

[The alternative would be a shift of our ways of seeing that would affirm the complexities and mutual integration of *both* sides of any interface. We reduce ourselves to such caricatures as "economic man," and we have reduced other societies and the woods and lakes that we encounter to potential assets, ultimately reducing them in still another sense as the prairie was reduced to desert, members of other groups to servitude, or the schizophrenic to the less than human by psychosurgery.

[What will it take to react to interfaces in more complex ways? At the very least, it requires ways of seeing that affirm our own complexity and the systemic complexity of the other and that propose the possibility that they might together constitute an inclusive system, with a common network of mind and elements of the necessarily mysterious. Such a perception of both self and other is the affirmation of the sacred.

[The way we act, the way we balance the complexities of freedom and responsibility, these depend on what answer we give to an ancient riddle, "What is man?" The Riddle of the Sphinx, which we encountered in chapter 13, is one of the many variants of that riddle. It asks, "What is it that walks first on four legs, then on two, and finally on three?" posing the question within the context of the interfaces that always exist within human society between infancy and adulthood and between adulthood and old age. What is it that is sometimes a bus, sometimes a tram, but never entirely "free"? And what is it to move through a larger and more complex mental system, involved in multiple encounters with other mental subsystems, each of which offers a certain possibility of wholeness? We are dealing with questions of the encounter between minds, encounters framed by even larger mental systems. In this context, such questions as the Riddle of the Sphinx should be asked two-sidedly, as Warren McCulloch did in his version of the Psalmist's question, "What is a man that he may know a number, and what is a number that a man may know it?"]

What do we think a man is? What is it to be human? What are these other systems that we encounter and how are they related?

Side by side with the riddle I want to offer you an ideal—not perhaps ultimately achievable but at least a dream we may try to approximate. The ideal is that our technologies, our medical and agricultural procedures, our social arrangements should somehow *fit* with the best answers that we can give to the Riddle of the Sphinx.

I do not think, you see, that an action or a word is its own sufficient definition. I believe that an action or the label put on an experience must always be seen, as we say, in *context*. And the context of every action is the whole network of epistemology and the state of all the systems involved, with the history that leads up to that state. What we believe ourselves to be should be compatible with what we believe of the world around us.

Notice that the ideal I offer you comes close to being a *religious* hope or ideal. We are not going to get far unless we acknowledge that the whole of science and technology, like medicine from Hippocrates downward, springs out of and impinges on religion. In two ways all health practitioners are religious—necessarily accepting some system of ethics and necessarily subscribing to some theory of body-mind relations, a mythology, for better or worse. [This should perhaps also be true of all those who act on living systems.] To achieve the ideal I have offered, all we have to do is to be consistent. Alas, to be consistent is excessively difficult and perhaps impossible.

It is to the Riddle of the Sphinx that I have devoted fifty years of professional life as an anthropologist. It is of first-class importance that our answer to the Riddle of the Sphinx should be in step with how we conduct our civilization, and this should in turn be in step with the actual workings of living systems.

A major difficulty is that the answer to the Riddle of the Sphinx is partly a *product* of the answers that we have already given to the riddle in its various forms. Kurt Vonnegut gives us wry advice—that we should be careful what we pretend because we become what we pretend. And something like that, some sort of self-fulfillment, occurs in all organizations and human cultures. What people presume to be "human" is what they will build in as premises of their social arrangements, and what they build in is sure to be *learned*, is sure to become a part of the character of those who participate.

And along with this self-validation of our answers, there goes something still more serious—namely that any answer which we promote, as it becomes partly true through our promoting of it, becomes partly irreversible. *There is a lag in these affairs.*

We must be doubly cautious in making assumptions about what sort of creatures we are dealing with. We have already created a nation of litigators by making a world in which harm and pain are given pecuniary value and in which it is unsafe to be undefended by insurance, unarmed and naked.

Furthermore, our ideas about how to answer the Sphinx's riddle are today in a state of flux. We are in extraordinary confusion at this very moment. Our beliefs are undergoing rapid change at a pace comparable to the rate at which things were changing in classical Greece, say between 600 and 500 B.C., or again in the beginning of the Christian Era. Ours is a strange and exciting world, in which the very premises of language are in question. What is the language of the heart? Or of the right hemisphere? Or of the psychoanalytic id? Is it Latin or English? Or Sanskrit? Is it prose or poetry, spoken or chanted? Is it expressed in the laying on of hands? Or in the discipline of the surgeon, the pharmacologist, or the masseur? And so on.

What is in question is the old matter of the relation between "body" and "mind"—the central theme of the world's great religions.

The old beliefs are wearing thin and there is a groping for new. It is not a matter, you see, of being a Christian or a Muslim or a Buddhist or a Jew. We do not yet have another answer to the old problems. We know only a little bit about the direction in which the changes are taking place, but nothing about where the changes will end up. We have to have in mind not an orthodoxy but a wide and compassionate recognition of the storm of ideas in which we all are living and in which we must make our nests—find spiritual rest—as best we can.

I suppose the American constitutional demand for religious "freedom" came out of a similar flux. By "freedom" the Founding Fathers meant the opportunity to worship and envisage God in variously contrasting forms, presented by the vagaries of a revolutionary period. Evolution and revolution and religion should go together. In spite of religious freedom, it was important to be religious. I think it was a mistake to prohibit religious teaching in state schools.*

But to return to more immediate aspects of the Sphinx's riddle, I have offered you two points defining answers to the riddle. The first point is that "human nature" is self-validating. The second is that the particular focus of the flux in which we all live today is the beginning of a new solution to the body-mind problem.

I assert that we know enough today to expect that the new understanding will be unitary, and that the conceptual separation between "mind" and "matter" will be seen to be a by-product of—a spin-off from—*an insufficient holism*. When we focus too narrowly upon the parts, we fail to see the necessary characteristics of the whole and are then tempted to ascribe the phenomena resulting from wholeness to some supernatural entity.

"Holistic" is a popular word today, occurring most often in phrases like "holistic medicine," referring to a multitude of views and practices, ranging from homeopathy to acupuncture, from hypnosis to psychedelics, from the laying on of hands to the cultivation of alpha rhythms, from Hinduism to Zen, from the bedside manner to the ultimate depersonalization of diagnosis by astrological typing. And so on.

Men have hoped for holistic solutions for a long time. The word itself goes back to Smuts in the 1920s and is defined in the *OED* as "the tendency in nature to produce wholes from the ordered grouping of units." The systematic thinking that makes it possible to give precise, formal, and nonsupernatural meaning to the word goes back to the nineteenth century. It is there we find the early contributors to this thinking about wholes and to the formal relations between information and organization, including Claude Bernard (the "milieu intérieur"), Clerk Maxwell (his "demon" and his analysis of the steam engine with a governor, 1870),

---

*Gregory's father, an atheist, had his sons read the Bible so they would not be "empty-headed atheists."

Russel Wallace (natural selection, 1858), and a man of special interest to doctors—the "Old Doctor"—Dr. Andrew Still.

Old Still was the founder of osteopathic medicine. In the late nineteenth century, he got the idea that the pathologies of the body could be due to disruption of what we today call communication—that the inner physiological organization of the body could be a matter of message transport and that the spinal cord was the principal clearinghouse through which all messages had to pass. He argued that by manipulation of the spine it should be possible to cure all pathologies. He went a little crazy, I think, as men do who have ideas a hundred years too soon. He came to believe that his ideas would cover not only the many defects whose focus indeed is related to the spine, its postures and its messages, but also that similar theories could be applied to bacterial invasions and so on. This got him into trouble, but still and all, he was an early *holist* in precisely the sense in which I want to use the word.

Today, of course, the idea of pathology as some sort of discord or discrepancy, a blockage or a runaway in the inner ecology of the body, is not at all unfamiliar. Even in such "physically caused" pathologies as broken bones, the focus begins to include the *idea* of the broken bone and the response to that idea. These changes fit with a great deal of contemporary thinking in all parts of biology.

The next step is to predict that within the next twenty years this sort of thing will be characteristic of the "man in the street" and will necessarily be the basis for a type of *credibility* that will be pervasive in the society, one in which both scientist and layman, both doctor and patient, will share.

The old credibility is wearing thin and the new is advancing at a surprising rate. We are learning in fact to deal with the world's tendency to generate wholes made up of units connected together by communication. It is this that makes the body a living thing, which acts as if it had a mind—which indeed it does.

·

I want to suggest that the word "holistic" has taken on an almost new and much more precise meaning since World War II, and that this new and precise meaning gives hope of a deep revision of occidental culture.

It is becoming clear that the mysterious phenomena we associate with "mind" have to do with certain characteristics of systems that have only rather lately come within the purview of science. These include:

—The characteristics of circular and self-corrective systems.

—The combination of such systems with information processing.

—The ability of living things to store energy (I use the word in its ordinary physical sense—ergs, foot-pounds, calories, etc.), so that a change in some sense organ (the receipt of news of a difference) may trigger the release of stored energy.

There are a few other points that go to make up the new ways of thinking about purpose, adaptation, pathology, and, in brief, life, and these are being explored in the fields of cybernetics, information theory, systems theory, and so on. But here I want to call attention to a condition of our time—that as the conventional ways of thinking about mind and life collapse, new ways of thinking about these matters are becoming available—not only to ivory-tower philosophers but also to practitioners and to the "man in the street."

Historically, the new developments, which became conspicuous in World War II and in the period following, have almost totally altered everything that we say and think about mental process and about the body-mind as a total, living, self-correcting, and self-destroying entity.

Cybernetics in its widest sense is, so far as I know, the only serious beginning of thinking about wholes in any formal way.

If we approach the phenomena of mind with these new tools, then genetics and the whole determination of shape and growth—that which determines the symmetry of your face, with an eye on each side of a nose—all of that which is steered by message material from DNA—can be recognized as a part of the mental organization of the body. A part of the *holism*.

If, then, we pose the double question, "What is a man that he may recognize disease or disruption or ugliness?" and "What is disease or disruption or ugliness that a man may know it?" the new ways of thinking provide a bridging answer, in the assertion that a self-recursive communication system may be aware of disruption of its own function. It may have pain and many other types of awarenesses. It may also be aware of harmony in its own function, and that awareness may become the basis for awe and an awareness of beauty in the larger and more inclusive system.

Finally—and here's the rub—the disciplines of the new ways of thought are still to be defined. To believe and act in the belief that there is no mind distinct from the body and (of course) no body distinct from the mind is not to become free of all limits. It is to accept a new discipline, probably more stringent than the old.

This brings me back to the notion of *responsibility*. It's a word which I don't commonly use, but let me use it here in all seriousness. How shall we interpret the responsibility of all those who deal with living systems? The whole tatterdemalion rout of the dedicated and the cynical, the saintly and the greedy, have a responsibility—individually and collectively—to a dream.

The dream is about what sort of a thing man is that he may know and act on living systems—and what sort of things such systems are that they may be known. The answers to that forked riddle must be woven from mathematics and natural history and aesthetics and also the joy of life and loving—all of these contribute to shape that dream.

I reminded you earlier that it is part of human nature to learn not only details but also deep unconscious philosophies—to become that which we pretend—to take the shape and character our culture imposes upon us. The myths in which our lives are embedded acquire credibility as they become part of us. Such myths become unquestionable and are built deep into character, often below awareness, so that they are essentially religious, matters of faith.

It is to these myths—and the future forms that they may take—that all of our mythmakers, our mythopoets, including scientists and politicians and teachers, owe responsibility. The doctors and the lawyers and the media share responsibility in the dynamic myths—the answers they offer to the Riddle of the Sphinx.

Let me then close with the Psalmist's answer to his version of the riddle:

"What is man, that Thou art mindful of him? . . . For Thou hast made him a little lower than the angels, and hast crowned him with glory and honor."

XVII *So What's*

a Meta For? (MCB)

THIS IS a book that has made me shun cocktail parties—shun, that is, those social occasions when friendly strangers, on learning that I am spending the spring working on a book, would ask me what it is about. First would I tell them how the book came to be, the task of completing a work my father was involved in at the time of his death. But still they'd ask, what is it about? "Well," I'd hedge, "it's sort of philosophical." A pause.

"Look," I say, "Gregory had been building up a set of ideas about the nature of mental process, ideas derived from cybernetics, which he believed formed the basis for a new understanding of the epistemology of living systems. He certainly didn't consider that the task was completed, but he was convinced that if this new understanding were widely shared, people would act differently on matters of ecological balance and war and peace. And he thought that the development of this sensitivity to natural systems had something to do with aesthetics and with the 'sacred.' "

Oh. I pause for air after the breadth of this claim, but I have said too much, too fast. You cannot say at a cocktail party that the book you are working on is about "nothing less than everything." And inevitably, when words like *epistemology* and *aesthetics* and *cybernetics* turn up in the same sentence, eyes glaze over. Beyond the complexity and ambition of Gregory's own project, I have added still another subject to the book (in addition to "everything"?). In trying to coax the very tentative and incomplete stack of manuscripts I received into coherence, to understand the direction Gregory was heading, to add or subtract material in ways that would clarify and develop, I have tried to shape the book so that it would show *how* Gregory thought and conversed. This is a book about mental process—and a book about the process of thought. Gregory's groping is evident at many points, but perhaps this will persuade the reader to think himself or herself into his questions and carry them further, using the tools and information available today.

The mental landscape in which Gregory moved is, to most of us, a foreign one, as foreign as the ways of thought we might have to explore in the study of a culture with different premises from our own, or perhaps the study of another species. I have consciously to shift gears when I want to work in Gregory's frame of reference. This is, of course, something that anthropologists often attempt to do. This shifting of gears, or adjustment of preconceptions, is central to the book's insistence on knowledge as artifact: knowledge necessarily depends on preconceptions which may sometimes be examined or altered.

It is strange, after all the years when Gregory has been regarded as having strayed from anthropology into other fields, to recognize his work as dealing with central anthropological issues. Anthropologists often try to enter, in some measure, the conceptual world of another culture. Readers of ethnography are used to learning, every time they read about a strange society, a few words of an exotic language, as the only way the writer can express a concept that has no place in Western thought, and some of these terms are even adopted into English: taboo, mana, suttee. Often there will be an explanation of an entire interlocking system: a pantheon of deities, a calendar, five generations of intertwined kinship terminology. On the island of Bali, for instance, directions are given in terms of the alternative between moving towards the sacred mountain at the center of the island or towards the sea. You cannot convey the way the Balinese conceptualize geography, therefore, without evoking not only the physical form of their world, but also its metaphysics, and these same spatial relationships structure relations between persons. The investigator who would move between mountain and shore in harmony with the Balinese must enter the world of their thought.

Most anthropologists find it necessary to practice more than one mode of thought and observation. On the one hand, they carry the instruments of ostensibly objective recording and measurement. On the other hand, they find themselves listening with total seriousness to tales of sorceries and gods . . . and between these two extremes attending to explanations of ordinary life in which other kinds of symbolic elements are given as causes: money, for instance, or honor, the communist menace, or hospitality, or sex appeal.

It is not possible to segregate fully these different kinds of discourse, for however clear the ethnographer may be that tuberculosis is "real" and sorcery is "not real," they are both involved in the causation of observable patterns of behavior. Without attending to both, you cannot interact effectively or account for what you see. In the same way, a physician cannot effectively heal if he deals with a patient only in terms of those variables that can be isolated in the laboratory. Indeed, in human events and interactions, it may be sorcery that is "real" and not tuberculosis. The idea of medication represented by the placebo may be effective against the idea of the symptom—and pain as we experience it is itself an idea, a kind of mental image.

This is the kind of diversity of reference necessarily present in anthropology, and it recurs throughout this book and throughout Gregory's work. Clearly, there is in the movement back and forth between humanly constructed meaning and physical reality a profound necessity for any anthropologist to think in terms of what Gregory came to call the interface between Creatura and Pleroma.* Where, in the clink of silver or the pangs of illness, do the mental and the material meet? And how does one construct a science able to speak, in a single, disciplined frame, of both reincarnation and protein deficiency?

But the issue is more fundamental than that. For Gregory is asserting that the same problem exists in the entire biological world. The ethnographer studies a community that lives by communication: without the transmission of learned patterns of adaptation, human beings are not viable. We as ethnographers study the messages and codes and organizational forms that bind a community together and regulate its daily affairs, and to do so we must move from one local epistemology to another, both human, both part of Creatura. If we study only those realities accessible to, say, physics and biochemistry, the picture will be inadequate. Gregory argues that all our descriptions of organisms or interacting communities of organisms must include the characteristics of their mes-

*There may be a temptation for anthropologists to associate the Creatura-Pleroma distinction with Kenneth Pike's use of emic and etic (*Language in Relation to a Unified Theory of Human Behavior*, Glendale, Calif., 1954–60). Etic descriptions do attempt to describe Pleroma; emic descriptions describe particular human cultural systems within Creatura, parts of local epistemology.

sage systems in the same way. He is in effect proposing that in order to understand organisms, one must understand them ethnographically.

The classic strategies of science are analysis, breaking down complex wholes into parts more accessible to study, and reduction, accounting for complex processes, like those of life, in terms of simpler processes that underlie them, reducing, say, the organismic to the molecular. But there are limits to these strategies. Although the physical reality of a chemistry professor could be exhaustively analyzed in the laboratory, this study of the professor as part of Pleroma could never determine whether he is wise or foolish, honorable or dishonorable, or indeed what it might mean to be a person or a professor. Only in Creatura, only when he is seen in the context of his communication and relationships, motivated by abstract goals and ambitions, can he be known, and so we need a Creatural science. We worry in anthropology about the difference between what the ethnographer perceives and what the natives perceive, about how well our descriptions *fit* their reality. Within the context of science, we are concerned about whether our descriptions will ever have the capacity to *predict*. Certainly they will never be able to do so unless we can identify causes—and these are generally abstract. Occasionally a biologist asks about what a cat or a bird or a frog* or even a bee perceives—but it is rare to ask the same question about a plant or a meadow or a single cell at a given point in the developing embryo, though each of these is a living system. Clearly in each of these cases it is important to know what information is available and how it is coded, in order to tease out the injunctions that determine the next step in growth or behavior. Can the concerns of an anthropologist perhaps induce more biologists to ask that question?

This approach to epistemology requires us to study our descriptions and our own nature as information-processing creatures even as we try to develop revealing descriptions of other systems with which we interact. Anthropology is often seen as a path to self-knowledge as well as a way of understanding what is strange and foreign. It becomes particularly important to consider language, that system of coding and communication that sets the human species off from others. We have in language

*Warren McCulloch, a key member of the group that did the original work in cybernetics, is referred to more often by Gregory than any other modern scientist, and it is worth noting here that he was one of the coauthors of a famous paper critical in the development of this line of thinking: "What the Frog's Eye Tells the Frog's Brain," by J. Y. Lettvin, H. R. Maturana, W. S. McCulloch, and W. Pitts, *Proceedings of the Institute of Radio Engineers* 47 (1959), 1940–52.

an extraordinarily flexible communications system, in addition to having the kinds of communicative and perceptual devices possessed by other mammals: chromosomal, hormonal, neurological, kinesic, and so on. We are also aware of an exceptionally large portion of our own information-processing activity—although only a minute fraction of the whole—through the various odd recursive loops of consciousness and proprioception, and all of this is intimately related to our reliance on learning and teaching as adaptive mechanisms. In language, the maps with which we work are cut loose from correspondence with "territory"; not only are we constrained, like all creatures, to deal with ideas of coconut palms rather than actual coconut palms, we can sit on a tropical island and imagine oak trees, lie about them, joke about them, or by simple linguistic transformation take any proposition about an oak tree or a palm and convert it to its opposite. Human language, alas, is rather like money—so flexible that it tends to falsify.

It is therefore not surprising that great human ingenuity has gone into finding ways to discipline this riot of potentiality, ranging from the Inquisition to the invention of the lie detector, and including the development of taxonomies of logical fallacy and rhetorical devices. Human communication is not a continuous fabric. Instead, we have defined a great variety of types of discourse, each with proprieties governing its use, each partly but not entirely circumscribed, each with the possibility of a different kind of correspondence to Pleroma. Even hallucination may be okay if you know you are doing it. Poetry is okay, but many have struggled to keep it in its place. Mathematics is elegant, but its application to the material world is always tentative. And so on. Much of the range of kinds of discourse we call science is an extension of the vastly successful system of discourse developed for describing material—physical and chemical—realities. Very elegant it is too, but perhaps inappropriate for eavesdropping on those portions of the material world that are also enveloped in a network of communications.

I believe that Gregory was more concerned with condemning the improper uses of particular forms of discourse or the breaching of boundaries between them than with condemning the particular forms outright. One way of interpreting his emphasis on unknowing is as an insistence that boundaries be maintained so that multiple forms of discourse will continue to be possible. Let not thy left hand know what thy right hand is doing, but strive to be ambidextrous. Avoid the errors of fundamentalism, scientism, and misplaced concreteness. Within a given sphere of discourse, strive for the consistency that fits the logic of that sphere. Take the reasons of the heart seriously, but do not treat them as if they were effective in Pleroma.

There is an irony expressed in the unlovely neologism "Pleromatize." Although language can only be a product of Creatura, it has been shaped, particularly in the sciences, for the task of describing Pleroma, to take us closer to material reality, which is nevertheless always known at second hand. It is our success in the one realm that leads us to use the same system where it doesn't fit. Sometimes accuracy is endangered by the effort of objectivity, and the social sciences are chronically in danger of being distorted by (physical) scientism.

Gregory returns again and again to the differences between the way communication must work in Creatura and the way we, having developed our language so that it fits Pleroma, tend to distort. The most important difference that he asserts is that language depends on *nouns*, which seems to refer to *things*, while biological communication concerns pattern and relationship. Thus, he asks of the genetic determination of the human hand: Does it specify five fingers (five things) or four relations between fingers? and of the cat mewing around its owner's ankles: Does it say, "Milk, milk" or "Dependency, dependency"? Even the shark, in its various adaptive programs, probably has information about how to relate to the ocean, rather than about the ocean (there may be no naming of "water," the matrix of life, any more than the embryo will refer, in its internal communications, to the womb). If it is true that there are *things* in Pleroma, then nouns (which are not things) are a useful invention for thinking about things—but with nouns we have invented the capacity for false reification. There are no things in Creatura—only ideas, images, clusters of abstract relations—but the vast convenience of talking about things leads us to treat any available idea—truth, God, charisma—as if it were thing-like. One way of looking at this would be to say that the semantics appropriate to Creatura must consist of relationships.

Having asked about the semantics of Creatura, it is reasonable to ask about the syntax. Gregory contrasts the general preference of biological communication for metaphor with the human development of a system organized around nouns set in subject-predicate relations. In metaphor, two complex propositions are set side by side and, to some degree, equated— the affirmation lies in juxtaposition. In language, it is possible to separate subject and predicate within a given proposition, so our affirmations lie in predication. Another way in which the internal structure of linguistic sequences apparently parallels external events is in logical argument, for logic has been developed in such a way as to allow the modeling of lineal causal chains, by the risky device of equating logical entailment (whereby ideas follow from one another) with physical causation (whereby events follow from one another). Elsewhere, Gregory also emphasized negation as a characteristic limited to human language, which is often replaced in communication between organisms by another kind of juxtaposition or by a manipulation of logical levels to achieve metamessages. (The dog cannot say, "I will *not* attack you." He can, however, use the behavior that signals the intention to attack in the context of contradictory signals, alternating aggressive and submissive behavior, thereby achieving the message "This is play, there is no need to be afraid.") Throughout Creatura the logical types are important, but the confusion of logical types also plays a part in the syntax. I suspect that confusions and contradictions of logical type limited to linguistic communication function differently from those that spill out into other types of communication, and this is why the double binds that create pathology always involve nonlinguistic and contextual elements.

Lastly, as compared to all other kinds of communication, human linguistic communication emphasizes messages whose primary function is referential, messages that report on the state of some "it" (which may, of course, be the "I" that is the source of the message), rather than messages of command and injunction—what one might think of as a preoccupation with messages in the third person, as opposed to "talk of thee and me." Humans, with their manipulative hands, have specialized in describing what they can affect.

Human language is thus very far from any other biological mode of communication, so it has properties that make it unlike those other modes—and more suitable to talking about Pleroma. Have we Pleromatized language? Or have we rather created a bizarre hybrid that is true to neither world? By a curious twist, the ultimate sophistication of Creatura is the capacity to communicate in a new way about Pleroma—and to *miscommunicate* about Creatura.

The basic thesis of the book, it seems to me, is the recognition that whereas it has been important in the evolution of language and the history of science to develop areas and styles of discourse that will fit the description of Pleroma, it is essential if we want to describe and respond to what goes on in Creatura to work with a semantics and a syntax that fit the subject matter. Since all of Creatura is within Pleroma, Pleromatic language will be strictly accurate—I do have five fingers, at the skeletal level my hand is made of separate *things* in batches of five, and these material objects are all sitting there capable of being dissected, counted, weighed, measured, and analyzed chemically. But none of those activities will be very illuminating if we wish to answer the other set of questions—what it means to have a hand, how an organism manufactures one in its epigenesis, how a hand resembles a foot or a paw or a flipper. To answer these questions, we need a semantics appropriate to Creatura, which must consist of differences, and a syntax appropriate to Creatura, which must at least be sensitive to metaphor and the logical types. A syntax, after all, is what we must have if ideas are to be combined in new ways, in a process which is something like deduction because it allows the generation of new combinations. As a scientist, Gregory was concerned to develop ways of talking about Creatura that would allow precision and clarity *and deduction*. He was interested in statements that were true and congruent and could be used in a process of thought with internal consistency and a potential for development. At the same time, he was concerned with ways of knowing that could be passed on.

·

The possibility of forms of discourse appropriate to Creatura that might become means of knowledge and decision making is not only hypothetical. On the one hand, this is a prescription for a biological science that might come to be, but it is also a prescription for recognizing what we have. Alongside his critique of our overreliance on modes of description more appropriate to Pleroma than to Creatura, Gregory also saw that within the existing range of human communication there are still registers or subsystems that come closer to the way the rest of the biological world does things. The patches of more purely Creatural communication, even in linguistic form, seem to occur in religion and in the arts, in interpersonal relations and in primary process in general: dreams, visions, imagination.

He also found that *Creatural communication has its own rigor*—must have, of course, if it is to be the medium of such vastly complex operations as epigenesis or the homeostasis within an organism—and is always at risk of distortion or failure. Indeed, he pointed out that pathology is itself a possibility only of Creatura, for at the level of Pleroma direct physical causation makes error impossible. It is never the physical universe that makes mistakes. The physical universe provides randomness and entropy, but error is a biological phenomenon—if by the term *error* we wish to suggest the existence or value of a possible something which would be "right" or "correct," the error being a *difference* between what is and what might have been. For looking at human beings, it becomes necessary to consider two types of pathology: the familiar kinds of pathology or distortion within Creatural communication, and the special kinds of pathology that have to do with consciousness and with the inappropriate translation or Pleromatizing of Creatural communication made possible by language. In the investigation of these matters, he followed during much of his career a path that has repeatedly been useful in the social and biological sciences, the study of pathology as a means to the understanding of the normal. In pathology he was able to discover patches of Creatural communication inappropriately coded or combined, and to ask about the nature of the inappropriateness.

If we want to be able to talk about the living world (and ourselves), we need to master the disciplines of description and reference in this curious language that has no things in it but only differences and relationships. Only if we do so will we be able to think sensibly about the matrix in which we live, and only then will we recognize our affinity with the rest of that world and deal with it ethically and responsibly. Not only do we misread and mistreat meadows, oceans, and organisms of all kinds, but our mistreatments of each other are based on errors of the general order of not knowing what we are dealing with, or acting in ways that violate the communicative web.

There is a bridge needed here between epistemology and ethics. In trying to understand that relationship I have always found Gregory's definition of love, offered at the Wenner-Gren Conference, especially useful, and worth repeating here:

"At least a part of what we mean by the word could be covered by saying that 'I love X' could be spelled out as 'I regard myself as a system, and I accept with positive valuation the fact that I am one, preferring to be one rather than fall to pieces and die; and I regard the person whom I love as systemic; and I regard my system and his or her system as together *constituting a larger system with some degree of conformability within itself.*' "*

This is essentially the assertion that love is based on metaphor, a

---

*M. C. Bateson, *Our Own Metaphor* (New York: Knopf, 1972), 279–80, emphasis added.

three-way metaphor that links self and other and also *self plus other*, and uses this recognition to assert the value of the relationship as well as the value of self and other.

The theme of metaphor runs right through Gregory's work. Indeed, the idea that was engrossing him in his last weeks was the idea of syllogisms of metaphor ("syllogisms in grass," see chapter 2). The use of syllogisms of metaphor, which he called abduction, was for him a basic intellectual strategy, the search for insight through analogy, as when he analyzed the process of evolution as analogous to the process of thought. His intention, of course, was to assert significant similarity, of the kind that permits further inferences, rather than identity. What we have in his equation of thought and evolution is an assertion of *homology*—a formal similarity that suggests a relationship, like that between a human hand and the wing of a bat, the metaphorical recycling of an old idea. It is often said in anthropology that cultural evolution has replaced biological evolution—can we perhaps say that the human version of mental process is precisely the recycling of an old idea? It was crucial for him, after emphasizing abduction as central to science for years, to begin to see it as a bridge to religion and a way to approach the question of how religion—and play—might have their own order of truth. Since he never spelled out that connection fully, the problem of this book has been to arrange the pieces of his thought and imagine links between them.

·

The description of *mind* gave Gregory a framework for beginning to define the disciplines of communication in or like or about Creatura, disciplines that the flexibility of human language has made it possible to violate. The key components of his thought began to be integrated in a single system: cybernetics and the logical types, the semantics of Korzybski and the efforts of the early psychoanalysts to describe the unconscious—all of these *coalesce* in the beginning of a Creatural grammar. Such a Creatural grammar should eventually make it possible to look at and think about organisms and meadows in new ways . . . and also about human beings. Gregory would like to see us able, for instance, to talk *as scientists*—ah, but as Creatural scientists—about aesthetics, for he suspects that most of what goes on under that rubric is an inappropriate form of discourse. Still he asserts that the matter is of first importance, because all organisms—not just art critics and philosophers—rely on aesthetics all the time.

Central to the effort to describe Creatura is the problem of a description consisting of multiple parts which is nevertheless *unified*, with a logical organization which in some way models the complexity of organization in living systems. Within the living system, myriad separate events occur, and yet somehow the whole hangs together. This is why it is important to see that each term of a metaphor is manifold—must have its own internal complexity. If "all the world's a stage," it is not a matter of identity between the parts of a theater and the parts of the wider world, but equivalence of the *relationships between* the parts of the metaphorical structure and that which it models. Similarly, one does not provide diagrams of a single point—or if one does, the meaning is in the relationship with the surrounding text, not in the single entity. The terms of a metaphor must each be both manifold and unitary: $A : B :: X : Y$, which explains Gregory's special interest in the place of ratios in perception.

Gregory focused especially on one kind of extended metaphor: the parable (or story). The distinctive characteristics of this kind of metaphor are its elaboration and its temporal framing in terms of narrative. A rose or a conch shell can be the basis of a metaphor—but both contain stories and both are constructed of multiple parts built on related ground plans. As with so many soap operas and heroic epics, the successive stories prove to be the same story, with small variations.

It is because a metaphor has multiple parts that we can use it to think with. This is even true of that family of metaphors referred to as the "pathetic fallacy." If I imagine a mountain grieving at the setting of the sun, I will not get far unless I elaborate and refine my sense of the mountain, including in my image the tree line, the bare rock above it . . . snow on the peak perhaps? And streams finding their way down toward the valley. . . .

Or to use a very different kind of example, we can consider a mental model that works rather like one of those computer programs that will immediately calculate the many interrelated implications of some small change (such as Lotus or Visicalc). I can set up a display that includes a very large number of variables about, say, a company I am interested in, and then insert a change in a single variable. Then I punch a key and let the effect of the changed variable be processed through all the other interrelated variables, so that after a few flickering moments I once again see a unified and integrated picture that tells me how a change in the cost of a single component will affect price, profit, tax, etc. Designers now do the same thing with, say, a tiny change in the span of a wing, working out its implications for other aspects of design and performance.

In theory we could have such models of the effect of a slight change in nutrition on the human body, or a new chemical effluent in a river, but in most cases, although we know a great many facts about each system, our capacity to construct a model of it as a whole is still primitive. Instead, we find an existing model that has within it the necessary complexity, necessarily perhaps a model that is alive—canaries in a mine shaft, rhesus monkeys in drug research.

Of all available metaphors, the most central and salient, available to all human beings, is the self. Here I mean not only the psychological construct of the "self," but the entire being, psyche and soma, for each of us the meeting place of Creatura and Pleroma. Central to the net of metaphor through which we recognize and respond to the world is the experience of the self and the possibility of reference to it. The evocation of self-knowledge as a model for understanding another, because of similarities or congruences that make the knowing possible, is properly called sympathy, but the current usage that seems to me to come closest is the term *empathy*. We need not limit ourselves here to the empathy between therapist and client, for surely the farmer whose crops are parched knows something of the death of his fields in his own body.

The knowledge or experience each person has of his or her own body-mind varies in profound ways and is partly accessible to deliberate alteration. A purely intellectual appreciation of one's own body as the home of vast numbers of microscopic creatures, for instance, can alter one's sense of relationship with the biosphere of this planet—that vast and complex being in whose gut each of us is a minute and transient bit of fauna, possibly benign. An imaginal identification with another kind of creature—a dolphin, a goose—can instruct a new degree of attention, as well as enrich and inform the sense of self, as in the exercises used by psychologist Jean Houston, who invites people to think themselves into the motion of other phyla—fly, swim, dive—as a way of discovering a new freedom of mental as well as physical motion.*

Again, one can use an imagined identification with another person to enhance one's understanding of an idea or event by asking, how would so-and-so see this? The mental model of another personality works like the computer program described above—one can introduce some novelty

*The Possible Human: A Course in Enhancing Your Physical, Mental, and Creative Abilities (Los Angeles: J. P. Tarcher–Houghton Mifflin, 1982).

and watch it ripple through the system, thinking oneself into the other person—and one can do this repeatedly, playing a question through alternate filters and seeing how it is processed each time. The same thing can be done with a group, a number of people whose interactions as well as their individual styles and voices are familiar, members of a conference, say, or a committee. For a time I used my memory of the Wenner-Gren Conference in 1968 in this way, asking, can I hear Gertrude discussing that? Or Tolly? And, of course, I have done it repeatedly in working on this book: How would Gregory respond to *that*? The names even become verbs in mental shorthand: Can I "Gregory" this idea? This methodology made this writing feel like a series of new encounters, as I met my father saying new things. One of the most basic forms of meditation in the Christian tradition has been the effort to imagine oneself (and the dilemmas presented by one's life) into the person of Jesus, *Imitatio Christi*, and other traditions propose related kinds of identification. Empathy is a discipline.

One can also use one's self as a basis for metaphorical thinking by shifting between different modes of expression, and this may bring us closer to some of the questions involving the aesthetic. Can I, for instance, change my understanding of something by *dancing* it? In which case my inferences, the way in which I move from one stage of thought to another, are disciplined by the structure of my body. Or can I change my understanding of something by *thinking* of dancing it? Is that the same kind of thing as "Gregory-ing" it or "Tolly-ing" it or "Gertrude-ing" it? And what about my limitations, the fact that I don't know as much mathematics as Tolly or as much biology as Gregory, and have never trained my limbs and joints—up to what point does empathy get me beyond these limits and at what point is it invalidated by them? How much does it matter that Lorenz cannot fly? And how will I protect myself from glossing over the dissimilarities in each of these identifications? For each of them proposes profound misunderstanding as well as insight.

Religions typically provide systems—mental models—that one can enter as I might try to enter the metaphor of thinking like Gregory or like a mountain or a goose. Playing something through such a mental model changes it; the outcome is different. For the believer, or for one who is willing to suspend disbelief, a religion is a rich, internally structured model that stands in metaphorical relationship to the whole of life, and therefore can be used to think with. The Australian aborigine had, in his totemic cosmology, a system that brought all natural species and forces and human institutions, plants and animals, wind and thunder, circumcision and the boomerang he used in hunting, into relationship and defined his place in that complex whole—and allowed him to use the sense of that multiplicity of relations in the decisions of his life. The European peasant in the Middle Ages went out to plow the fields in the presence of a great crowd (or cloud) of witnesses, patron saints and powers and principalities, and, of course, angels. The truth that the aborigine and the peasant share is the truth of integration. By contrast, we must be concerned today because, although we can persuade our children to learn a long list of facts about the world, they don't seem to have the capacity to put them together in a single, unified understanding—there is no "pattern which connects." For most human beings through history, the pattern which connected their individual lives to the complex regularity of the world in which they lived was a religion, an extended metaphor, which made it possible for ordinary people to think at levels of integrated complexity otherwise impossible. It is no wonder that the unity of God has so often been the focus of meditation.

In general, in human cultures there are partially circumscribed cognitive subsystems that privilege Creatural thought, such as religions shaped and passed on across the generations. Under certain contextual rules, and even while using language, the very potentials of language that make it possible to talk about Pleroma may be suspended. We may choose to find ourselves in a world of mystery and ambiguity where objective reporting is not primary, for suddenly secrecy and what we have called unknowing become important, and certain ideas are unquestionable—or rather immune to validation and invalidation. Can that possibly be a good thing? What is being protected is surely not the individual bits and pieces, which are often a sort of grab bag of historical remnants, but the *relations between them*. There must be some "stuff" on which those complex relations can be hung, but a quilt is not the history of the odds and ends from which it is sewn. It is their combination into a new fabric that provides warmth and color.

The example I use to approach this matter is the question of whether a tree is more like a dryad or a steel pylon.* Interestingly, the question becomes clearer if the quaint and mythic "dryad" is replaced with "woman," reminding me of what I know of myself. The dryad metaphor is a way

*For a full discussion of love and the dryad, see my essay "Daddy, Can a Scientist Be Wise?" in *About Bateson*, ed. John Brockman (New York: Dutton, 1977).

of saying a tree is like a person, like *me* (after all these pages in which "man" has meant human, perhaps readers will be able to generalize "woman" to the same degree).

Is it possible that the dryad metaphor allows me an order of knowledge about trees which a Ph.D. in botany might not? How important is it to have a metaphor uniting all the odds and ends of knowledge about trees into a whole that can sustain such love? Most foresters and many botanists start with the holistic love, and in a few it survives the disintegrative effect of their educations, just as a surprising number of physicians manage to continue to care about persons even after the rigors of medical training. Woodworkers, too, continue to love and be attentive to the living textures of wood and the trees it comes from, perhaps because their knowledge is coded in muscle and fingertip, matched to their own bodies.

There is another very important sense in which religion sometimes protects the communications appropriate to understanding Creatura, and that is by functioning as a kind of therapy for certain distortions or pathologies in communication that commonly arise in human beings. At this point we need to examine the uses of paradox in the quest for enlightenment, the play of logical types and shifts of context, the deliberate search for revelation in contradiction, and the direct attacks on purposiveness and the sense of time. Interestingly, meditation is often proposed as a way of handling stress, but it is also a way of unlearning the addiction to entertainment and its accompanying vulnerability to boredom.

It is striking that religious metaphors are so largely paradoxical. If it is the case that logic has inadequacies in describing the natural world, inadequacies that have to do with circularity and recursiveness, then these are rather ancient barriers to human understanding. It seems likely that double binds are not simply a human artifact but pervasive—perhaps every organism is caught in the incapacity to bridge all the logical levels involved in any given message, so these must somehow be collapsed, but language may make this harder rather than easier. This would mean that double binds are both natural and necessary, immanent in the living world. Put somewhat differently, this would mean that the task of learning to trust Epimenides (the Cretan who said, "All Cretans are liars") is essential to life. The paradoxes of religion may have been the metaphors that have made it possible to live within a double bind. A great deal of adaptation, including unsuccessful adaptation, could be seen as efforts to deal with double-bind situations, as when embryos develop extra limbs and the organism somehow improvises circulation, possessing not only the information for normal growth but the ability to make the best of a bad deal.

It is not always immediately clear how the notion of metaphorical thinking might apply to other kinds of organisms, or systems consisting of multiple organisms, beyond the recycling of ideas in epigenesis and evolution, but for Gregory clearly it did. In a letter to the ecologist John Todd (October 24, 1978), Gregory speculated about the "view that a field of wheat (or better . . . a meadow of mixed species) can have of the death of its controlling farmer. Not the *new* value of 'gallons of irrigation per week' but the *change* in this value is what will affect the field. . . . Let me assume that [the life of the field is characterized by a dynamic pattern], a sort of dance, rather formal, say a minuet. And that the purpose, functioning, etc., of this minuet is to *detect* and *classify* other patterns of dance. The meadow with its interacting multiplicity of species is unendingly dancing and thereby being bumped by information (i.e. news of change and contrast) 'about' the environment, i.e. dynamic pattern is a sort of unlocalized sense organ. Ha!

"Of course, there is, in these primitive examples, no information *about* anything. The clover lives, like a saint, only in that dx/dt which is the eternal synchronic present. Information *about* (i.e. the *report* aspect of information) is completely irrelevant and of interest only to Metazoa. Plants, I assume, receive only the command or injunctive—restraint or release—aspect of information. . . ."

We can perhaps take this discussion of the field of wheat and combine it with the notion that a field, like a person, is its own central metaphor—uses its own internal structure to understand its environment, or rather to organize and generate its response to its environment. But there is a suggestion of a different way of looking at the same matter in the notion that the dance of the field might be analogous to a sense organ. Perhaps meditation or participation in a religious ritual is comparable to a dance of this kind, which must clearly therefore be rather formal—or at least the formal characteristics will be the ones that matter. The dance—the metaphor—must have the appropriate complexity so that some other complexity can be mapped upon it. Will it prove to be essential to human adaptation that we preserve at least patches of that kind of dancing as ways of knowing for which other kinds of description are so far inadequate?

Gregory believed that art, like religion, represents an area of experience that privileges Creatural ways of thinking. A work of art is the outcome of mental process, like the conch or the crab or the human body. The thought that enters into its creation generally involves multiple cycles of self-correction, repeated testing and listening, correcting and editing. Sometimes we may see the results of calibration in the swift curve drawn by the practiced hand of the Zen master, as sure as the hawk stooping to its prey after eons of evolution. On the one hand, there is the text that has been polished and honed, "tuned and tuned and tuned again," and on the other, a pot thrown with certainty and confidence by an illiterate potter held and informed by centuries of tradition.

Every work of art depends on a complexity of internal relations and can be seen as another in that family of examples that can be looked at to understand "the pattern which connects" and the nature of Creatura. "It took a lot of thought to make the rose." Aesthetic unity is very close to the notions of systemic integration and holistic perception. And arguably the appreciation of a work of art is a *recognition*, perhaps again a recognition of the self.

This book is really a double argument, an example, like so much else that Gregory wrote, of double description. It moves in a sort of pincer maneuver from formal abstract thought on the one hand and natural history (including ethnography and biology) on the other, closing in on the questions of aesthetics and the sacred. This double argument echoes two important and recurrent religious ideas: one, that deity can best be identified with timeless abstract truths; the other, that deity pervades all of nature, perhaps *is* nature or life. Gregory is affirming and at the same time denying both of these, identifying deity with the abstract relationships recognizable in nature—not the pigs and coconut palms but the fearful symmetry of both and of the tiger as well.

He is also drawing on another argument that has become newly important in the last fifty years or so, after a few centuries in which it was believed that science would answer all possible questions, namely the argument that there are limits on what science can know. It has become common to refer to Werner Heisenberg and the "uncertainty principle" to argue that the existence of limitations on knowledge makes particular kinds of nondemonstrable belief more credible. Yet few of those who assert casually the limits on scientific knowledge have troubled to understand them, but simply take them as license for speculative or occult thinking. Instead Gregory was asking the functional question of how organisms adapt to the necessary limits of communication/knowledge, and what are the economies that make it possible to do much with little . . . metaphor, abduction, homology . . . religion. Gregory's answer to the question "why religion?" is, like Durkheim's, a functional one, but it is one that treats religion as addressing unavoidable epistemological problems: the limitations on knowledge, the unavoidable gaps in every description, the paradoxes produced by recursiveness. He suggests that certainly through human history, and perhaps necessarily into the future, religion has been the only kind of cognitive system that could provide a model for the *integration* and *complexity* of the natural world, because these are the characteristics that must persistently elude even the most meticulous efforts to describe.

In the introduction to *Steps*, Gregory describes a student coming to him, very much perplexed by the direction of the course, and asking, "Do you want us to *learn* what you are telling us? . . . or is it all a sort of example, an illustration of something else?" Exactly the same questions might be asked about Gregory's approach to religion: Do you want us to *believe* in religion—in any particular religion? Oh no. Gregory wants us to "believe in" the sacred, the integrated fabric of mental process that envelops all our lives—and the principal way he knows that has allowed men and women to approach this (but not necessarily the only way) has been through religious traditions, vast, interconnected metaphorical systems. Without such metaphors for meditation, as correctives for the errors of human language and recent science, it seems that we have the capacity to be wrong in rather creative ways—so wrong that this world we cannot understand may become one in which we cannot live. But it is important to remember in this context Gregory's commitment to the principle of double description. The richest knowledge of the tree includes both myth and botany. Apart from Creatura, nothing can be known; apart from Pleroma, there is nothing there to know. Gregory, convinced that the artist and visionary sometimes know more than all our science, might have ended with this fragment of prayer embedded in a poem by William Blake:

> May God us keep
> From Single vision & Newton's sleep!*

---

*Letter to Thomas Butts, November 22, 1802, lines 87–88, quoted in *Blake: Complete Writings*, ed. Geoffrey Keynes (London: Oxford UP, 1966), 818.

XVIII Metalogue:

Persistent Shade (MCB)

FATHER: Still awake and working?

DAUGHTER: How about you? You're a remarkably persistent shade, you know. Sometimes I wish you were properly dead.

FATHER: As well you might. Certainly I always argued that the civilization is in trouble unless we can accept the fact of our dying. But such immortality as we have is in our ideas, which is why I left you the chore of finishing this book.

DAUGHTER: And a nasty, manipulative trick it was, too. A kind of huge lever to pry me away from other kinds of work. But you know what really bothers me as I work on this? It's the mediocrity of what gets attributed to ghosts at séances, as if vivid and splendid people went into a mode of being that thins them out to banality. That's what I want to avoid. Incidentally, an excess of piety doesn't help. And then I'm going to close up shop. At least among the New Guinea Manus the Sir Ghost dwindles away and finally floats out to sea, after running everyone's life for a generation or so.

FATHER: I told you about that psychic that turned up at Esalen, didn't I, who would go into a trance and paint and sign mediocre Monets?

DAUGHTER: Quite. A friend of mine has a room in her house where Margaret used to stay, where people still report dreams of Margaret. They dream that she comes and tells them to get on with the job, finish the research, take up some responsibility. She bullies them, as, of course, she would have, but they don't dream the other side of it, the way she would have coaxed them into clarity and awareness of the next step.

FATHER: Hmm. Ever sleep there?

DAUGHTER: Yes, but I had other things on my mind and she didn't turn up in my dreams. Anyhow, she has lost her otherness for me, so I no longer think of her as a vis-à-vis. But you have always had a quality of otherness. Strange.

FATHER: Yes, well, you can't get around the unconscious. I never quite managed to lay my father's ghost, but, of course, it made me rethink the nature of evolution.

DAUGHTER: That's a pretty one, because you picked up the new dialogue with your father with the paper about beetle teratology. W. B. had discovered that when a beetle has a freak extra leg, what it has is two legs in place of one, one a right leg and one a left leg, "Bateson's rule." And what you discovered was that this represented not the *addition* of an extra degree of bilateral symmetry, but a loss, the *loss* at some stage of epigenesis of the information needed to determine the asymmetry of right or left in the instruction to grow a leg in that particular position. And *that* was critical for you in the whole move to thinking about Creatura, the biological world, as the world of information.*

FATHER: Cap, I don't think I ever told you about—

DAUGHTER: No, but that you cannot do. You cannot provide new pieces to the puzzle. I can pull some out of tapes of yours that I never heard or writing I haven't read, or I can get pieces from my experience, often experience that has nothing at all to do with you. But maybe you can remind me of parts of the argument that I have heard somewhere along the line, and I can do what I have done before, pulling them together and making connections that were never made. A lot of that happened at the Wenner-Gren conference, where I made a book† by drawing the connections between pieces of thinking that the participants had perceived as disparate, even as dissonant.

I had an image once, of the "angel" of *Angels Fear*, as a nude male figure (because, after all, the unconscious is always up to all sorts of other business) marked with points of light, like the diagram of a constellation. That's what you can do with this whole body of

*Steps, 379–99.
†Our Own Metaphor.

ideas I'm trying to work with—you can point to a symmetry here, an asymmetry there, a gracefulness in the predestined curve of the spine, even though your own spine was all squunched over in the effort to conceal your height in your youth.

FATHER: Yes, well. It's all in the connections. It is, after all, a tautology that we are trying to map out.

DAUGHTER: So it will all in the end seem as simple as "If *P*, then *P*"?

FATHER: There are the basic ideas, which are probably mathematical in form and which are *necessarily* true but need to be discovered, and there are the connections between them. And there are the bits of data that allow you to see the connections when you try to map them onto the necessary truths. A beetle, perhaps. I wish you had gone on in maths instead of getting distracted by all that nonsense about the Middle East and academic administration.

DAUGHTER: Mmm. You're a bit of a bully in your own way, you know. And sometimes I have this image of, say, Euclid—not the real Euclid, who probably existed but built on the work of others, but a sort of mythical Euclid, who might have worked out the whole of the *Books*— and one of his disciples comes up to him and says, very proudly, "Look, I've worked out three new theorems." And Euclid says, "Yes, *that's all in there*. You have recognized something that was in there, in the axioms, all along." And then the theorems are just stitched into the whole. Well, you see, they aren't *new* theorems, the theorems are immanent in the axioms. That's how the whole business grows.

FATHER: No, no, that's exactly the point. Growing is precisely what a tautology doesn't do. Theorems may get added but there is nothing *new* in them. They are only the same old axioms and definitions blown up bigger and recombined. The Pythagoras theorem is all there in the axioms. Mathematicians spend their lives trying to show that there is nothing new—trying to "prove" the four-color theorem—trying to reduce it to fit the axioms. No "self-evident" propositions—but self-evident *links*. The essential requirement of tautology is that the *links* between the propositions shall be empty—i.e. shall contain no information about the subject of discourse.

DAUGHTER: I tell you it *grows*.

FATHER: No! The whole idea is that the axioms shall *not* grow!

DAUGHTER: All right. Don't shout at me. So the axioms and stuff don't grow. But in that sense a seed does not grow. It only gets blown up, as you call it; and its DNA consists of commands or "injunctions" that tell the embryo—the seedling—how to grow. Isn't it the same with the tautology? the axioms telling the tautology how to grow?

FATHER: All right. In that sense, yes. The seedling doesn't add anything new as it grows—or not much. . . .

DAUGHTER: So now I start thinking of myself as a gardener. A gardener with a word processor. You know what your problem is? You may not believe in the existence of ghosts, but you do believe in the existence of ideas. Bloody hovering.

FATHER: Hmm.

DAUGHTER: You know, you never gave me the good lines when you were writing the metalogues.

FATHER: There's still the other problem for *Angels Fear*, the problem of the misuse of ideas. The engineers get hold of them. Look at the whole god-awful business of family therapy, therapists making "paradoxical interventions" in order to change people or families, or counting "double binds." You can't count double binds.

DAUGHTER: No, I know, because double binds have to do with the total contextual structure, so that a given instance of double binding that you might notice in a therapy session is one tip of an iceberg whose basic structure is the whole life of the family. But you can't stop people from trying to count double binds. This business of breaking up process into entities is pretty fundamental to human perception. Maybe correcting for it will turn out to be part of what religion is all about. But you became so grumpy about it, and rather nasty to people who admired you immensely.

FATHER: I kept trying to get people to think straight, Cap, to clean up their premises.

DAUGHTER: It *looks* like possessiveness. And just as you can't count double binds, you really can't own ideas.

Look, I just saw a connection, I think. You know how you were always asking audiences to look at their hands—how many fingers do you have? No, perhaps you have not five fingers but four *relationships between* fingers?

FATHER: And then I suggested that that might make them think rather differently about possessiveness. How do you own an idea, a relationship?

DAUGHTER: See, what I think is going on is the same process that produces the monstrous beetles with extra limbs, the same thing is creating a monstrousness in the family-therapy industry, and other places too.

Some of the information has been lost, an essential part of the idea. Now that's useful. Instead of scolding those who have to work out their epigenesis with essential ideas or connections missing, we can try to identify the missing pieces. At least leave them with the right questions. Maybe *Angels* can help on that.

FATHER: When you start talking about being useful, you sound like your mother. I'm going to take a nap and let you get back to work. Good oatmeal they have here in Hades, but the coffee is pretty dreadful.

Glossary

The following glossary has been limited to two kinds of terms: a) terms defined by GB in the glossary of *Mind and Nature* that are used with substantial frequency or relate to significant concepts in this volume, e.g. "adaptation" (these definitions are reproduced verbatim); and b) terms used frequently in this volume whose meaning for GB is somewhat idiosyncratic but possible to capture in succinct definition, e.g. "learning"; these definitions, written by MCB, are enclosed in brackets. Terms used idiosyncratically by GB, but with a degree of inconsistency or tentativeness that shows he was still struggling with their meanings, e.g. "sacred," are not included here. The best way to approach these terms, short of an extended essay, is to pursue their various usages through the index. This glossary also assumes that the reader has access to a good dictionary for technical terms that may not be known to all, but which are used in conventional ways and often easily interpretable in context, e.g. "lobotomy," "chelae".

[**Abduction**   That form of reasoning in which a recognizable similarity between *A* and *B* proposes the possibility of further similarity. Often contrasted by GB with two other, more familiar types of reasoning, deduction, and induction.]

Adaptation   A feature of an organism, whereby it seemingly fits better into its environment and way of life. The process of achieving that fit.

[**Aesthetics**   That branch of philosophy that provides a theory of the beautiful. For GB, the study of the processes in creator and onlooker whereby beauty is created and acknowledged.]

Analogic   See *Digital*.

[**Character**   That aspect of personality assignable to experience, particularly the learning of cultural premises conveyed through repeated sequences in child-rearing.]

Co-Evolution   A stochastic system of evolutionary change in which two or more species interact in such a way that changes in species A set the stage for the natural selection of changes in species B. Later changes in species B, in turn, set the stage for the selecting of more similar changes in species A.

[**Consciousness**   A reflexive aspect of mental process that occurs in some but not all minds, in which the knower is aware of some fraction of his knowledge or the thinker of some fraction of his thought.]

[**Creatura**   A gnostic term borrowed by Jung, which GB used to refer to all processes in which the analog of cause is information or difference. Sometimes GB used the term to refer to the entire biological and social realm, necessarily embodied in material forms subject to physical laws of causation as well as the distinctive processes of life. See also *Pleroma*.]

Cybernetics   A branch of mathematics dealing with problems of control, recursiveness, and information.

Digital   A signal is "digital" if there is discontinuity between it and alternative signals from which it must be distinguished; "yes" and "no" are examples of digital signals. In contrast, when a magnitude or quantity in the signal is used to represent a continuously variable quantity in the referent, the signal is said to be "analogic."

[**Double bind**   Communication in the context of an emotionally important relationship in which there is unacknowledged contradiction between messages at different logical levels; proposed by GB and his colleagues as a possible etiology for schizophrenia.]

[**Dualism**   Any system of thought that recognizes two independent principles, such as mind and matter or good and evil, is "dualistic." Contrasted with "monism," in which reality is conceived as a unified whole.]

[**Ecology**   The science of interrelations and interdependence between organisms and between organisms and their environments. For GB contemporary ecology errs in overemphasizing energy exchange and attending insufficiently to information exchange.]

Energy In this book, I use the word "energy" to mean a "quantity" having the dimensions: *mass times velocity squared* (MV^2). Other people, including physicists, use it in many other senses.

Epigenesis The process of embryology seen as related, at each stage, to the status-quo ante.

Epistemology A branch of science combined with a branch of philosophy. As science, epistemology is the study of how particular organisms or aggregates of organisms "know," "think," and "decide". As philosophy, epistemology is the study of the necessary limits and other characteristics of the processes of knowing, thinking, and deciding.

[**Feedback** "Negative" feedback is the central mechanism of cybernetic explanation whereby in recursive systems a report of the outcome of previous functioning is used to adjust the mechanism governing future functioning, allowing for corrections that are apparently goal directed. In "positive" feedback (or schismogenesis), the effect of the feedback message is to move the system further in the direction of its previous movement, thus increasing instability rather than returning to stability or homeostasis.]

Genetics Strictly, the science of genetics deals with all aspects of the heredity and variation of organisms and with the processes of growth and differentiation within the organism.

Genotype The aggregate of recipes and injunctions that are the hereditary contributions to the determination of the phenotype (q.v.).

[**Holism** The tendency in nature to produce from the ordered grouping of parts complex wholes with properties that are not present in or predictable from the separate parts. GB frequently uses the term and its adjective "holistic" to refer to modes of acting and observing that are attentive to holistic properties.]

Homology A formal resemblance between two organisms such that the relations between certain parts of A are similar to the relations between corresponding parts of B. Such formal resemblance is considered to be evidence of evolutionary relatedness.

Idea In the epistemology offered in this book, the smallest unit of mental process is a difference or distinction or news of a difference. What is called an "idea" in popular speech seems to be a complex aggregate of such units. But popular speech will hesitate to call, say, the bilateral symmetry of a frog or the message of a single neural impulse an idea.

Information   Any difference that makes a difference.

[**Interface**   This general term for a surface that forms the meeting place between two regions serves to replace the notion of boundary when speaking in three dimensions. In GB's usage, dealing with the interaction of systems that may not be entirely enclosed or bounded, it typically refers to system boundaries defined by information exchange and by changes in coding, rather than to enclosures like skin. As such, "interface" becomes the term for the locus of systemic interaction.]

[**Learning**   GB included within the notion of "learning" all those events in which a system responds to some external stimulus, including as a limiting case examples in which the system adjusts but is unchanged (e.g. a thermostat switching on the heat in response to falling temperature: zero learning), but focusing on those cases in which the system is modified in response to the information received. The concept thus becomes an umbrella concept to include adaptation, character formation, habituation, acclimation, addiction, etc., as well as more familiar forms of learning, and can refer to different logical types. Notably, learning in which the learning capacity of the system is modified ("deutero-learning") is referred to as learning II, being of a higher logical type than learning in which the organism is changed without an alteration in learning capacity.]

Linear and lineal.   "Linear" is a technical term in mathematics describing a relationship between variables such that when they are plotted against each other on orthogonal Cartesian coordinates, the result will be a straight line. "Lineal" describes a relation among a series of causes or arguments such that the sequence does not come back to the starting point.

Logical types   A series of examples is in order:

1. The name is not the thing named but is of different logical type, higher than that of the thing named.
2. The class is of different logical type, higher than that of its members.
3. The injunctions issued by, or control emanating from, the bias of the house thermostat is of higher logical type than the control issued by the thermometer. (The "bias" is the device on the wall that can be set to determine the temperature around which the temperature of the house will vary.)
4. The word "tumbleweed" is of the same logical type as "bush" or "tree." It is not the name of a species or genus of plants; rather, it is the name of a

class of plants whose members share a particular style of growth and dissemination.

5. "Acceleration" is of a higher logical type than "velocity."

[**Metalogue**   A metalogue is a conversation dealing with some aspect of mental process in which ideally the interaction exemplifies the subject matter.]

[**Metaphor**   Strictly, a literary device in which a description is extended from some item to another with which it shares certain characteristics. Sometimes contrasted with "simile," in which comparison is explicit, whereas metaphor, by not making comparison explicit, proposes a degree of identity. For GB, metaphor includes all processes of knowing and communicating that depend on assertions or injunctions of similarity, including "homology," "empathy," and "abduction".]

[**Mind**   A mind is a system capable of mental process or thought. GB's criteria for recognizing such systems are listed on pages 18 and 19. They do not include consciousness nor do they require association with a single organism.]

Mutation   In conventional evolutionary theory, offspring may differ from their parents for the following sorts of reasons:

1. Changes in DNA called "mutations."
2. Reshuffling of genes in sexual reproduction.
3. Somatic changes acquired during the individual's life in response to environmental pressure, habit, age, and so forth.
4. Somatic segregation, that is, the dropping or reshuffling of genes in epigenesis resulting in patches of tissue that have differentiated genetic makeup. Genetic changes are always digital (q.v.), but modern theory prefers (with good reason) to believe that "small" changes are, in general, the stuff of which evolution is made. It is assumed that many small mutational changes combine over many generations to make larger evolutionary contrasts.

Ontogeny   The process of development of the individual; embryology *plus* whatever changes environment and habit may impose.

Parallax   The "appearance" of movement in observed objects, which is created when the observer's eye moves relative to them; the difference between the apparent positions of objects seen with one eye and their apparent positions as seen with the other eye.

[**Pattern**   The term pattern refers to an aggregate whose members are arranged in such a way that they can be economically specified (or, put slightly differently, whose arrangement is highly redundant). Five dots arranged in a quincunx (as on a die) are more economical to describe than five dots randomly dispersed, and therefore may more efficiently be copied.]

Phenotype   The aggregate of propositions making up the description of a real organism; the appearance and characteristics of a real organism. See *Genotype*.

Phylogeny   The evolutionary history of a species.

[**Pleroma**   The material world, characterized by the kinds of regularities described in the physical sciences. The sharp contrast between Pleroma and Creatura (q.v.), the world of communication, is blurred by the fact that human knowledge of Pleroma is entirely mediated by Creatural processes of response to difference].

Random   The sequence of events is said to be random if there is no way of predicting the next event of a given kind from the event or events that have preceded and if the system obeys the regularities of probability. Note that the events which we say are random are always members of some limited set. The fall of an honest coin is said to be random. At each throw, the probability of the next fall being heads or tails remains unchanged. But the randomness is within the limited set. It is heads or tails; no alternatives are to be considered.

Reductionism   It is the task of every scientist to find the simplest, most economical, and (usually) most elegant explanation that will cover the known data. Beyond this, reductionism becomes a vice if it is accompanied by an overly strong insistence that the simplest explanation is the only explanation. The data may have to be understood within some larger gestalt.

Somatic (Greek *soma*, body)   A characteristic is said to be of somatic origin when the speaker wishes to emphasize that the characteristic was achieved by bodily change brought about during the lifetime of the individual by environmental impact or by practice.

Stochastic (Greek *stochazein*, to shoot with a bow at a target; that is, to scatter events in a partially random manner, some of which achieve a preferred outcome)   If a sequence of events combines a random component with a selective process so that only certain outcomes of the random are allowed to endure, that sequence is said to be stochastic.

[**Structure**   In GB's usage, structure refers to characteristics of systems that define the systems' responses to environmental events and regulate their internal balances. They correspond to the thresholds and landmarks of functioning as outlines in a drawing define the depicted solids.]

[**Subsystem**   Properly speaking, this term refers to any system that can be seen as part of a hierarchically related larger system, so that for instance the single cell is a subsystem of the organism. However, GB most frequently uses the term subsystem in reference to human beings; this is primarily a way of underlining the mental characteristics of larger systems that include individual human beings, such as families, societies, or ecosystems.]

Tautology   An aggregate of linked propositions in which the validity of the *links* between them cannot be doubted. The truth of the propositions is not claimed, e.g. euclidean geometry.

Notes on

Chapter Sources (MCB)

It seems useful to reiterate here that all sections of manuscript drafted by GB have been edited and reworked in the name of coherence and clarity, sometimes very extensively.

I. *Introduction.* GB's portion of this chapter is based on one of three sections that he had designated as introductions for this book. "The Manuscript" appeared in *The Esalen Catalog* 20, no. 1 (January–June): 12.

II. *The World of Mental Process.* This chapter, which was also labeled by GB as a possible introduction, is based primarily on a lecture given by GB at San Francisco's Jungian Institute on February 29, 1980. The written text was stolen from the podium at the end, so the version here is based on two prior drafts and a transcript of the lecture itself, prepared by Rodney Donaldson. An earlier version edited by Kai Erikson and myself was published in the *Yale Review* 71, no. 1, Autumn 1981: 1–12. I have added a long insert, including the list of criteria for mind from *Mind and Nature* and a final paragraph adapted from a lecture which GB recorded for the Lindisfarne Fellows a month before his death ("Men are Grass: Metaphor and the World of Mental Process," ed. M. C. Bateson, *Lindisfarne Letter*, no. 11, 1980).

III. *Metalogue: Why Do You Tell Stories?* The discussion of the conch is a sequence GB used repeatedly in teaching and writing, alternating with a comparable discussion of a crab. Some of the phrasing here is drawn from a seminar with the Work Scholars at Esalen.

IV. *The Model.* This chapter was created by combining three draft fragments grouped together by GB: the first on the house thermostat, the second on calibration and feedback (both discussed at greater length in *Mind and Nature*), and the third on the triad of learning.

V. *Neither Supernatural nor Mechanical.* Another section drafted for a possible introduction, which has been fleshed out with related comments from "Health: Whose Responsibility?" GB's keynote address to the Governor's Conference on Health, May 3, 1979, at Berkeley, Calif., published in *Energy Medicine* 1: 70–75, 1980.

VI. *Metalogue: Why Placebos?* The comments on GB's experiences of illness are also taken from "Health: Whose Responsibility?"

VII. *Let Not Thy Left Hand Know:* This chapter was drafted by GB, and it was he who inserted his previously published account (*CoEvolution Quarterly*, no. 9 [Spring 1976]: 82–84) of the Governor's Prayer Breakfast, with the included quotations. At one time GB thought of putting together a book entirely of his most frequently used parables and stories.

IX. *Defenses of Faith.* This section is made up of two draft fragments and a portion of the "Remsen Bird Lecture," given by GB at Occidental College on October 25, 1978. One of the draft fragments, that dealing with Lamarck and the Ancient Mariner, was rejected by him, except for the point about short cuts, with the label *n.b.g.* ("no bloody good"), but retained in the file.

X. *Metalogue: Are You Creeping Up?* The portion of this metalogue dealing with action and free will is based on fragmentary notes by GB, associated with materials used in chapter 9, and the remarks on synchronic and diachronic time are drawn from an uncompleted draft metalogue by GB.

XI. *The Messages of Nature and Nurture.* This section is based on a presentation prepared for the Conference on Ontogenetic and Phylogenetic Models of Development held at Abbaye de Royaumont near Paris, October 10–13, 1975.

XII. *Metalogue: Addiction.* Most of GB's comments in this metalogue are based on transcripts of two seminars he conducted with the Esalen Work Scholars on November 3 and 15, 1979.

XIII. *The Unmocked God.* This chapter has been constructed from related sections of a much longer chapter by this same title drafted by GB for this volume.

XIV. *Metalogue: It's Not Here.* Several of GB's remarks are based on remarks in letters to Patrick Bateson (1980) and Brian Smith (1979).

XV. *The Structure in the Fabric.* This chapter incorporates most of the remainder of the draft, "The Unmocked God."

XVI. *Innocence and Experience.* The first half of this chapter was contained in a lecture given by Gregory under Esalen auspices to a University Extension Conference of the University of Michigan, March 18, 1979, titled *From Childhood to Old Age* (excerpts appeared in *Psychology Today* 13 [June 1979]: 128). The bracketed section that follows page 176 was inserted as a transition to a heavily adapted excerpt from "Health: Whose Responsibility?" reshaped to extend Gregory's phrasings from medicine to other spheres of action and interaction between systems.

XVII. *So What's a Meta For?* Written by MCB on completion of the book in 1986.

XVIII. *Metalogue: Persistent Shade.* The quarrel about tautology was actually written by GB, and was found in a discarded section of draft.

Glossary. Wherever possible, definitions have been used as they appeared in *Mind and Nature.* New definitions written by MCB are bracketed.

Index

Abduction, 37, 90, 174–75, 192, 206
Aborigine, Australian, 108, 195–96
Acquired characteristics, 54, 90–92.
  See also Lamarck
Acrobat, 119
Actaeon, 80
Actions
  knowledge of, 102–103
Adam, 80, 101
Adams, Joe, 69–70, 87
Adaptation, 42, 130, 147, 197–98, 207
Addiction, 125–34
Addition, operation of, 159
Adji Darma, 77–79, 83–84, 87
Aegisthus, 137
Aeschylus, 140
Aesthetics, 63, 70, 75, 183, 192, 195,
  199, 207
Agamemnon, 139
Albinos, 110
Alcoholics, alcoholism, 77, 125, 128,
  131
Alcoholics Anonymous, 128
Algebra, 22, 152
Algorithms, 158–60
Aloneness, 171
Amanuensis, 3
Ambition, 169
American Indians, 72
Ames, Adelbert, Jr., 92–94

Analogic communication, 39, 121, 207
Analytic geometry, 59
Anangke (necessity), 137–38, 141, 142,
  151
Ancient Mariner, 73, 76, 77, 79, 83
Angels Fear (G. Bateson and M. C.
  Bateson), 1–5, 183–85, 202–204
Anggara-Kasih, 171–72
Anthropologists, anthropology, 9, 22, 71,
  177, 184–85
Anthropomorphic supernaturals, 55
Antigone, 139
Apical dominance, 154
Aquinas, Saint Thomas, 11
Archetypes, 10, 25
Ares, 139
Aristotle, 11, 14
Arithmetic, 23, 152, 156–57
Arms race, 127, 130, 133
Art, 49, 132, 163, 199
As if mode of communication, 29
Ashby, Ross, 119, 120
Athena, 137, 140
Atomic weaponry. *See* Arms race
Atreus, House of, 137
Attachment, 106–108, 130, 170–72
Augustine, Saint, 10, 21–22, 156
Australian aborigine, 108, 195–96
Avoidance of communication. *See* Non-
  communication

Awareness. *See* Consciousness
Axioms, 9, 157, 203

Bach, J. S., 49
Balance, beam, 62–63
Balinese, 25–26, 77–79, 106, 141, 171–72, 184
Barong, 141
Bateson, Gregory, 1–9, 184–90
Bateson, Mary Catherine, xi–xii, 1–9
Bateson's rule (William), 202
"Battle of Blenheim, The" (poem), 162
Beam balance, 62–63
Believing, seeing as, 96–99
Bell-shaped curve of random distribution, 112–13
Berkeley, Bishop, 24, 155
Bernard, Claude, 179
Berry, Wendell, 32
Bias, 38–42, 134
Bill W., 128
Binge alcoholics, 131
Biological evolution, 152
Biologists' descriptions, 154–56
Biosphere, 36, 99, 142, 153, 194
Blake, William, 18, 36, 97, 161, 170, 200
Blood sugar, 111–12
Body-mind problem, 50–52, 124, 178. *See also* Dualism
Boredom, 127
Bread and Wine. *See* Communion
Breaking point of chain, 116, 117
Brown, Gov. Jerry, 71, 75
Burning chaparral, 107–108
Bus *vs.* tram, 167–68, 170, 174
Butler, Samuel, 60, 98, 126, 129

Cadmus, 80, 139
Calibration and feedback, 42–46
Cameras, 72, 76
Carroll, Lewis, 21, 161
Cartesian coordinates, 59, 60
Case of the Midwife Toad, The (Koestler), 58
Chain, breaking point of, 116, 117
Change, 91, 106–107, 119, 155, 178
Chaparral, burning, 107–108
Chapter sources, 213–15

Character, 46–49, 108, 207
Cheating (in conversation), 33
Chladni figures, 47
Chlorine, 61
Christianity, 23, 25, 141, 146
Chrysippus, 137
Cigarette pack, Lucky Strike, 93
Circular causation, 14, 18–19, 37
Circuits, self-correcting. *See* Self-correction
Civilizations, interface between, 175–76
Clams, ridges on, 112–13
Classes, 13, 21, 27, 61–62, 91, 152–53
Cleo (nurse), 66
Clytemnestra, 137
Co-evolution, 207
Cogito, 61, 94–96
Coincidences, 57
Coleridge, Samuel Taylor, 73
Collingwood, R. G., 127
Color, skin, 110–11
Communication(s), 21, 28–29, 31–34, 62, 151–56, 180, 186–91, 197. *See also* Information; Messages; Non-communication
Communion (of Bread and Wine), 29, 77. *See also* Mass
Commutative law, 159
Computers, 34, 51
Computer programs, 193–94
Conch, 34–35
Concurrence, 86
Conflicting themes, 138–41
Conscious Purpose and Human Adaptation conference. *See Our Own Metaphor*
Conscious(ness), 19, 69, 76, 81, 90–97, 100–105, 109, 146, 207
Conservative devices, 97
Consistency, 58, 68, 177, 188
Constitution, U.S., 163, 179
Context, 13, 48–49, 73, 83, 87, 98, 168, 173–74, 177, 189
Contradictory themes, 138–41
Control, 37–45, 88, 106, 154, 168, 170, 207. *See also* Homeostasis
Coordinates, Cartesian, 59, 60
Counterculture, 4, 51–52
Crabs, appendages of, 114–15

Cratylus, 40
Creatura, 13–14, 16–28, 33, 50, 61, 66, 123, 146, 149, 166, 185–94, 198–200, 207
Cremations, 78–79, 172
Cretan paradox, 143, 197
Cromwell, Oliver, 29
Cross-sex knowledge, 80, 84, 169–70
Crystallization of liquid, 116
Cultural relativity, 22
Cultural transmission, 99
Culture, 97, 184
Culture contact, 176
Curiosity, 80
Cybernetics, 11–14, 102, 117, 121, 136, 144, 181, 183, 207. *See also* Communication; Control

Dangers of knowledge, 80. *See also* Non-communication
Darma, Adji, 77–79, 83–84, 87
Darwin, Charles, 61, 91, 117
DDT, 107
Deadly Sin, 11
Death and dying, 1, 57, 101, 108, 170–72, 201
Deduction, 23–24, 190
Definitions, 7, 157–58
Deity, 6, 8, 12, 141, 199
Delirium tremens, 76–77
Dependency, systemic, 132–33
Descartes, René, 10, 11, 14, 58–61, 94–95, 147
Description, 17, 18, 62, 114, 146, 151–56, 162–65, 191, 199–200
Determinism, 168–71
Deutero-learning, 13, 46. *See also* Learning
Diachronic time, 106–108
Differences, 14, 18, 40, 62–63, 121–22, 157, 191
Digital communication, 39–40, 119, 122, 207
Dinesen, Isak, 173*n*
Ding an sich, 32, 95, 152, 164
Discontinuities, 24, 84, 121, 165
Disease, 181
Distributive law, 159
Dizziness, 96

DNA, 85, 88, 113–14, 120, 154, 158, 163
Dolphin training, 129
Dormitive principle, 86
Double binds, 126, 128–29, 146–47, 173, 197, 203, 204
Double description, 146, 199, 200
Dryad metaphor, 196–97
Dualism, 11–12, 16, 18, 58–63, 141, 149, 161–62, 207
Durkheim, Emil, 200
Dyadic comparison, 98

Eco, ecological God, 142–43, 145, 148–49
Ecology, 8, 142, 207–208
Economic man, 175, 176
Economics, 59–60, 175–76
Editing, 2, 82
Education, 45, 127
Eggs
  frogs, 118–19
  hens, 98
Einstein, 11
Electra, 137
Eliot, T. S., 106, 171
Embryo(logy), 16–17, 85, 115, 120, 160
Emic descriptions, 185*n*
Empathy, 33, 56, 194–95
Endorphins, 127
Energy, 18, 36–37, 55, 117, 181, 208
Entertainment, 127, 131–32
Environment, 37, 100, 110–24, 133
Epigenesis, 98, 208. *See also* Embryo(logy)
Epimenides, 143, 197
Epistemology, 8–11, 15, 19–23, 32, 50–53, 61–63, 69, 93–94, 97, 142, 183–87, 191, 208. *See also* Perception
Error, 43–45, 147, 155, 191
Esalen Institute 4–5, 51, 68, 132, 201
Escalation, 12, 133
ESP (extrasensory perception), 54–55
Eternal Verities, 10, 22–23, 24, 144, 156–58
Ethics 9, 177, 191
Ethnography, 184–85. *See also* Anthropology
Etic descriptions, 185*n*

Euclid, 203
Eumenides (Aeschylus), 140
European peasant, 196
Evil and good, 149
Evolution, 7–8, 14, 16–17, 34–35, 90–
    92, 147, 152, 192, 207
Extinction, 147
Extrasensory perception (ESP), 54–55

Faith, 10–11, 95–96
Fechner, Gustav, 123–24
Feedback, 11, 12–13, 42–46, 127, 208.
    See also Control
Fertilization, 98, 118–19
Fey state, 170–72
Field (meadow), 198
Flexibility, loss of, 86, 92, 119–20
Flux, 39–40, 103, 166, 178. *See also*
    Structure
Form. *See* Structure
Four-color theorem, 203
Fracture plane, 120
Frazer, Sir James, 56
Free will, 103, 168
Freedom, 21, 166, 168, 179
Frogs, 118–20, 186
Functional(ism), 147, 200
Fundamentalism, 77, 142, 187
Furies, 137, 139, 140

Gaia hypothesis, 149
Galatians, epistle to, 135
Gaps, 39, 95–96, 150, 162–66
Gaussian curve, 112–13
Genesis, 142
Genetic(s), 68, 100–101, 114–15, 208.
    See also DNA; Genotype
Genotype, 34, 110–24, 208
Gertrude (Hendrix), 194
Ghosts, 6, 54, 201–202, 204
Glossary, 206–12
    of *Mind and Nature,* 206
God, gods, 8, 10, 12, 25–26, 55, 74, 83,
    86, 96, 128, 135–36, 141–43, 149,
    151, 160–61, 200. *See also* Anthro-
    pomorphic supernaturals; Deity
Goethe, J. W. von, 27
Good and evil, 149
Grammar, 28, 192. *See also* Language

Greek language, 147
Groups *vs.* classes, 152–53
Growth, 35, 130, 203
Guilt, 76, 92

Haddon, Alfred, 169–70
Hallucination, 187
Halogens, 153
Hamlet, 97
Hand, human, 188, 190
Hardness, 157
Healing by visualization, 66
Hecht, Selig, 121
Heisenberg, Werner, 199
Hens and eggs, 98
Hera, 84
Heraclitus, 40
Heresy, concept of, 12, 23, 54, 68
Hierarchy, 13, 19, 40, 85–86, 99, 165,
    169
Holism, holistic, 52, 179–81, 199,
    208
Hologram, mental, 47
Homeostasis, 119–20, 134
Homology, 16, 30, 152–53, 192–208
Hospitalization, 66
Houston, Jean, 194
Hubris, 141, 142
Human potential movement, 52
Hume, David, 53
Humphrey, Nick, 27
Hysteresis, 46–47

Iatmul (New Guinea). *See Naven*
Ideas, 27, 32, 57, 65, 67, 70–71, 94,
    157, 185, 187, 204. *See also* Differ-
    ences
Images, mental, 53, 88, 92–96, 102,
    185, 202
Incarnations, previous, 57
Information, 14, 17, 47, 54, 85–86, 88–
    89, 100, 117, 118, 122, 146, 187,
    198, 205, 209. *See also* Communi-
    cation
Inheritance, Lamarckian, 54, 58, 90–92,
    101, 105
Initiation, 77, 86
Inset stories, 83
Integration, systemic, 196, 199

Interfaces, 19, 39, 121–23, 167, 175–76, 185, 209
Invention, 80
Involuntary actions, 103
Iphigenia, 137
Islam, 146, 149

Jamming of traffic, 116
Jehovah, 77, 149, 161
Jesus, 25, 141, 195
Job, 74, 83
Jocasta, 139
Judeo-Christian God, 149
Jung, Carl Gustav, 13–14, 16. *See also* Archetypes; Synchronicity; Bill W.

Kali-Durga, 172, 173
Kant, Immanuel, 32, 152
Karma, 137–38, 151
Kevembuangga, myth of, 34–35
Kipling, Rudyard, 58
Knowledge, 20, 80, 84, 102–103, 146. *See also* Epistemology; Perception
Koestler, Arthur, 57–58
Korzybski, Alfred, 13, 20

Lag, cultural, 178
Laius, 139
Lamarck, J. B., Lamarckian, 60, 90–92, 101, 105, 134
Language(s), 27–30, 37, 161, 166, 186–89
Latin language, 94, 95, 147
"Laws," 159
Learning, 13, 46–49, 99, 131, 133, 178
Lethalness of consciousness, 105
Lewis, C. S., 106
Limericks, 167–68
Lineal (logic), 144, 209
Liquid, crystallization of, 116
Lobotomy, 173–74
Logic, 32, 143–44, 158, 189
Logical types, 11, 13, 19, 32–33, 40, 43–46, 91, 94, 100, 105, 111–13, 147, 189, 209–210. *See also* Class
Lord's Prayer, 25, 28–29
Lorenz, Konrad, 33, 195
Love, 63, 87, 171, 191, 197
Lovelock, James, 149

LSD, 69–70, 75
Lucky Strike cigarette pack, 93

MacBride, Judge, 71, 75
Machine, schizophrenic, 125–26
Macy Conferences (on cybernetics), 12–13
Magic, 55–56, 58
"Manuscript, The" (poem), 5–6
Manus (New Guinea), 201
Map, territory and, 14, 20, 122, 152–56, 161, 187
Marxism, 12, 115–17, 118
Mass (ritual), 29, 77, 108
Materialism, 6, 51, 60–62, 64
Mathematics, 22–23, 187
Matriarchy, 140
Matter, mind and, 6, 58–63. *See also* Dualism
Matthew, Saint, 69
Maxwell, Clerk, 179
McCulloch, Warren, 12, 21, 22, 25, 95, 114, 145–46, 177, 186*n*
Mead, Margaret, 171, 201–202
Meadow (field), 198
Mechanists, 51, 68
Medicine, 65–68, 177, 179, 180, 185, 197
Memory, 47
Mental processes, 16–19, 25, 36, 47, 65, 69, 85, 99, 135, 138, 174–75, 183–85, 200. *See also* Mind
Messages, 13, 32, 62, 113, 180, 185, 189. *See also* Communication
Metalogues, 3, 34–35, 204, 210
Metamessages, 32, 189
Metaphor(s), 25–30, 35, 125, 188, 191–98, 210. *See also* Abduction; Empathy; Stories
Mind, 7–8, 11–12, 18–19, 58–63, 85, 136, 192, 210. *See also* Dualism; Mental processes
Mind and Nature: A Necessary Unity (G. Bateson), 1–3, 5, 7–8, 14, 18–19, 27, 52, 166; glossary of, 206
Miracles, 51, 53, 142
Mittelstaedt, Horst, 42–46
Models, 35, 36–49, 194
Monet, Claude, 54

Mongoose, 76–77
Monism, 7, 11–12, 146
Monotone changes, 119
Morphine, 127
Morphogenesis, 114–15
Multiplication, operation of, 159
Murray, Margaret, 173n
Mutation, 210
Mystics, 10, 174
Mythology, 138–41

Native American Church, 72
Nature, nurture and, 110–24
Naven (G. Bateson), 12, 137–38
Nemesis, 141, 142
Networks of propositions, 98
Neurons, 95, 120–21
Newton, Isaac, 200
Ngglambi, 137–38
Nonattachment, 170
Noncommunication, 79–81, 86, 88–89,
    101, 135. *See also* Secrecy
Normal curve, 112–13
Nouns, 28, 188
Number, 113–15
Nurture, nature and, 110–24

Obedience strike, 120
Objects, images of, 102
Obsolescence, 52, 68
Oedipus, 139–40
Oedipus at Colonos (Sophocles), 140
Old age, 167–68, 171
On the Origin of Species (Darwin), 12,
    61
Ontogeny, 210
Oppenheimer, Robert, 128
Order. *See* Sequence
Orders, silent, 81
Orestes, 137, 140
Orpheus, 80
Ostensive communication, 155
Osteopathic medicine, 180
Otters, 31–32
Our Own Metaphor (M. C. Bateson),
    Wenner-Gren Conference on Con-
    scious Purpose and Human Adap-
    tion, 42, 50, 76, 86, 191, 202
"Out-of-body experiences," 55

Pain, 181
Paley, William, 12
Palliatives, immorality of, 126
Parables. *See* Stories
Paradox, 69 143, 146, 197. *See also*
    Contradictory themes
Parallax, 93–94, 210
Pathetic fallacy, 193
Pathology, 89, 155, 175, 180, 190
Patriarchy, 140
Pattern(s), 59–60, 115–17, 154, 158,
    188, 210
Peasant, European, 196
Pentagon, 84
Pentheus, 80
Perception, 62, 88, 92–97, 102–103,
    121–23, 199. *See also* ESP
Percipio, 94–96
Percival, John, *Percival's Narrative* (G.
    Bateson), 128
Peyote, 72–73
Phenotypes, 110–11, 114, 211
Photography, 76, 83
Phylogeny, 211
Picasso, Pablo, 161
Pike, Kenneth, 185n
Placebos, 51, 65–67, 185
Plato, 60
Pleroma, 11, 13–14, 16–28, 50, 123,
    149, 166, 185–91, 194, 196, 200
Pluralism, 68
Pluto (planet), 132
Poetry, 27, 29–30, 174, 187
Polybus, 139
Power, 59–60, 169, 176
Practice, 45, 46, 49, 163, 199
Prayer, 25, 28–29, 57, 71, 83, 128
Prayer breakfast, 71–76
Preconceptions, 99, 184
Present, 106–108
President of United States, 169
Presuppositions, 92–94, 98–99
Pretending, 178
Pribram, Karl, 47
Process, 36–42, 91–92, 158, 166
Programs, computer, 193–94
Projection, religion and, 105–106
Proliferation of species, 101
Prometheus, 80

Propositions, 98, 158
Protestants, 29
Psychotherapy, 77, 80, 83, 129, 132, 204
Purpose, 56, 79, 90, 105–106, 171–72
Pythagoras, Pythagoreans, 23–24, 60, 160

Quality, quantity, 119, 175
Quantity, 59–60, 115–17, 119, 175
Question, 117–18

Rain forests, 176
Random(ness), 112–13, 211
Rangda, 141, 172–73
Rappaport, Skip (Roy A.), 148
Recognition, 35, 105, 199
Recursiveness, 161, 181, 200
Redefinition, strategy of, 7
Reductio ad absurdum, 23–24
Reductionism, 99, 211
Redundancy, 163
Regents (University of California), 127, 169
Registers, 190
Reincarnation, 57
Relation(ships), 33–34, 37, 113, 129,
    147, 157, 188, 193
"Relaxation-oscillation," 120–21
Religion, 2, 11, 29, 50, 55–56, 64, 72–
    77, 95–96, 105–106, 135–36, 142,
    146, 148, 177–79, 190, 195–97,
    200, 204
Reproduction, 97–98
Responsibility, 26, 84, 168, 182
Riddle of Sphinx, 139, 176–78, 182
Rifle and shotgun shooting, 42–46
"Rime of the Ancient Mariner, The," 73
Rituals, 56, 198. *See also* Initiation; Mass
Rosita (Rodriguez, healer), 67
Russell, Bertrand, 13

Sacred, 2, 8, 11, 29, 50, 64, 69, 80–81,
    86, 143, 145, 148, 149, 176, 183, 200
Sacrilege, 83
Sangha (clergy), 68
Santa Claus, 55, 57, 77
Satan, 74
Scheherazade, 83
Schismogenesis, 12
Schizophrenia, 27, 83, 109, 125–26, 129
Schizophrenic machine, 125–26

Schools, religion in, 179
Science, 6, 10, 14–15, 58–64, 186,
    187–88, 192, 199
Scientism, 187–88
Screwtape Letters (Lewis), 106
Séance, 54
Secrets, secrecy, 24, 80–87, 196. *See
    also* Noncommunication
Seeing as believing, 96–99
Self, 56, 176, 194–97, 199
Self-consciousness. *See* Consciousness
Self-correction, 11, 19, 40, 143–44, 181, 199
Self-evident truths, 156, 158
Self-healing tautologies, 150
Semantics, 188, 190
Sense organs, 17, 40, 46, 62, 122
Sequence, "laws" of, 159
Sex(es), sexuality, 97–98, 101, 169–70
Shakespeare, William, vii, 97
Shamans, 25–26, 58
Shooting, rifle and shotgun, 42–46
Shortcuts, 91, 127
Shotgun and rifle shooting, 43–46
Silent orders, 81
Similes, 29
Sin, 11, 142, 147
Skin color, 110–11
Skulls, 170
Snails, 101. *See also* Conch
Socrates, 159–60
Somatic characteristic, 211
Sophocles, 140
Southey, Robert, 162
Sparagmation, 80
Species, proliferation of, 101
Sphinx, riddle of, 139, 176–78, 182
Spinal column, human, 34–35, 153, 180
Spirals, 35, 101
Steps to an Ecology of Mind (G. Bate-
    son), 2, 13, 46, 202
Still, Dr. Andrew, 180
Stochastic sequence, 27n, 211. *See also*
    Question
Stories, 31–35, 53, 69–70, 76, 80, 82–
    83, 163, 193
Strategy of redefinition, 7
Strike, obedience, 120
Structure, 36–42, 103–105, 134 151–56,
    160–66, 211

Subject-predicate relations, 27, 30, 188
Subsystems, 211–12
Subtractive differences, 63
Sufi choir, 75
Sugar, blood, 111–12
Supercooling, 116
Supernatural(s), 53, 55, 58–61, 64. *See also* God, gods
Superstition, forms of, 51–61
Syllogisms, 26–30, 143–44, 192
Symmetry, 118, 181, 191, 202–203
Sympathy, 194
Synchronic time, 106–108
Synchronicity, Jungian theory of, 57
Syntax, 146, 189, 190
Systems, 8, 19, 37–41, 85, 89, 99, 105, 108, 125, 131–34, 135, 141–43, 179–81, 199, 211. *See also* Cybernetics; Mind

Tanning, 110–11
Taoism, 108
Tautology, 90, 124, 147, 150, 156–57, 203–204, 212
Tax, Sol, 72, 75
Taxonomies, 143
Templates, 98
Territory. *See* Map
Theorems, 203
Thermometers. *See* Thermostat
Thermostat, 37–42, 166
Theseus, 140
Things, 27, 61, 151–52, 157, 161, 188, 190. *See also Ding an sich*
Thought, 16, 21, 94–95. *See also* Mental processes
Thresholds, 38–41, 121–22. *See also* Structure
Thyestes, 137
Time, 48, 85, 91, 106–108, 172
Tiresias, 84, 139
Todd, John, 103, 198
Tolly (Anatol Holt), 86, 195
Totemism, 56, 108, 195–96
Toxicity, 68, 85, 105, 122
Traffic jams, 116
Tragedy, Greek, 80, 136–41
Tram *vs.* bus, 167–68, 170, 174

Transcendence, 129, 149
Transmission, cultural, 99
Triadic patterns, 47–48
Truths, 6, 34, 63, 95, 156–57. *See also* Epistemology; Verities
Tuberculosis, 185

Uncertainty principle, 199
Unconscious. *See* Conscious
Unity, 64, 102, 136, 199
Universe, determined, 168
University of Californira, regents of, 127, 169
Unknowing. *See* Noncommunication

Verities, Eternal, 10, 22–23, 24, 144, 156–58
Versailles, Treaty of, 111, 148
Veterans Administration Mental Hospital, 173–74
Vision. *See* Perception
Visualization, healing by, 60
Von Domarus, E., 27
Vonnegut, Kurt, 178

Wallace, Russel, 117, 180
Warner, Sylvia Townsend, 173*n*
Weaponry. *See* Arms race
Weber-Fechner laws, 121–23
Weismannian barrier, communication across, 88
Wenner-Gren Conferences, 75, 195, 202. *See also Our Own Metaphor*
Whitehead, A. N., 11, 13, 152
Wholes, 52, 181. *See also* Holism
Wiener, Norbert, 12, 122, 125
Wine and Bread. *See* Communion
Witches, 172–73
With a Daughter's Eye (M. C. Bateson), 1
Wolves, 28

Young, Thomas, 36
Youth, 167–68

Zen (Buddhism), 45, 146, 199
Zero-learning, 45, 46, 133
Zeus, 140

About the Authors

Gregory Bateson (1904–80) was an anthropologist by training who pursued his interest in pattern and communication in New Guinea and Bali, then conducted research on psychiatry and schizophrenia and later on dolphins. He played a major role in the early formulation of cybernetics and in introducing systems and communications theory into the work of social and natural scientists. His influence has been most conspicuous on the contemporary understanding of learning, the family, and ecological systems. His previous books include *Steps to an Ecology of Mind* and *Mind and Nature*.

Mary Catherine Bateson, daughter of Gregory Bateson and Margaret Mead, is the author of a highly acclaimed book about her parents, *With a Daughter's Eye*. She has done research in the Middle East and in the Philippines, and is professor of anthropology and former dean of faculty at Amherst College. She lives in Cambridge, Massachusetts.